Edwardian Accrington

Observed

First published in 2011
by
Thornham Local History Society
Red Brick House
Hall Lane
Thornham
Norfolk
PE36 6NB

ISBN 9780955333347

The publisher wishes to acknowledge the kind permission given by Lancashire County Library and Information Service for the reproduction of many of the photographs in this book and also the help and assistance of John Simpson and Katherine Walsh in providing access to the Accrington Observer and Times bound files at Accrington Library.

Printed and bound in the UK by the MPG Books Group, Bodmin and King's Lynn

FOREWORD

For more than 60 years during the 20th Century, the Accrington Observer and Times published a weekly column under the heading "Ladies' Chain".

Written by a succession of lady journalists, the column featured reports of and observations on the social life of the town.

Its heyday, arguably, was the Edwardian era from 1901 to 1911 during which time the mantle of "Stella" was taken on by Florrie Crossley the daughter of the "Observer's" proprietor and editor Richard S Crossley.

Besides recording details of the social life of the town's emergent middle classes, the column also provided a platform for "Stella" to express her own often quite decided views on local affairs and a variety of contemporary issues, particularly where they affected the lives of her fellow women.

The content is arranged in chronological order and each entry is dated to the Saturday issue of the Accrington Observer and Times in which it appeared.

Richard A Crossley

November 2011

PREFACE

Before embarking on the diary, readers may wish to acquaint themselves with the Accrington of 1901 through this somewhat "tongue-in-cheek" article contributed to the "Observer" by a visitor to the town in that year.

Rattle—rattle—bump! With, an extra-sized jump the train stopped at Accrington station. It was a wretched November day; rain and mist everywhere. The sky was one great threatening cloud of slaty-grey, and the ground was in a state of sodden hopelessness. The only feeling one had besides that of dampness was a pronounced sensation of deep, dark, and despondent misery. The dampness prevailed everywhere—it invaded the very railway carriage, and even creeped in between your back and your shirt—and the misery seemed to hang like a wet blanket over everything and everybody. In the train coming from Manchester—the train by the way was termed by the Railway Company an " express," and I will say it did its level best to deserve the title —all the passengers sat in silence, brooding over the weather and their sins. Instead of a cheerful carriageful of men passing away the time in hearty conversation and smoke, everyone seemed to be suffering from a bad attack of the "sulks," and sat there glaring at one another in a way that gave me the shudders. It was a cheerful journey!

Anyway, we got to Accrington at last, and, after a day's journey—from the far South of England—I had reached my destination. Collecting all my travelling impedimenta, I stepped on to the platform, with a feeling of utter loneliness and misery at my heart. Was this really the town of Accrington? With a station like that? I groaned in spirit as I satisfied myself that it was.

But I had my loneliness, at least, soon dispelled by the sight of the friend whom I had journeyed North to visit. Even the prevailing cloud of misery could not moderate his hearty grip and still more hearty words of welcome; it was like a gleam of brilliant sunlight through the darkness of the storm-cloud to me. With his assistance I got my "tackle" safely to a cab, and in less than twenty minutes I was sitting at tea in a bright, cheery room with my host. Is that station the central station for Accrington?" I asked, as I took a third helping of toasted muffin.

"Er—yes," he said, "of course, you know it is the original station, built when the railway was first opened here. It was only intended to be a temporary structure."

"How long ago was that?" I enquired. "Oh! about sixty years. I should say." he replied. "But they are talking about building a proper station shortly." I have some little acquaintance with railways and their management, and I understood fully the real meaning of those last words. I extend my sincere sympathy to Accrington: it may possibly get a properly built and fitted station some time. It has been said that Mr.

Cecil Rhodes thinks in territories. That may be so, but English railway companies think in centuries.

After tea, my host proposed that we should take a walk in the town.

"I want to show you the lions of Accrington," he said. "I should like to hear what you think of the town." The rain had ceased when we ventured forth, but it had been succeeded by an oily and altogether unpleasant mist. The gas lamps shone faintly through the dampness, and seemed to only intensify the general murkiness. It was a peculiar sort of illumination, too. An ordinary self-respecting candle would have been ashamed of itself for giving a light like those gas-lamps. I looked round for the electric arc lamps, or even for a triple-jetted gas lamp, but I couldn't see any.

Apparently, like the station, they are still being thought about. So far as the weather was concerned, my first impressions of Accrington were "depressions." But my friend was quite cheerful about it."We get nearly six months of continuous rain and mist in the winter," he said, "but we make up for it all in the summer."

I congratulated him: so far as I could see it would want some "making up."

The first thing that struck me—almost literally—was an Accrington tram, and I confess I was staggered. It came about in this way. We were walking along, looking at things generally, when suddenly I heard a noise some distance behind me which reminded me of a cross between an express and a traction engine. I gripped my friend's arm.

What's that," I asked. "Why," he said, "it's only a tram coming."

I felt relieved, and we waited to see it go by. With a terrific noise—clatter and puffing—it loomed suddenly through the mist. I escaped just in time, and stood in silent admiration. I have never seen trams like that before, and they take some getting used to. I noticed that the people of Accrington did not seem to mind, so I concluded that their appreciation, like tomatoes, was an acquired taste.

But in my opinion electric cars are quite as good as these, and I really advise Accringtonians to try them. When you get quite used to comfort, the absence of noise and dirt, I am sure you will like them, and perhaps even prefer them to the ones at present running. One thing I was impressed with, and that was the businesslike aspect of the town. Everybody seemed busy, intent on the work in hand. It is a good sign, and always speaks well for any place. Evidently Accrington is one of the prosperous towns, and I am glad of it. "Go-ahead," my friend said, and I heartily agreed with him, though I made certain reservations. The traffic in the streets, in the Market—which the town can be proud of—the never-ceasing clatter of the clogs on the pavement, and the busy look of the shops, impressed me, even more than the weather. And I say with, all my heart, "Advance, Accrington."

So we went home and to bed. And in my sleep I dreamed that I was trying to knock down a railway station with a steam tramcar for a battering-ram.

R.H. EVERITT
January 1901

v

1901

January 5th

That all readers of the Ladies Chain may live to see many years of the New Century, have good health and plenty of money to go to market, is my sincere wish. Not one of us will live to see another Century, and my advice is — make the best of this one. I had hoped that before the Century closed some practical step would have been taken towards the establishment of decent tram cars driven by electricity, and also for the better lighting of our town.

Well, let us hope that we shall see many long talked-of improvements accomplished in Accrington before the New Century is much older.

* * *

The disfigurement of our railway station approach by huge advertising boards is bad enough, but the nuisance arising from the water which percolates under the boards is much worse. The footpath in Eagle Street opposite the Liberal Club is invariably wet, and in bad weather such as we have had of late the water runs down the footpath like a stream.

That our authorities should tolerate such a nuisance is beyond my comprehension. It would not be very difficult to rectify the matter. An open drain on the other side of the hideous hoarding would he necessary, and since the "contemplated" improvements at the station may take years to accomplish, perhaps it would be well to call the Railway Co's attention to the nuisance.

Perhaps some wide-awake Town Councillor will take note of this: I am beginning to think that a few ladies on our Town council might after all be a blessing. They could not neglect affairs any more than some of our male local senators

February 2nd

Every English woman, nay every English boy and girl to-day knows how good, true and noble our Queen has been. One can scarcely realise that we shall see her no more. That she will be heard of, that her influence for good will be felt generations to come is certain. To sing "God save the King" seems awkward to us, but I suppose we shall get into it by and by. I am glad to notice that so many people in Accrington have gone into mourning. On Saturday, I trust, very little, if any colour, in dress will be seen in our town.

* * *

The postponement of the Mayoral reception and dance was naturally a disappointment to many of us but there was no option in the matter. The Mayor and

Mayoress had practically completed their work, and this will have to be done over again.

* * *

The Mayor of Accrington, Alderman David Sprake proclaiming Edward VII as King

Recently the craze for big hats has been growing more and more. Not long ago I was at a concert in Accrington, and, unfortunately, seated behind an enormous black hat. No doubt the creation was very pretty, but somehow its beauty did not appeal to me when I wished for a view of the artiste on the platform. Ladies have entirely their own way in this matter at present, but surely their own common sense would suggest a small toque rather than an outrageously large hat.

February 9th

An Accrington lady writes a few jottings on her visit to London for the funeral of our beloved Queen. She writes:

Have you ever seen a London crowd? The one I was jammed in on Saturday was something to remember. On Saturday there was black or purple on every hand. Certainly purple was the prevailing decoration of the houses and shop fronts; but if anything this shade lent a more solemn, if a little lighter, appearance to the surroundings than even black would.

Many were the touching incidents that could not fail to impress me. Close by my side stood an old lady, grey almost white, with some three score and ten years, who had journeyed a long distance to see the King. She had taken up her position there four hours before the procession was timed to pass, and was waiting quite alone and contentedly, her only wish being to see her Sovereign. Poor old lady, how could she hope to see anything but the backs of the mighty throng in front of her? But, as the coffin bearing the remains of Victoria passed, a good Samaritan in the shape of a brawny Scotchman came to her rescue, and, lifting her high above the heads of those in front, the old lady was able to obtain a glimpse of the coffin, and probably her first and last look at Edward the Seventh.

* * *

My hearty congratulations to the ladies and gentlemen of the Accrington Amateur Operatic Society who are taking part in "Falka". It must be very gratifying to them to know that their efforts are so much appreciated, and that there will again be a good round sum to hand over to local charities. Will the amount come up to last year's? I hope so, though I have my fears

* * *

Bull Bridge—King-Street, is one of the busiest but most neglected throughfares in our town. There are difficulties in the way, I understand, but surely something can be done temporarily to make the street decent.

February 19th

Many things militated against the success of the Conservative Ball on Friday evening, and the dresses, like the attendance, were disappointing.

The ladies were perplexed what to wear. Dresses of mourning in a ball room always seem out of character somehow. And yet the guests could not forget our recent national loss. The result was that while very few new dresses were worn, many of them had received additional trimmings of black and purple.

The Misses Appleby wore rich black lace overdresses without any coloured trimmings. Their mourning, it may be assumed, was out of respect for their late uncle, Mr. Edgar Appleby, and they looked very becoming.

Miss Bertha Chapman was robed in a pretty pale-blue brocaded silk, with black and white lace insertion; Miss Cunliffe wore a flame-coloured silk, trimmed with black velvet. Mrs. G. W. Grimshaw (Lytham) was attired in rich yellow satin, and Miss Grimshaw in a lovely pale blue silk with cream lace overdress, while Mrs. K. Horne wore a beautiful pink and white overdress.

A black brocaded silk worn by Mrs. Dr. Hanna looked very genteel, and a handsome white brocaded silk elaborately trimmed with silver sequins was that of Mrs. J. B. Ormerod. A novel gown in heliotrope crepe-de-chene was shown to advantage by Mrs. G. W. Pickup. Mrs. B. J. Sims, in white silk with lace over-dress, was much admired. The Mayoress (Mrs. D. L. Sprake) was attired in a violet silk robe, and Miss Schofield in a dainty muslin over-dress with pale-green background. A smart dress was that of Mrs. H. Wilkinson (Clayton), composed of ivory duchess satin trimmed with cream.

The room itself looked very pretty, and, thanks to the electric light, never became uncomfortably hot.

March 23rd

Next week D'Oyly Carte's Opera Company will visit Accrington. "Mikado," "Yeomen or the Guard" and "Rose of Persia," I believe, are amongst the operas to be performed.

* * *

Last Friday's Chamber Concert was an excellent finish to the series. The chief feature was the Brodsky Quartet, who played with great skill. Beethoven's quartet in C major was undoubtedly their best effort. The amount of technique and pathos introduced into this, one of Beethoven's finest compositions, was very remarkable. The vocalist, Miss Grace Shorrock, sang with excellent taste, and added not a little to the evening's entertainment.

April 20th

The Mayor and Mayoress (Mr. and Mrs. D. L. Sprake), following up a pleasant custom inaugurated several years ago, held two receptions in the Town Hall on Wednesday and Thursday evenings, entertaining their guests in an admirable manner. Though not on the same lavish scale as the brilliant gatherings given by Mr. J. S. Higham to commemorate the attainment of the borough's majority, the Mayor and Mayoress rose to the occasion with commendable taste and discrimination, with the most happy results, the functions socially and artistically fulfilling the highest expectations. Originally, the receptions were arranged to take place in January, but their postponement was brought about by the period of gloom and sorrow which overwhelmed the nation immediately after the death of Queen Victoria.

Alderman D.L. Sprake, Mayor of Accrington 1900-1901

The gatherings proved in every way a great success, and Mr. and Mrs. Sprake must have been delighted at the gratifying response. The Mayor and Mayoress received the guests in the anteroom adjoining the entrance to the platform, whence they passed through into the large assembly-room which, in itself artistically decorated, was further adorned with flowering plants, mirrors, folds of drapery, designs of flags, etc. The floor of the room, like the entrance steps and vestibule, was covered with thick red felt, on which were arranged suites of drawing-room furniture, with here and there small tables, which bore dainty confections, etc., afterwards partaken of when the room was given over to the possession of a small army of attentive waitresses who had charge of the refreshments. Thursday's gathering was more for the younger folk,

The Mayoress, Mrs Sprake

as it comprised dancing. Miss Smith, Plantation-street, catered for Wednesday's gathering, and Mr. John Turner for Thursday's.

There was a fashionable company on Wednesday evening. The platform was occupied by Mr. George Thornton's band, who discoursed selections during the reception.

High-class artistes were engaged, and no one had room for complaint at the musical portion of the evening. Madam Annie Grew, contralto, in a rich, sympathetic voice, extremely full and tuneful, was eminently successful, her renderings of "Kathleen Mavourneen" and "Angus Macdonald" being particularly fine. Mr. Astley Weaver thoroughly deserved the title of humorist. He gave several items of his own composition, and they evoked hearty appreciation. Miss Marie Raynor was the favourite. She gave her recitals with such refreshing warmth and feeling that it was impossible not to feel agreeably impressed. On the whole it was a most delightful entertainment.

April 27th

The weather during the last week has been splendid, for cyclists and others who have a fondness for long rambles. Many are the delightful spins I have already had on my machine.

How beautiful everything looks in the country just now! On every side plants and flowers are springing up in answer to the sun's beams. The budding trees and the greenness of the surrounding fields are most refreshing, while the birds from the tree-tops and hedges are warbling and twittering their glad welcome to the spring all day long.

* * *

I wish some generous person would provide suitable swimming baths for the benefit of the people of Accrington. Surely there is nothing more delightful in the hot summer weather than a visit to clean, cool baths. I held that every child should be taught to swim, and I think if decent accommodation were only provided, there would be a great demand for this enjoyable recreation. Of course there are baths in Accrington — of a sort. Have you ever visited them? If not, avail yourself of the first opportunity of doing so. You will realise then how terribly inadequate they are, and compared with the baths in other towns, how sadly deficient. The vile odour which greets you as you descend the stairs is not suggestive of a healthy atmosphere. But do not let this deter you from your purpose. Proceed and view for yourself our swimming baths.

* * *

A group of Edwardian Accrington Tennis Club members

The members of the Accrington Tennis Club are anticipating another enjoyable season. The club will be formally opened on the second Saturday in May. By that time, the secretary informs me, the ground will be in condition.

Miss M. Peters, I hear, has taken on the tea-secretaryship for the coming year. Many new members have already been enrolled, so that the courts this year will be in greater demand than ever.

May 11th

Quite a crowd of people gathered in Oak Hill Park on Sunday afternoon. The weather was all that could be desired, and the park looked at its best.

The Old Band played selections and hymn tunes, the birds overhead and around rendering a novel and charming accompaniment. The music on the whole was fairly well rendered, though not free from defects.

Beautifully dressed ladies were seen here and there or pausing for a moment to listen to the music under the shade of the trees. One black and white check costume with short bolero finished with white revers was very becoming. A white toque relieved with a touch of yellow was worn with it. Two white muslin dresses over pale blue, trimmed with lace and insertion, looked very nice. Another particularly charming dress was in palest blue shade of cashmere with tucked skirt and deep collar, a large White hat completing the costume. A hat trimmed with heliotrope chiffon, with a tie of the same shade bowed trickily at the left hand side, worn by a girl in mourning, looked charming. A tiny child clad in a pretty silk smock over pale blue looked very sweet.

We strolled all round the park in the hope of finding a vacant seat. But no, they were

The Accrington Old Band

all occupied, and the majority of them by the male sex. One can scarcely call them gentlemen, for they hadn't even the courtesy to give up their seats to elderly ladies who were obviously more entitled to them. And yet we are told that "Manners make the man".

* * *

On Sunday evening Cannon-street Chapel was filled with people who had come— some from a distance—to hear the Rev. Charles Williams preach his last sermon as pastor of that church. For fifty years Mr. Williams has filled the pastorate and has earned the love and respect of his congregation, and the admiration of his townsfolk. At the close of the sermon he spoke briefly but most pathetically of his life's work, and was evidently much moved as he gave the congregation his last message. The quiet way in which he spoke of the time when he should be called to another home went straight to the hearts of his listeners.

May 18th

I have received the following lines from "Un-gallant," and am pleased to note that he is in agreement with me on the need for more seats in the Park:—

A WORD WITH "STELLA."

A section of "creatures"—once "gentlemen" styled,
At your last week's remarks are astonished.
For you hint they have yet to learn "park etiquette,"
And they're feeling unduly admonished.

That we've just about half enough seats in the Park,
Is with most folks a settled conviction;
To keep walking about, till you're just "tired out,"
Is a most aggravating infliction.

But we wretched "ungallants" who thus commandeer,
This inadequate handful of benches,
Feel, somehow, we must say your censure's unjust;
Your taunt each ungallant heart wrenches.

We don't think we're to blame, in fact, think it unfair
That our manners should thus be corrected;
And beg to protest, and politely suggest
That your efforts are wrongly directed.

Though the "rude" sex endeavoured to "keep on the move,"
And were courteous to those who were "tired,"
In spite of their tact, t'would not alter the fact
That more seats in the Park are required.

Do our Councillors know of this long-felt want?
Do they visit the Park on a Sunday?
Do they notice the mass that reclines on the grass,
And reminds one so much of Whit-Monday?

We are glad this matter's been publicly broached;
Though it seems to us quite a pity,
That you didn't "lash out" and " lay it about"
The ears of the Parks Committee.

Had "more seats in the Park!" been some candidate's cry
At the last Municipal Election,
He'd have stood at the poll, "streets ahead " of them all,
Irrespective of "party connection."

" UNGALLANT."

May 25th

No small amount of pleasurable anticipation is being experienced just now amongst members of the Tennis Club. The membership of the Tennis Club numbers, I believe, nearly a hundred, and, strange to say, the gentlemen are in the majority. Never before has the club been so prosperous, and the company on the whole are very amiable. Of course, like all other clubs, it has its exceptions, who, in their zeal to have what they term "a good set," often outstep the bounds of courtesy. Fortunately these are in the minority.

* * *

A splendid substitute for tennis in wet weather is that new game, Ping-pong, or table tennis as it is often named. A good, big table and plenty of room are required to make the game a success, but in any case it is most exciting, though the grovelling on the floor in search of balls is calculated to make one very hot. I think for beginners it is a splendid idea, as it enables one to learn the count and rules of tennis without any trouble. I am told that this delightful game can be purchased from a shilling upwards.

June 8th

Sunday was anniversary day at Altham, and, as usual, the Church was crowded in the morning, and the graveyard well thronged afternoon and evening. There is no more picturesque scene hereabouts than Altham Churchyard on Anniversary Sunday. The sight on Sunday evening was most impressive. There was the Vicar, in his white surplice and hood, surrounded by hundreds of people—some seated on forms, others gravestones, some standing or leaning against the trees. Old and young were there— veterans who knew the old church half a century ago or more, with their children or grandchildren, all earnestly following the words of the pastor. Not a sound, save the chirping of the birds, and an occasional rustling of the foliage, disturbed the peaceful scene, and the commanding voice of the preacher rang out true and pleasant in the evening air. Not many preachers can gather together such an appreciative audience, and I am sure the Vicar must have felt a glow of satisfaction as he gazed upon the vast crowd who had come, some from a great distance, to the service.

June 29th

Favoured with charming weather the cricket match for the Children on Wednesday was a very enjoyable affair. This annual contest between the police and gentlemen of the district is becoming quite an important social function. Wednesday's attendance broke the record easily, and I was told that the pavilion stand rarely looks so gay as it did on Wednesday. That I can well believe, for the seats were almost entirely occupied by ladies, and the scene was very picturesque. The early afternoon was dull, but later on the sun shone brilliantly, and everybody seemed to be in the best of humour, save, perhaps those who were unfortunate enough not to secure tea early. Everybody eventually succeeded in gaining possession of a refreshing cup, let us hope. It was a big task to serve afternoon tea to so many people and when one takes into account the unsatisfactory accommodation and the fact that a much larger number of persons turned up for tea than was expected the arrangements went off well.

A few members of the Ladies' Committee of the National Society for the Prevention of Cruelty to Children had undertaken the management of the tea, and they were assisted by about a score of pretty young ladies, who carried the tea on small daintily-covered trays. Some of the covers, by the way, got badly stained, and I would suggest that it would be wiser in future to leave the cloths at home. I don't know how many cups of tea they served — anything between one and three thousand, but they did their work well. Some people on the stand were very impatient; others who thought they had come to a banquet were disappointed (in nine cases out of ten these were the people who had tickets given them by friends). The strawberries and cream were a pleasant innovation, and by many were enjoyed better than the sandwiches and the bread and butter. By the way, sandwiches, bread and butter, sweet cakes, tea, admission to the ground and stand, with a band thrown in, and all for sixpence. It was too cheap; it ought to have been a shilling.

July 6th

There was certainly an improvement in the performances of the Old Band, under the conductorship of Mr. Gray in Oak Hill Park on Sunday. He seemed to liven the performers, the consequence being the music did not drag as it generally does, and it is rather a pity Mr. J Gray is not the permanent conductor. What with glorious weather, crowds of gaily attired people, and last, but not least, the exquisite scenery presented from the green in the Park, made the afternoon an exceedingly pleasant one.

There were several pretty dresses which attracted attention. One in brown had three rows of stitched strappings on the skirt, giving a nice fullness. The bodice was adorned with White silk under pretty cream lace made in the shape of a vest and collar; a becoming hat of white chiffon trimmed with chiffon and black velvet completed the toilette. A rather conspicuous dress was in dark green under black net, the hem of the skirt consisting of frills of black chiffon ruched at the edge, and made to sweep the ground at the back.

The bodice was made with, a black chiffon fichou, worn with a white straw hat adorned with chiffon and black velvet, a string of velvet from the back of the hat hanging over the right shoulder. A neat and pretty gown was of purple cloth, the bodice having saddle and collar of white silk under cream lace, flounced skirt, the waist-band purple velvet. Purple seems to be a popular colour among the young ladies of Accrington, and if it is the right shade and made properly, nothing could look prettier or simpler.

As a rule I do not care for grey, but one gown last Sunday took my fancy. It was an uncommon shade and exceedingly becoming to the wearer. On the skirt were two frills edged with black velvet, the skirt being allowed to sweep the ground. The bodice was also trimmed with black velvet, a collar of the same giving the dress a very effective appearance.

August 3rd

The Saturday band concerts in the Park are over. The more the pity. They have been most enjoyable, and we all hope that next season another series will be arranged. The crowds have been large, but the collections, unfortunately have not been correspondingly great. I do not know what the collections work out to per head per concert, but I hear the amount is very paltry. This is not right. When people go to the Park to enjoy a band, employed by a number of gentlemen, not for their own edification but for the public good, they ought to contribute liberally. A copper or two would not be missed individually, but it is astonishing how much is collected if every person contributes his or her share.

Thanks to the generosity of a few guarantors, we have had the privilege of listening to some of the best brass bands the country can boast of. The Wyke band, which played on Saturday is one of the most successful combinations ever got together, having taken prizes valued at not less than £7,000. From Accrington the band went to Blackpool to take part in a sacred concert at the popular watering place. There can be no two opinions as to the performance of the Wyke Band. They play with a precision that is truly remarkable, and the programme was one of the most entrancing I have listened to this season.

August 31st

Most Accrington young ladies have adopted the low neck band, and despite the fact that some people consider it "rather vulgar," it is eminently more satisfactory than the very high collar band of last year. Though why the absence of a collar band in summer should be considered more unladylike than a low-necked dress for evening wear passes comprehension.

* * *

Very soon now we shall have the electric light in the Mechanics' Institute, which will be a decided improvement. At the Liberal Club the electric light, I understand, has been a great success.

* * *

Those of you who have not already done so should journey to Blackburn on the new electric cars. Of course you will be obliged to go as far as Church in our miserable, lumbering cars but the ride from Church to Blackburn will fully compensate for your trouble. They are delightful, and I don't see why we cannot substitute similar ones in Accrington for those we now possess.

There was some talk a little while ago about cars going to Whalley, but, like many other sensible projects it seems to have died away.

September 21st

It is to be hoped that the new Literary and Philosophical Society will be a greater success than the last society formed in Accrington of that kind, some 18 or 20 years ago now. The meetings were held in the court-room of our Town Hall, and for a time all went merrily until some of the ambitious ones wrote papers which were only understandable to an exclusive few, and so the interest of the members waned. There is no reason why such a society should not flourish in Accrington as in other towns, if only the subjects discoursed on are suited to the understanding of the multitude and not reserved for the "select" few.

October 8th

Bravo, Jennie Hoyle! Mr. Langham's old scholar seems about to achieve for herself what a host of Accrington admirers always hoped and predicted she would—a reputation and a name among the front rank of our English lady violinists. Miss

Hoyle, as Observerites will recollect, came over here from America about a couple of years ago to complete her musical education. Prior to that she had travelled the whole American continent as soloist with the famous Sousa combination. Now Sousa has brought his orchestra to England, and Miss Hoyle again assumes the former role of violinist.

Sousa and his orchestra made their first appearance in this country at the great Albert Hall, London, on Friday evening, and created quite a furore. The big hall was packed, and "The March King," as Sousa is often

Miss Jennie Hoyle, Accrington violin soloist with the De Sousa Band

popularly described, scored a veritable triumph, befitting America's most popular musician. Miss Hoyle played a couple of solos, one of them Saint Saen's "Rondo Capriccioso," and the London papers speak in the very highest terms of her performance. No less an authority than the musical critic of the "Daily Mail" says of her that "she created a great sensation." Local admirers will watch with interest her future career.

October 26th

My congratulations to the young ladies who promoted the "Cafe Chantant." The affair was unanimously proclaimed a success, and reflected great credit on those who had the arrangements in hand.

It is surprising how much can be attained by curtains, plants, flowers and pretty girls. Never before has the Liberal Club assembly-room looked so sweet and inviting as on Wednesday. The young lady waitresses, about fourteen in number, clad, some in white muslins, others in silk, but all wearing white aprons and black velvet bows in their hair, presented a pretty sight as they glided here and there amongst the tables, attending to the wants of the visitors, one and all smiling and chatting gaily as they dispensed tea, coffee, and sweets. At intervals artistes appeared on the platform and afforded a pleasant musical entertainment, a welcome respite from the gay chatter.

Miss Nettie Livesey was particularly graceful in a skirt dance, and though there wasn't much room at her disposal owing to the scenery erected for the sketch, she went through the steps with apparent ease. The limelight effect added greatly to the charm of her appearance.

Messrs. Kenyon and Haywood made two delightful old bachelors. 'Captain Pigeon's' "get up" was a sight to behold.

Mr. W. S. Walker and Mr. James Crossley shared the duties of accompanist. All the artistes, I believe, gave their services, and their efforts met with we'll merited applause.

From beginning to end the ball was kept rolling, and the conversation never flagged for a moment. The financial results, I hear, are very satisfactory, amounting to £20 or more, so that the Misses Wilkinson need have no fear should they, at any future time, desire to repeat a welcome novelty. The electric light gave the finishing touch to the scene.

Next Wednesday another section of Liberal bazaar workers intend having a similar cafe, but dancing will be introduced as a variation during the evening. Assuredly "imitation is the sincerest form of flattery."

* * *

On Monday Mr. Hill, of Burnley, read an interesting paper on "Oliver Cromwell" in the Mechanics' lecture-room. It was rather a pity that the paper was so lengthy, as had it been shorter we would have had a most enjoyable debate, for more than one gentleman appeared to have his "fighting armour" on.

Next week the reading of separate papers will only take about twenty minutes' time, so that the debaters will have a better chance.

Might I suggest to whoever has the arrangements of the desks in hand that they would be far more comfortable if the backs were arranged differently? All those who were unfortunate enough to be sitting on them either had to lean forward at an uncomfortable angle or to use cloaks or books to prevent the contact with the hard wood from becoming painful. T'would be an easy matter to unscrew them and make them more suitable.

November 9th

Oh for a few generous Landowners! When shall we have a Carnegie in our midst? An idea. The Scottish-American millionaire has been squandering his thousands in various towns for the establishment of free libraries and similar institutions. No town is more in need of a Library building than Accrington, though for preference— seeing that we have a library in embryo—I should prefer that Carnegie, or some other rich man, gave us public baths. Our library, young though it may be, is passable; our baths execrable.

* * *

Execrable! I am reminded of Alderman Garsden's description of our trams — a monstrosity. I am not surprised that Mr. Garsden spoke so strongly about our trams. It is my misfortune to live on the tram route, and as I write I hear an approaching car. The noise is horrible. Everybody condemns our trams, even the tramway shareholders and directors. Now, surely, it is possible for the Tram Company and the Corporation representatives to put their heads together and end this miserable business. "Give and take" ought to be the policy. Our trams are bad enough now; what shall we think about them when the Church-Blackburn electric trams begin to run a few weeks hence?

One of the old steam hauled tram cars pictured in Infant Street, Accrington

November 30th

First of all my hearty congratulations to the ladies to whose efforts the magnificent display in our Town Hall is due. As Mr. Riley put it in his opening speech, the Liberals of Accrington owe everything to the ladies. And not the Liberals only, but the Conservatives too, for how would the debt on their beautiful club have fared without the timely help of the fair sex?—(no pun intended). A bazaar is essentially a woman's show. To give them their meed of praise, the men help to fix up the stalls, to get off the raffles, and to do the shouting. But without the ladies there would be no bazaars, and the £13,000 Mr. Riley mentioned would never have been got together but for the dexterous fingers and the energy and perseverance of the women. It is not often that I am tempted to pat my own sex on the back, but this week I think we may all shake hands with ourselves.

The Bazaar should have been opened at one o'clock on Wednesday. Long before that time the Town Hall Assembly-room was literally packed with people who had come to see and hear the Liberal Leader. But once started the proceedings were commendably brief. Sir Henry Campbell-Bannerman's speech was brief but very happy; indeed it was one of the best bazaar speeches I've ever heard. Those who expected a political speech were disappointed, and I am glad they were. (Sir Henry recognised that he was in a place of business, that the one aim of the bazaar was to make money— to sell and be "sold" as he humorously put it. The whole proceedings occupied less than half an hour, and by two o'clock the sales had begun. Sir Henry patronised some of the stalls; I sincerely hope he was "sold".

The stall-holders wore lovely dresses, the majority of them suffering somewhat from the terrible crush. A rose-coloured satin dress, profusely tucked, was worn by a petite and active lady. Another very pretty gown was in pale blue silk with white embroidered collar. A charming grey silk, with vest and under- sleeves of crepe de chine and zouave of tucked silk was worn to advantage. Very beautiful also was a dress of cream elaborately-tucked satin, and equally lovely was a rose-coloured silk, abundantly trimmed with black lace. A pale green with draped vest of pink satin worn with black hat formed a pretty combination. But why all those trains in a bazaar of all places in the world?

The flower girls were nearly all attired in white with large hats, and very nice they looked too against the green plants on their stall. The chrysanthemums were lovely, the centre stand especially contained large and exquisite blooms. Scarcely a person in the room was without a flower, so assiduous were the girls in their flower selling task.

The most irksome work fell undoubtedly to the tearoom waitresses, and though not decked out in finery, they were attentive and obliging. Each wore a sensible white apron and worked with right good will.

December 7th

Bravo, ladies! The most sanguine bazaar enthusiast would scarcely have predicted such a result from an Accrington bazaar of but six days' duration in times of such depression. It only shows what can be done when determined people set to work. Fancy, nearly £5,000! It is splendid. The Liberal ladies deserve all praise, for they have worked early and late during this last week to make the bazaar a success, to say nothing of the efforts expended during the summer months by many willing hands.

Excitement ran very high on Tuesday night as the bazaar drew to a close. The stalls, stripped of their pretty and dainty articles, looked very cheerless and had no charms for the anxious waiting people. Nearly everybody had a share in the bicycles and watches, and the sense of hearing was strained to its utmost tension as the numbers and names were given out from the platform. Not a sound was heard in the room, every eye was turned expectantly towards the speaker as the names of the lucky members fell from his lips. Sighs were distinctly audible when the raffling was ended, and a look of disappointment appeared on more than one face.

* * *

What has been the matter with, our gas lately? In doors as well as in the streets the illuminant has been exceedingly poor. Our streets, I think, never looked so dark and dismal as they have done this winter. Either the gas is shockingly bad or the lamps want a good cleaning. The mantles of some of the incandescent lamps certainly want renewing. I have heard many complaints about the defective lighting of our streets. Cannot something be done to remove all this grumbling?

* * *

My congratulations to Miss Jennie, or, as she is now known, Miss Dorothy, Hoyle, who had the distinction last Sunday of playing before the King and Queen and many members of the Royal family. Miss Hoyle, who belongs to Accrington, and who, I am glad to hear, is engaged to an Accrington young gentleman, has been solo violinist in Sousa's band for a number of years, and has travelled with Sousa pretty well over the American Continent, and also visited many of the large centres of England. She does not form part of the orchestra, for Sousa's band does not include any strings but is a most acceptable accompaniment, her violin playing having given delight to thousands of Englishmen during the past few weeks.

It was with Sousa's band that Miss Hoyle went to Sandringham on Sunday—the Queen's birthday. Dinner was served on the train, and the party reached Sandringham soon after eight o'clock. Two hours later their Majesties entered the large ball-room, which had been converted into a concert hall. The Prince and Princess of Wales and the Duke of Cambridge and several invited guests were also present.

The whole affair had been kept a profound secret until Sunday afternoon, as the King was most anxious to give his Royal consort a surprise on her birthday. Accordingly not even the members of the 'band' knew of their destination until they were actually on the platform at Liverpool-street station. All they knew until then was that they were going to play at a private house, in the country.

The King and Queen appeared to greatly enjoy the lively music of the famous American combination, and at the conclusion of the programme His Majesty sent for Mr. Sousa, congratulated him, and presented him with the Victorian medal. The King demanded no fewer than seven encores, and in most cases stipulated what they were to be.

December 14th

My congratulations to Miss Alice Heap, B.A., on her recent success at the London University. Very few ladies have earned such a distinction; and in the first division too. I confess I am not an authority in these matters, but, if I am not mistaken, Miss Heap is the first young lady in these parts to receive her B.A. She deserves the high honour, for no student has worked more diligently.

* * *

The Infirmary Ball held in Blackburn Town Hall last Friday was a great success. The large assembly-room looked extremely pretty. In front of the orchestra was a large jardiniere cabinet, and at either side were tastefully draped mirrors and beautiful plants. The fireplaces were adorned with flowers, and the mantelpieces hidden by clusters of chrysanthemums. A drawing room was arranged at the Victoria end of the hall, and the cosy seats there were seldom vacant during the evening. The large entrance hall, as in previous years, was improvised as a supper room, the catering again being in the hands of Mr. Agar, of Manchester. Herr Vetter's band played the dance music in excellent style.

The Mayoress of Blackburn (Lady Hornby, wore a beautiful trained gown of handsome moire silk, of lovely heliotrope shade, the skirt and bodice being draped with old lace. The tabular was cut with a point in front, edged with netted silk fringe of exactly the same shade as the dress. A large knot of black velvet and handsome plumes looped up the lace drapery at the left side of the skirt, while a corresponding, but smaller, bow and plumes adorned the right side of the bodice. Lady Hornby wore diamond ornaments.

Lady Coddington was handsomely gowned in a black silk, of French make. The trained overdress was edged with silver sequin embroidery, disclosing an underskirt of soft chiffon frills. The bodice was trimmed with chiffon and sequins. A beautiful diamond tiara and necklace was worn with it. Miss Wade (niece of' Lady Coddington) wore a dress of thin spotted muslin de soie over white silk, with a multitude of frills round the bottom of the skirt. The bodice being trimmed with black velvet and rose leaves. Miss Thwaites had a lovely ivory lace dress over white satin, with black velvet belt and shoulder straps. The bodice was trimmed with dainty little drawings of black bebe ribbon velvet, and creamy lace. She wore pearls. Miss Mary Thwaites was robed in spotted mousseline de soie over white satin with tiny frilkins edged with narrow black lace. Black lace was also introduced in the bodice with good effect. Miss Robinson (Skipton) looked nice clad in ivory white satin, with soft frilkins edged chiffon. The bodice of white satin and chiffon, with silver belt, was very dainty. A pearl necklace was worn with it.

Mrs. A. Appleby (Clayton-le-Moors) looked very graceful in a Brussels point robe over crimson silk, with charming necklace of pearls and diamonds. Miss Nellie Smith, a tall debutante, was gowned in white. And very bonnie she looked too. Miss Lily Smith wore a gown of pale pink satin. Mrs. Dr. Ramsey wore pale pink silk with chiffon flounces, the bodice trimmed chiffon and black lace applique. Miss Eastwood's dress was of cream lace with knots of moss green velvet. Miss Gertie Fielding wore a striking gown of poppy coloured chiffon. Mrs. Baynes (Samlesbury) was dressed in a rich yellow satin, with deep white flounce and net embroidered in gold, and Miss Baynes was attired in a green crepe de chine.

December 21st

Before my next contribution is due, Christmas will have come and gone. I sincerely hope that Christmas may be a happy time for all the readers of the Ladies' Chain, and that the year upon which we are about to enter may be one of great prosperity for Accrington district. Trade has been none too good during the past twelvemonth, and many shopkeepers have suffered acutely. Let us hope we have seen the last of bad trade for many a year to come.

* * *

We are certainly having very seasonable weather, and at the time of writing there seems every prospect of a white Christmas, for the snow abounds everywhere. In some parts indeed there has been rather too much snow and wind, with the result that Accrington and many other towns have been cut off from telegraphic and telephonic communication with places south of Manchester.

* * *

Long before half-past seven on Wednesday the Town Hall was packed with people eagerly waiting for the commencement of the "Messiah" Many were unable to gain admittance, so packed was the room. Such a crowd speaks much for the popularity of our Choral concerts; but with such names as Ada Crossley, Madame Esty, Andrew Black and W Green figuring on the programme as principals, one could scarcely be surprised.

The star of the evening was undoubtedly Miss Ada Crossley, who charmed her audience. Especially beautiful was her interpretation of "He shall feed his flock". Perfect silence reigned below as her voice, rich, mellow, well-trained and pathetic, filled the room. One felt sorry at the conclusion of this solo that encores were not permitted. By the way, I never before saw such a cool, unappreciative audience; whether the heat of the room affected their tempers or they were dissatisfied with the performance I do not know; at any rate, they failed to give the artistes, and choir too, half of the applause they merited.

1902

January 11th

In consequence of the popularity of "ping-pong" in Accrington, some lady members of the Mechanics' Institution are desirous of utilising the ladies' room for that most fascinating game. The table there is admirably suited to the purpose and, as one lady remarked, "There is no reason why such a table should not be used for "ping-pong." Upstairs the gentlemen have billiards, cards, chess, books, and what not provided, while the ladies are expected to be satisfied with a few —a very few—magazines. A 'ping-pong' set would not be a very expensive item, and think of the enjoyment to lady members which would be derived from this small outlay suggested having a piano there, to make the ladies' room worth visiting, but that would be too much to expect. If there were a few ladies on the Mechanics' directorate we should soon have the ladies' room improved.

* * *

The Literary and Philosophical Society's second course of lectures commences on Monday. One can call them lectures much better than debates, as, so far, very little debating has been indulged in, and what little there was fell to the lot of about half a dozen gentlemen. The intellectual wealth of the town is not surely confined to six middle-aged heads! What of the youth of Accrington? All those young people who flock to the billiard room night after night? Have they no desire to improve their minds by debate? Apparently not, or they would have taken advantage of the splendid opportunity offered to bring forth their latent capabilities. One does not like to think that they have no ambition beyond knocking billiard balls about or playing a game of whist, and yet..... The subject chosen for next Monday evening is "Mountaineering at home and abroad," by Mr. W. Lancaster, junr.

* * *

Again we are indebted to the gentlemen for a jolly dance. I wonder why the gentlemen's subscription dances are always jollier than any others. Is it because the gentlemen feel their duty is to make themselves as agreeable as possible? Or does the fact that nearly everybody knows everybody else account for it? At the commencement of the dance, the ladies and gentlemen in groups in the centre, instead of being ranged round the room. It is certainly a good idea and makes one feel at home immediately. The affect too, of the ladies' dresses was beautiful. Many of the gowns and many of the girls looked lovely by themselves, but when the dresses were viewed all together- white, pink, blue and yellow, all harmonising— their beauty was considerably enhanced.

The draperies, mirrors and pictures added to the beauty of the scene. One young lady wore an exquisite trained gown of delicate grey; the bodice consisted of a square tucked bolero edged with cream insertion, adorned at the neck with very beautiful lace; the vest and under-sleeves were of green chiffon, while the skirt was elaborately tucked and finished with two rows of wide lace insertion. It was one of the nicest gowns I have seen this season.

Charming was a dress of pale blue silk, covered with a white muslin robe, trimmed at the neck with blue ribbon. A blonde looked sweet in a neat blue cashmere; the narrow turned-down collar was trimmed with insertions the three frills on the skirt being edged with white piping. Equally pretty was a pale green cashmere, with plain skirt and elbow sleeves, worn by a slim petite figure. Still another lovely dress was of white soft silk over pale blue; the ruched skirt, with alternate rows of insertion, was finished with frills and train, while blue chiffon adorned the bodice. Handsome also was a gown of emerald green silk, with zouave covered cream piece lace; above the plain circular flounce were two rows of insertion. A pink satin, trimmed with knots of pink bebe ribbon was much admired. A simple, but pretty, pearl grey blouse, trimmed cream insertion, and long sleeves was worn with a black tucked skirt. Another, emerald green adorned with a profusion of cream lace, looked very nice. Several of the ladies were gowned in white muslin, and as usual looked neat and fresh.

The decorations were not all reserved tor the ballroom; the refreshment-room looked particularly nice. Little tables covered with dainty white tea cloths were used; the large table at one end was temptingly laden with sweets and adorned with mimosa bush and flowers. Tiny paper serviettes, with "Gentlemen's private subscription dance" printed in one corner were a decided novelty. I meant to take and keep one as a souvenir, but, alas, the next time I entered the room they had all vanished.   Apparently some of the other people had thought likewise and appropriated them. It is a pity the ante-room, used as a refreshment room, is so small, as many were obliged to wait at the interval, the room being so crowded. Parringtons supplied the refreshments. Those who had the arrangements in hand had not forgotten the stairs either; plenty of chairs and lounges there were, and curtains warded off the draught.

The secretaries and M.C.'s looked after the dances splendidly, though I think two or three of the gentlemen who disappeared at the interval would have been much better employed attending to those ladies who had no partners. All praise to Mr. Harry Heap and Mr. "Bob" Crossley, the two secretaries, though, the latter says Mr. Heap did most of the work. Mr. George Thornton's band supplied the music, and as usual the dances were a success. Nearly all the lancers were encored. But our lancers are hard work.

February 15th

We have been treated to a touch of real wintry weather this week; and in spite of the heavy downfall of snow some enthusiastic skaters have had a good time on the ice. Though the snow adds much to the discomfort of wayfarers, there is no doubt that it transforms the landscape into a thing of beauty which, if not a joy forever, is a thing of delight to many. Even in the town the newly- fallen snow is a pretty sight, but it is necessary to go out a little way into the surrounding country to thoroughly realise the majestic beauty of the snow-clad landscape. The sunsets, too, are particularly grand just now, and well worth the climbing of the Coppy to witness.

* * *

Thanks to the untiring zeal of our local Opera Society, still another success has been achieved. When I heard that the "Yeomen of the Guard" had been chosen I was not a little dubious about the result, as everyone knows it is by no means an easy opera to put before the public. SO very much depends on the singing and acting of the principals, while but two or three choruses are introduced. SO far as the principals are concerned, "Yeomen" is undoubtedly one of Sullivan's best efforts. The simple, but sweet, music appeals to many, while the note of pathos running through the piece captivates the least appreciative of audiences. And surely Accrington audiences are to be placed in that category. Less demonstrative people I never met with anywhere. I believe a lot of them go to the amateur opera expecting the performers to improve on professionals, never taking into account the hard work necessary to produce even a third-rate performance. As a natural consequence they restrain their applause, which, this last week at any rate, should have been given freely enough. No wonder one of the actors observed that it was worse than thawing an iceberg. But instead of administering boiling water, a little tomfoolery suffices to thaw in many cases.

The first and second nights the orchestra was far from satisfactory. If the instrumentalists had been sight-reading they couldn't have made a worse attempt. It was horrible! The struggles of the cornet player produced most unearthly sounds which rose above the jumble and murmur of several violins. Later in the week a piano was substituted for the harmonium, and, thanks to Mr. "Teddy" Whittaker's efforts, a marked improvement was shown in the accompaniments.

Mrs. Saul makes a charming Phoebe. Her bright red velvet corsage against the white overskirt is pretty and effective; the jauntily placed red and gold cap sits well on her fair wig, with its long plait. She sings the opening song very well indeed, receiving very little applause at its conclusion, however. But the thawing process hasn't begun so early. "Were I thy bride " is more appreciated. Her wooing of Wilfred and his grimaces during the process are most amusing, and, like him, one feels rather sorry when this playful lovemaking is at an end. In the succeeding quartets she is equally successful, and plays the part of the wilful, impulsive, yet loving girl splendidly.

As Elsie Maynard, Miss Nellie Pickup is a decided success. Her graceful stage carriage is the admiration of everybody. The wig she wears is much too heavy for so small a face, and I'm sure her own hair would have suited her much better, especially when wearing that pretty white satin bridal gown. " I have a song to sing, oh!" is, to borrow one of the warder's phrases, well sung and well danced by Elsie and Jack

Point. But that very pathetic song, " 'Tis done, I am a bride," is perhaps Elsie's best effort.

What a dear, motherly Dame Carruthers Mrs. Shorrock is, to be sure! It seems a pity that such bonnets, with white strings, neat white aprons and quiet costumes are not in vogue in the 20th century, for none can deny their unobtrusive charm, and they're so becoming, too. At least, Mrs. Shorrock's is. I was delighted with her deep "Warders are ye, whom do ye ward?" and there is no doubt that in "When our gallant Norman foes" she excels. I don't think she is troubled with stage-fright, either; her demeanour appears so cool and collected.

Wilfred (Mr. Will Kenyon) is splendid. His facial contortions are very funny. It's a good thing Jack Frost doesn't overtake him while he wears one of those hideous grimaces, or I tremble to think of the result.

All praise to Mr. Phil Roberts. A better jester one could not wish for. His acting and expression throughout are remarkably fine, and he gets about the stage with the agility of a cat. For an amateur actor, he's wonderful. "A Private Buffoon" is very well sung, though I think a few local jokes, judiciously introduced, would amuse many of the audience, as it is the only song which could possibly be termed topical.

Mr. Critchley, as usual, takes his part well, and scores every time with "Fairfax's" songs, "Is life a boon " and "Freed from his fetters grim."

Mr. Dobson makes an admirable Sergeant Meryl, and knows his part to the very letter. The Lieutenant's part is well performed by Mr. H Entwisle, and that of Leonard Meryl by Mr. Bamber.

The chorus has comparatively little to do except look pretty and smile often—referring, to the female portion at any rate. "Night has spread her pall," etc., goes very well indeed.

The dresses are pretty, and a credit to the ladies' committee, who, I hear, made them all.

The finale is an admirable wind-up to one of the best performances our amateurs have yet given us. In the last scene the death of Jack Point is full of pathos. How people can leave their seats in the midst of such a scene is beyond my comprehension.

February 22nd

The Mayoral receptions this week have been, delightful and well-managed functions. The guests were received in the ante-room adjoining the ballroom. The Mayoress looked charming in an elaborate amber brocaded satin gown, appropriately trimmed on the skirt with wide black lace, with vest and high collar of white tucked silk. She wore the Mayoress's chain, and very well it looked too. The Mayor also had on his chain.

The ball-room looked very inviting: plants were arranged all around, a number of lighted Japanese lanterns were suspended from the electrolysers with good effect, several large paper "sunshades" were placed here and there in the corners, also paper fans arranged on the various mirrors.

On Wednesday musical selections were played by Mr. E. Whittaker's orchestra from 7-30 to 8 o'clock followed by a short programme including choruses sung by the New Church choir and several songs.

Dancing commenced at 9-30, and for the non- dancers a comedietta and farce were arranged in the court-room. Light refreshments were provided on long tables on the platform.

Many lovely gowns were worn with trains, which, as usual, were sadly in the way of clumsy people. Miss Bell was dressed in a very pretty trained gown of heliotrope satin, a lovely deep lace collar adorned the decolletage, while the vandyked over skirt of satin disclosed a flounce of chiffon on the same shade. Miss M. Bell was gowned in salmon pink satin; festoons of white lace decorated the skirt, the bodice having pearl trimming.

A charming dress was worn by Miss B. Lupton—a pale blue clinging material, with flounced skirt edged with ruching, vertical rows of cream insertion, together with the elbow sleeves and tiny White satin pouch produced a very girlish, but altogether graceful, dress. The skirt just cleared the ground. Another dainty creation of muslin clothed Mrs. Osbaldeston, a tiny zouave edged with lace and insertion of pure white muslin, and a profusion of tucks and frills upon the skirt.

The Mayor, James Cunliffe

Miss Blake was attired in a plain white satin gown, relieved with a spray of red flowers. Mrs. Fox wore black silk with transparent sleeves, and Miss Appleby, black with many little frills; she also wore red flowers. The Misses Sandeman (Church) were garbed in white satin, and Mrs. Sandeman in black satin trimmed with transparent black lace and long sleeves.

Miss C. Edie was gracefully robed in a soft cream material; equally sweet was Miss F. Edie's dress off soft silk with fichu. Mrs. W. Smith was gowned in green and white striped silk, with deep collar of white lace. Miss Smith's also was a most charming dress— orange coloured chiffon with overdress of white lace trimmed with velvet. A very striking dress was Mrs. D. Dewhurst's, pale heliotrope bengoline silk; a snow white feather boa was worn with it. Mrs. (Dr.) Clayton wore a black, with zouave, adorned with gold trimming.

Here are a few more; I have not time to particularise: ——Mrs. Lee, white satin, with stripes of black lace insertion and black velvet trimming. Mrs. (Dr.) Hanna, black dress, with square of pink ruching. Mrs. (Dr.) Brooke, soft white silk, very prettily tucked. The Misses Chapman: White silk. Miss M. Grimshaw, pearl grey, with green net vest and undersleeves, trimmed cream insertion. Mrs. Greenwood, very stylish black sequin gown. Mrs. A. Higham, white silk dress, trimmed pale blue band and streamers. Miss Fox, white satin. Miss Burgess, elaborate gown of ivory satin, with chiffon flounce. Mrs. Beckett, heliotrope, trimmed deep cream lace, and velvet. Mrs. Barlow, black silk with neat embroidered turned-down collar of white silk; a bow of white silk worn in the coiffure. Miss Riley, delicate rose pink silk, with overdress of pink net. Mrs. J. Barnes, bronze green adorned with velvet and cream silk vest.

Miss Cunliffe, a very appropriate black silk trimmed with pretty insertion. Mrs. K. Cunliffe, blue material, trimmed white silk. Miss Grimshaw, pale blue silk, with overdress of white lace. Mrs. Barnes, black, with transparent yoke and sleeves. Mrs. Bagnall, pink silk, trimmed white lace. Miss Heap, white silk with net overdress, trimmed rows of white satin ribbon. The Misses J. and E. Barnes, white silks with pretty fichus. Miss M. Rendall, white muslin.

Miss Kearns, white. Miss Barr (Rishton), white satin trimmed deep pink flowers. Mrs. Kenyon, grey, with crinkled flounce, trimmed, with white piping. Mrs. Cheney, black velvet, with pale blue silk collar under black lace. Mrs. Rolfe, white silk. Mrs. Bunting, black silk with lace cap.

The ball-room looked very inviting: plants were arranged all around, a number of lighted Japanese lanterns were suspended from the electrolysers with good effect, several large paper "sunshades" were placed here and there in the corners, also paper fans arranged on the various mirrors.

On Wednesday musical selections were played by Mr. E. Whittaker's orchestra from 7-30 to 8 o'clock followed by a short programme including choruses sung by the New Church choir and several songs.

Dancing commenced at 9-30, and for the non-dancers a comedietta and farce were arranged in the court-room. Light refreshments were provided on long tables on the platform.

Many lovely gowns were worn with trains, which, as usual, were sadly in the way of clumsy people.

* * *

It is hoped that a balance of £100 at least will be the result of last week's Amateur performance. What a pity "An Old Patron" didn't make his suggestions concerning the price of seats earlier, then there would have been a still larger balance to hand over to local charities. And his remarks, too, anent the balloting, methinks, should have been made a fortnight ago. Some people were waiting to book seats considerably after eleven o'clock on the balloting night. Some of the ladies were positively wearied out with their long wait, and vowed that next year they'd risk getting a poor seat rather than endure another such night.

* * *

I was glad to notice that on Saturday night, at all events, the Accrington people showed a keener appreciation of the "Yeomen". Bouquets of roses were presented to the principal ladies—Miss Pickup, Mrs. Saul, Mrs. Shorrock, and Miss Hope—and never were such favours more justly earned. There isn't a town for miles around can produce such clever amateurs. May they live long to give us many more productions such as last week's.

* * *

The "Mechanics' Powet" has once more earned my gratitude by sending the following lines, which I print with pleasure: —

THE COMING OF PING-PONG.

Dear "Stella," news for you I've got,
Just listen. The Mechanics' lot,
Methinks, have straight gone off their dot,
They've taken now to Ping-Pong!

They say that YOU advised the deed,
And in your columns gave a lead
To those who unto you pay heed,
And now they've got a Ping-Pong!

No more the boys "camp" round the fire,
Or rouse a keen opponent's ire
By "potting white" or "fluking" dire,
They've all gone mad on Ping-Pong!

"Shell out" and "fifty-up," alas!
Are dubbed by ev'ryone "no class!"
His "3d's" now doth each amass;
A right cheap game is Ping-Pong

The "General's" face wears quite a frown,
As daily his receipts go down,
He swears the club'll be "on the town"
If we stick to that Ping-Pong

No longer "check" and "mate" are heard,
"Your pard's ace trump"—a thing absurd,

Is ne'er done now. For 'pon my word,
They'll nothing play but Ping-Pong!

Yes, old and young, and golfers, too,
Have deemed it best to humour YOU;
They've all gone mad and true as true,
They're dotty, now, on Ping-Pong!

The girls, I hear, the pretty dears,
Sit down below, all bathed in tears;
But "Stella", bid them calm their fears,
They, too, shall have a Ping-Pong!

So up, my braves, just raise a shout,
Quick! Hang the flags and banners out;
And quaff its health in ale and stout,
Here's to the reign of Ping-Pong.

P. PIP!!!

March 1st

I have previously complained about people leaving concert rooms before the performances were ended, and even at the conclusion of the amateur performance in our Theatre, while witnessing the most pathetic part in the whole opera—the death of Jack Point—many people rose from their seats and began bustling about in search of wraps. At the Minnehaha minstrel performance on Saturday a number of people had the bad taste to enter the Town Hall during the progress of some item, and quite half an hour after the entertainment had commenced. By so doing they not only caused much annoyance to the artistes, as well as the audience, but completely spoiled the first four pieces on the programme. The concert was advertised for seven o'clock. What pleasure people can find—knowing this—in coming at 7-30 I fail to see. The programme boys, too, walking up and down the aisles during a performance are most irritating.

The concert itself was a decided success. The Minnehaha minstrels are undoubtedly the best we have ever had in our Town Hall— either professionals or otherwise. There were seventy performers. The "Cloister voices" was exquisite, only an organ accompaniment being needed to make the song perfect.

Mr. John Allen was answerable for a fund of merriment which kept the audience in a continual roar of laughter. His stump speech was only equalled by his mimicry of "The baby." In fact, so true to life was the picture that one lady remarked that "he'd evidently gone through it." Certainly he did it very well. Mr. H. Critchley's whistling solo was extremely clever and received much applause. Indeed the performance throughout was most enjoyable, though some of the jokes I've known from my cradle.'

* * *

In continuation of the receptions given by the Mayor and Mayoress (Mr. and Mrs. James Cunliffe) in the Town Hall on Wednesday and Friday of last week, another attractive party, the last of the receptions, was given in the Town Hall on Tuesday evening, the guests on this occasion being the juveniles and right well the little ones appreciated the good-things provided for them. It was quite a pleasure to see their bright faces and trim little figures, as they tripped gaily through the dances. They will long remember such an enjoyable evening, for, as one little girl remarked, "It's the very nicest party I've ever been to."

THE GUESTS

James Ashworth, Fred Ashworth, Sylvin Arthur. Marion Bardsley, Alice Bardsley, Mary Bardsley, Marjorie Bolton, John Bolton, M. Bolton, Dorothy Bury, Harry Bury, Harold Beckett, Eleanor Beckett, Alice Broughton, Fanny Broughton, Alwya Brown, Humphrey Brown, Mary Barnes, Norman Barnes, Gladys Barnes, Ida Bradley, Ellen Beattie, Thomas Burt, Geo. Burt, S. Briggs, John Bury, Phyllis Bury, Frank Britcliffe, Kathleen Britcliffe, Sallie Bamber, Robert Bradley, Nellie Bullock, Nicholas Bentley, Amy Bentley, Alice Burrows, James Burrows, A. Barton, May Barnes, Arthur Barlow, Rennie Broughton, Clara Bardsley, Donald Barlow, Doris Clayton, Nellie Clayton, Ethel Coupe, Annie Critchley, C. Critchley, Marie Critchley, Dorothy Crabtree, Ernest Cronshaw, Phyllis Cronshaw, Harry Carley, Nellie Carter, D. Carter, Janet Cunliffe, Herbert Cunliffe, Marjorie Cunliffe, Wilson Cunliffe, Alice Carter, Lizzie Carter, Maggie Crawshaw, Herbert Crawshaw, Jno. E. Crawshaw, C. Crawshaw, Jno. .H. Chadwick, H. Cowie, A. Cowie, Allan Cowie, Jack Cowie, Nellie Clayton, Mary Cronshaw, Alice Cronshaw, Arnold Chadwick, Isabel Croft, John Croft. Ethel Dean, Nellie Diggle, Jessie Diggle, John H. Driver, Gertrude Driver, Mary Driver, Annie Duckett, Tom Dean. Lizzie Duxbury, H. Dickenson, Jennie Duckworth, Ethel Dickenson, Florrie Dickenson, Nellie Eastham, J. E. Ecroyd, R. Ecroyd, Sarah Entwisle, Norman Entwisle, Florrie Eccles. Grace Foster, Hilda Foster, Nellie Foster, Geoffrey Frankland, Reginald Furness, Dorothy Furness, Ernest Fayer, Gladys Foster, Nellie Foster, Annis Firth, Ernest Fayers. Frank Grace, Lizzie Grace, Burgess Geddie, Dora Greensill, Cuthbert Greensill, Gertrude Gill, Stanley Gill, C. Greenwood, M. Greenwood, Kathleen Grimshaw, Ivy Grimshaw, Alan Grimshaw, Miss Gill, Lizzie Grimshaw. Peter Holden, C. Holden, B. Holden, Charlie Holgate, Flora Holgate, M. C. Holden, F. Holden, D. L. Holden, C. Harrison, Kathleen Harding, Gertrude Hodgson, Molly Hanna, Bob Hanna, Eli Higham, Thos. Higham, Hannah Higham, Ann Hargreaves, Dorothy Haworth, Reginald Haworth, Herbert Haworth, Sydney Heywood, Douglas Haywood, Alan Haywood, R. R. Haworth, Miss Haworth, Walter Heap, Walter Hayhurst, Winifred Hulme, Richard Hurst, J. R. Hurst. Tom Harwood, Fred Haworth, J. Hindle, W. Holgate, Arthur Hesketh, Ellen Heap. Nellie Hacking, Thos. Hayhurst, Willie Harold, Connie Hartley, Alan Hartley, Dorothy Hartley, Arthur Hurst, J. E. Hindle, Lizzie Harrison. Amy Ingham, R. J. Ingham. Spencer James, Alec Jardine. Gilbert Kenyon, Mona Kenyon, James Kenyon, Leo Kearns, Henry Kauntz, Nora Kauntz, Elsie Kauntz, Jas. Kenyon, Kathleen Kenyon. Dolly Kenyon, B. Kenyon, Nina Kenyon, Lillie Kirkman. Nellie Kemp. Edith Lord, Arthur Lightfoot, Frank Lightfoot, L. Layland. Bessie Moore, Norman Moore, Marjorie Macalpine, Geoffrey Macalpine, Alec McKernan, G. Moore, Maud Morris. Hilda Millward, Teddie Millward. Miss McKernan, Roland Millward, L. Mason, Florence Millward. Mabel McConwell, Annie Mitchell. Pollie Marland, Minnie Maden, Nellie Morn, Colin McRae. Bessie Newton, Ruth Nightingale. Jack Oldham, D. Ormerod. Constance Pickup, Alice Parker. Harry Parkinson. Norah Peat, Geo. Pratt. Martha Pilling, Roland Priestley, Alan Priestley. Bob Ramsbottom, Maggie Ramsbottom, E. Rawson, Arnold Rushworth, Olive Ruttle, Connie Rauth, Frank Rushton, Ellen Robinson, Joe Ramsbottom. Mary Riley, Mary Ann Riley, Herbert Riley, Jas. Riley. Willie Saul, Colin Sandeman, Geo. Slinger, Willie Slinger, Gilbert Sprake. Harry Smith, Hilda Smith, Alice Southworth, Percy Smith, U Smith, Geo. Spiers, Rachael Sinclair, Maggie Sinclair, Jos. Shorrock, Mildred Shorrock, Jas. Spiers, Maggie Spiers. Gilbert Thornber, Chrissie Tough, John Tough, Arnold Tough, Gertie Tough, Arthur Thompson, Norman Tootal, Fred Thompson, Lillian Thompson, Lillie Tomlinson, Nellie Tomlinson, Lucy Taylor. Walter N. Walmsley, Thomas. H. Walmsley, Alan Walmsley, Nellie Welch. Fred Welch, Absolem Westwell, Jennie Westwell, Lucy Whittaker. E. Whittaker, Roland Wood. Prudence Whittaker, Emily Wood. Cassie Wood. Gladys Wolf, Charles

Wolstenholme, Nellie Whittaker, Arthur Walmsley, Hilda Whittaker, Jos. Whittaker, Mildred Whittaker, Elsie Whittaker.

March 8th

Apropos of last week's remarks anent the late arrival of some people at theatres and concert rooms, I notice that Mr. George Alexander has announced that all late comers to his theatre will be obliged to wait till the conclusion of the first act before they are admitted. A very good thing, too. What a pity such a plan is not adopted unanimously by theatre proprietors and concert promoters.

* * *

Accrington is, up to the present, free from that terrible scourge, smallpox; but the authorities, I see, are taking active measures for isolation in case of an outbreak. It is said that much harm has been done to London trade by the creation of quite unnecessary apprehension on the part of nervous people in the country. The fact that the King and Queen, the Prince and Princess of Wales, the members of the Court and Royal Households, not only remain in town, but go frequently to the theatres, should, it is said, in itself be a convincing proof that there is no real cause for alarm.

March 15th

This miserable March weather, with its monotonous rotation of drip, drip, blow, blow and cold east wind, varied occasionally by odd spring-like days— sent from the weather office by mistake— such is our miserable lot. How one envies those who can escape it. To say nothing of our regular seasiders who come from the Fylde coast every morning, what of the thrice-blessed ones who are able to get away to the land of the Sun God, to Egypt, the Mediterranean, the Riviera?
Mr. and Miss Williams returned this week to Accrington having completed their trip round the world; while Mr. Langham and party are still enjoying the delights of Egypt. Several other fortunate Accringtonians are at Madeira and the South of England, and I hear that Mr. and Mrs. T. Higham and friends left Accrington on Monday for the Riviera. Lucky folks!

* * *

My correspondent of a fortnight ago will be pleased to learn that two ping-pong tables have been provided at the Mechanics', and, as far as I can gather, ladies are not excluded from the room at all. Why doesn't some enthusiast promote a tournament there I wonder?

* * *

Many people flocked to the Mayoress's "At Home" on Tuesday—rather too many, in fact, and at one time the Mayor and Mayoress were bewildered how to accommodate their unexpected guests. Women who had been marketing took advantage of the occasion to have a cup of tea with the Mayoress. And right well did they enjoy her hospitality. Several were heard to remark to their friends, "Aye, but tha mon hev a cup o' tay; it's reight good." By the time fixed for the arrival of guests, the vestibule was crowded with women, some carrying string bags packed with oranges and baskets, with all sorts of things inside. If a slight check had not been put upon them there would have been no room at all for the elite. Taking the "At Home" literally, some of the women took off bonnets and jackets, and made themselves quite comfortable, for, having finished their marketing for the day, they were in no hurry to forsake such a generous host and hostess.

A gentle hint was passed round that the reception was not intended for them, but, as one woman remarked, "Id wor in th' papper as all as hed abeawt two heawrs to speare would be med welcome by th' Mayor and Mayoress." The Mayor and Mayoress received all comers with an outward show of cordiality at any rate. Some of the ladies quite enjoyed the diversion caused by the advent of these "at homers;" while others were apparently disdainful. Will this unique "At Home," I wonder, be the first of many? After all, I see no reason why the masses should not take tea with the classes, and they show far more appreciation of the good things provided for their entertainment. To use one phrase I overheard, "We'd a reight good do."

March 22nd

Music lovers of Accrington are looking forward with, pleasurable anticipation to next Wednesday's Choral Concert. That their highest expectations may be realised is my sincerest wish. It is to be hoped that the people who habitually leave before the conclusion of a concert will have the good taste this time to wait until the finish, and it is just as well to remember that the concert commences at seven o'clock sharp. Nothing is more disconcerting to a conductor than the bustle of late arrivals.

* * *

Talking of matters musical, I am glad to learn that Friday's Chamber Concert was so generally appreciated. I am not such a tyro as to say that all the patrons of these Chamber Concerts attend because of their love of high-class music. Some of them, I fear, have no music in their souls, and cannot enjoy even a Brodsky quartette. It is interesting to watch these peolpe, the effect is so varied. While some frankly admit that the music is too "high" for them, others yawn and fidget on their chairs, wearing an expression of boredom, and to others a whiff on the staircase is infinitely more enjoyable! On the other hand there are those in Accrington who can really appreciate good music, and I am glad to think the number is increasing. The fact that the Chamber Concerts have continued so long here, while in much larger towns they have languished long ago, speaks well for Accrington, and I sincerely hope they may continue to flourish.

April 5th

I understand that Mr. and Mrs. H. L. Wilson, Clayton-le-Moors, have arrived home this week from the Canary Isles, where they have been spending the winter. The rather hard winds and damp weather we have had during the last few days will come somewhat severely to anyone who has become accustomed to a semi- tropical climate.

April 19th

One or two ladies have recently become members of the Golf Club. I wonder why more ladies do not embrace this healthy exercise. Are they afraid of appearing too masculine in the eyes of their fellow creatures?

* * *

The members of the Accrington Tennis Club are making preparations for the coming season. Some of the more enthusiastic ones have already had a fair amount of practice on the gravel court, while others have paid visits to the club to ascertain the state of the grass courts, which, I am glad to learn, will be in condition early in May. How very clumsy one feels handling a tennis racquet after the small ping-pong bats. Mr. "Teddy" Whittaker has undertaken the duties of secretary to the club, and Miss Alice Broadley is in charge of the teas for this season.

* * *

Great interest was manifested in the marriage of Mr. Hubert Blake and Miss Marie Fox, on Thursday. Long before the time fixed for tying the nuptial knot, two o'clock, the Church of the Sacred Heart was filled by an expectant crowd, who greatly admired the charming decorations of the altar, which was adorned with choice lilies, daffodils, ferns and palms. The moment the bride appeared the sun shone forth in all its glory, lighting up the beautiful stained windows in the sanctuary, and the glistening folds of the bride's gown as she knelt in front of the altar. Tall and stately, the bride was exquisitely attired in white duchesse satin with transparent yoke of lovely lace and long flowing train. Her veil of white tulle was adorned with orange blossoms and white heather; she carried a shower bouquet of white flowers. The bridesmaids, five in number, were prettily attired in white voile dresses over white silk, profusely tucked, with yokes of green chiffon and lace; they wore white picture hats, with shower bouquets of azaleas. Miss W. Marsden (the bride's niece), a tiny bridesmaid in white carried a basket of flowers, and very sweet she looked.

* * *

Another interesting wedding took place at Blackburn, on Wednesday, at St. James-street Congregational Church, the contracting parties being Mr. Edgar Appleby, of The Grange, Wilpshire, nephew of Mr. Arthur Appleby (Clayton-le-Moors), and Miss Bickerdike, of Bryers Croft, Wilpshire.

May 3rd

Mr. and Mrs. Tom Higham returned home this week after a tour on the Continent where they have had many enjoyable journeys and escaped the biting winter winds of this district. It must be very nice to spend one's winter in warmer climes, and to return to old Accrington in the spring.

* * *

To-day the Mayoress (Mrs. Jas. Cunliffe) has a novel task to perform, novel to Accrington at any rate. She is to present war medals to members of the St. John Ambulance Corps who have served in the South African War. This, I should think, will be the first time a Mayoress of our borough has been able to present war medals, and I sincerely hope that the weather may favour the Ambulance men and those friends who attend Oak Hill to witness the ceremony.

May 17th

It is hard to realise that the first great summer holiday commences to-day. One naturally associates rain with Accrington holiday times, but a combination of rain, hail, snow and east winds is not a pleasant prospect for Whitsuntide. Despite the miserable weather we have had, though, the country is assuming a summer appearance. In the parks most of the trees are in leaf; daffodils have given place to tulips and crocuses, while the birds make the wooded places ring with their joyous twittering from morn till dewy eve.

* * *

The decline in the ladies' membership at the Mechanics' is a matter for regret. Do ladies generally know, I wonder, that a six shilling fee covers all? It is a pity Miss Bright declined her nomination on the executive, for a more ideal representative the ladies couldn't wish for. The newly-elected directorate might try to develop the ladies' side of the Mechanics', though. A ping-pong room, for the use of ladies would be much better than the present one, for no lady is fond of playing the game through a cloud of cigar smoke, and then, as one of the lady members observed, "If we had a room to ourselves we could go there and stay without feeling that we were intruding on the gentlemen's rights, and, above all, be free from any reflection as to any other motive than that of ping-pong playing.

June 7th

Wednesday turned out a bad day, as far as the weather was concerned, for the garden party at Arden Hall, in aid of the Nurses' Association. There was no rain, but the sun, a necessary attribute to a successful garden party, persisted in remaining behind a bank of sullen clouds.

The arrangements were very complete. A number of tiny tables, tastefully covered with white tea cloths, were arranged on the lawn on one side of the hall, where several young ladies attired in neat costumes, catered for the wants of the guests.

Arden Hall, the home of Mr and Mrs J.E. Riley

Mr. Robert Cunliffe's band discoursed sweet music on the lawn in front of the house, the tennis court and croquet ground were at the disposal of the guests, and a ping-pong table was provided indoors. In fact, everything was done to make the enjoyment of the guests complete. It is very good of Mr. and Mrs. Riley to place their beautiful grounds at the disposal of the public for these gatherings, and to make such excellent arrangements.

June 28th

When the news of the King's serious illness and the postponement of the Coronation reached Accrington on Tuesday afternoon people utterly declined to believe it. One of the earliest intimations was a telegram from a London news agency to the "Observer and Times," intimating that His Majesty was seriously ill, and that an operation was necessary. So important was the message that its terms were at once communicated by telephone to the Town Hall, where the Mayor and Town Clerk were quickly in attendance. Copies of the "Observer" telegram were printed, and sent round to the public buildings, clubs, hotels, and principal business places, and everywhere the news came as a great and unpleasant surprise. People in the streets talked of nothing else, and confirmation was anxiously looked for. Between two and three o'clock a second message was received at the "Observer" Office, stating that the operation had been successfully performed, and that the Coronation ceremony had been postponed until the autumn. It bore the official stamp, and there was no longer room to doubt the authenticity of the news. In a little while came other telegrams, one of which announced that it was the King's wish that the provincial celebrations should proceed. All over the town Corporation workmen, private tradesmen, and householders were busy getting out their decorations for Thursday, and, though there were many speculations as to whether the local celebrations would' proceed or would be postponed, the work of laying out bunting and flags was continued. The Mayor found himself in rather a dilemma, and probably it was a great relief when an "Observer" representative handed to him a copy of the telegram in which it was intimated that it was His Majesty's wish that local festivities should proceed. The situation was one such as was not easy to determine. To have abandoned everything would have been to sorely disappoint the children and the old people, and there was all the local decorations to consider, and a hundred and one arrangements that had gone too far to be cancelled, without serious loss.

Eventually it was decided to summon a meeting of the Town Council to consider the matter, and notices were hurriedly despatched to every member of the Council, calling a meeting for seven o'clock. In the hope of receiving some official hint as to the proper course of action, the Mayor telegraphed to the Home Secretary, but no reply had been received at the time fixed for the meeting. The Council meeting was private, and the Council unanimously expressed the opinion that the local celebrations as arranged should proceed, in view of the King's earnest hope, as expressed in the message from the Earl Marshal, that the celebrations in the country should be held as already arranged. It was, of course, understood that this proposed course would be subject to re-consideration in the event of bad news about the condition of the King being received.

July 5th

A more perfect night than Monday for bonfires, fireworks, and torchlights couldn't be wished for. It was a splendid treat to watch the bonfires on the hills around Accrington blaze forth just as the sun sank, leaving the sky bathed in an exquisite sunset glow. Thousands of people clambered up Moleside, while Whinney Hill bonfire and searchlight had many enthusiastic admirers. The torchlight procession to Moleside was a grand sight.

True, there were many complaints of the conduct of some of the younger torch-bearer while passing along the streets, but up in the hills, the two thousand torches winding in and out of the plantations made up a scene as unique as it was pretty. From the golf links, I hear, the scene was particularly brilliant. The straggling line of torch-bearers wending their way upwards, together with the silhouetted figures and the glowing fire above, formed a strangely weird picture. And near the top of Moleside the sight was simply grand. Rockets and balloons shot up in all directions, making a gorgeous display as they descended to earth again.

The bonfires around were plainly visible. That on the top of grand old Pendle, lighted soon after that on Moleside, shone very brilliantly, and in the direction of Colne was

Bunting in Blackburn Rd, Accrington erected for the Coronation of Edward VII in 1902

another big light. The Darwen fire seemed very dull by comparison, and the Blackburn flame was at least a quarter of an hour behind the rest. Young and old thoroughly enjoyed themselves. Two or three enterprising people sold mineral waters in the firelight on Moleside to the crowd, and some apparently hungry folks sat munching their suppers contentedly. A number of boys occupied an enviable position in a high tree until a hard-hearted policeman swooped down upon them and they very reluctantly descended.

Everybody on Moleside seemed to agree that bonfire night was a great success. Excitement ran high, the shouting was loud, and dancing, to the strains of the band, was freely indulged in.

* * *

It is no exaggeration to say that Saturday's cycle parade was a brilliant success. The weather, for a wonder, smiled approval on Accrington, and the sun lit up the gay costumes of the cyclists with exquisite effect. Some of the characters were most amusing. By the way, what an unappreciative crowd lined Blackburn-road. I don't think there was a cheer raised loud enough to be heard by the cyclists. The collections, too, were very small, considering the vast numbers in the crowd. Let us hope that when such efforts are made in future they will meet with something like due appreciation.

August 16th

Last week was the Accrington pleasure fair, the children's playground, and this week the pot fair, the housewives' paradise. The Accrington market ground has been given over to the pot man whose reputation for wonderful (?) value always draws hundreds of wives, mothers and sisters, all intent upon making some splendid bargain in crockery. Perhaps there have been bargains this week, but in almost every case the potman has come best out of the deal. In the glaring light of the gas jets, or electric lamps I noticed that some of the fairmen were so enterprising as to have their stalls illuminated by means of electricity a piece of "Doulton" may appear good and sound, but after the purchase has been carefully carried home, and more carefully examined, a flaw is very frequently discovered. But then I suppose that the majority of visitors to the pot fair go there anticipating a little gamble, and if by chance one of them should get a good specimen, so much more the pleasure afforded in recounting the fact to her friends.

* * *

Although, the Accrington Coronation celebrations were held in June, those of the neighbouring villages of Whalley and Clitheroe (I am afraid I shall be taken to task for describing Clitheroe as a village, but it always gives one the impression of being an overgrown hamlet) reserved their junketings until, last Saturday. Even though the holidays had commenced, and numbers of the townspeople had left for the various pleasure resorts, Clitheroe was full to overflowing, for hundreds of visitors helped to swell the crowd. In the early part of the day an ox was roasted, and the Mayoress

(Mrs. Aspinall) cut the first slice, a ceremony witnessed by several thousands of residents and visitors; in fact, it looked as if all the country side had turned out to "have a. piece." At Whalley sports were held on the cricket ground in the afternoon, and in the evening the whole village took part in the torchlight procession. Of course, Accrington, Clayton, and Harwood people flocked down to Whalley in hundreds on Saturday afternoon and evening, and—well, they were well repaid for their walk. I heard a whisper about several parties having to "do" the five miles home in the rain, and on foot too. Their enthusiasm would be considerably damped, especially when they arrived at the top of the Canal Brow to find that the last tram had just left.

August 23rd

Was ever holiday weather so changeable? Certainly it was never quite so tantalising as during the last two weeks. One day began with brilliant sunshine and a clear blue sky but, ere noon the clouds had gathered and down came the rain in pitiless showers, just as we had donned some summerlike apparel and started for a good, long walk! Another day would be cloudy and miserable, but as soon as we were suitably clothed for a wet trudge, the sun shone out bewitchingly, making our macintoshes, short skirts and that abomination, an umbrella, look ludicrous. In vain we sighed for the finery left behind at our "digs." But if we Accrington people aren't temper-proof against this most variable climate by now— well, we ought to be.

September 6th

The garden party at Bank House on Saturday was a pleasant function. Considering that a number of people are away holiday-making the turn-up was good, and afforded Sir George Cotton, the new Conservative candidate for Accrington, an opportunity of becoming acquainted with many of his future friends and a few (political) enemies. The grounds, though not very extensive, are well laid out and presented a charming picture in the sunlight. Unfortunately the orchid-house was not open to the public. It is rather early yet to see these delicate flowers at their best, but it is well known that some of the finest blooms to be found hereabouts are grown at Bank House.

September 13th

I regret to hear that there is little improvement in the condition of Mrs. E.J. Riley, who has for some time past been lying dangerously ill at Arden Hall. Mrs. Riley counts friends in nearly every portion of the Accrington Division; few ladies have thrown themselves more actively than she into the social, political and religious life of the town, and all will, I am sure, join me in wishing that she may soon be among us again fully restored to health and vigour.

* * *

Can nothing be done, I wonder, to put an end to the wretched practices a cheeky band of youngsters indulge in Whalley-road? Visitors to the "Little Man Island" will not need reminding that one of the most pitiful impressions left on one's mind after traversing the island is that of the "Hi Kelly" gang. As one drives along the road there, bands of children run tumbling after the conveyance, tipple somersaults, and even stand on their heads, with noses scraping the mud. "Hi Kelly! Hi Kelly!" they shout, and thoughtless tourists foolishly scatter pence among them.

The filthy practice has been taken up here, and several times this summer I have noticed a gang of Clayton, Harwood or Rishton boys behaving similarly on the road between Harwood Bar and Whalley. Only the other day I came across several dirty lads, who ought to have been at school, sharing their muddy earnings. With faces caked with mud, shoeless, wearing no stockings, and torn garments that even the rag and bone man would disdain, they made a sorry figure. I wonder whether the county police couldn't take steps to put an end to this state of things.

* * *

A recent visit to the Accrington plunge baths has only served to convince me that the arrangements are altogether inadequate. Can't something be done towards pushing on the erection of new baths, or at any rate improving those we have? The odour which greets one at the present St. James-street establishment is not suggestive of new-mown hay; the boards around the bath may, or may not, have been raised since the baths were erected, but they certainly don't appear to have been. They ought to be replaced by some substance that would not absorb the moisture. The boards which lead from the cabins, too, might be kept cleaner, and the water—now we come to the most important item—ought to be cooler and cleaner, than it is at present. Swimming is one of the best exercises imaginable, but when indulged in such a rank atmosphere and in warm—almost hot—water, the result is generally not a happy one. A bad atmosphere is not conducive to good health, while hot water for swimming is positively ridiculous.

September 20th

From Tuesday's "Observer" I gather that harvest thanksgiving services were conducted last Sunday in at least half-a-dozen places of worship in and around Accrington. There is great similarity in these services, and it is almost impossible to say anything new about them. But for me, and for many hundreds besides, judging from last Sunday, there is always a fascination about the harvest festival at Altham Church. To spend a few hours in the old sanctuary, to see the really beautiful floral decorations, to take part in the go-ahead service, and to listen to a sterling address from the pulpit, is positively refreshing. I have not enjoyed a service like that of Sunday evening for many, many months.

Good music, an impressive service, a. vigorous well-thought-out sermon from the Vicar — everything was in good taste. "As a man sows, so shall he reap" was the burthen of the sermon—I am not sure that that is a literal quotation, but no matter.

It was an excellent discourse admirably delivered. Gifted with a splendid voice, a man of fine presence, Mr. Green commands big congregations wherever he goes, and it was not surprising that Altham Church was packed to the doors. Chancel and aisles were crowded, and people were standing at the back of the church; and yet scores were unable to gain admittance. It was a very unusual thing to see a long procession anxiously awaiting the opening of the church door prior to the service—it seemed more like a London theatre than a church.

September 27th

Accrington is poorer by the death of Mrs. Riley. She will be sorely missed. Scarcely a charitable movement in our town but has had her active and cordial support in the past. She was the Lady President of the Accrington branch of the N.S.P.C.C., and a more generous one the Society will never have. Many are the occasions on which the grounds at Arden Hall have been thrown open to the public for that and other worthy objects. The Charity Ball loses one of its promoters, the Nurses Home a good friend, and many other institutions an energetic supporter.

October 4th

Like "Th' Little Owd Chap," whose tribute I was glad to read in Tuesday's " Observer," I was one of many who waited in the wrong place to see the funeral cortege of Mrs. Riley on Saturday. It was generally thought that the route taken would be along Whalley-road and through Clayton to Altham, and scores of blinds were drawn as the hour of the funeral approached, and many people gathered along the line of route. To them it was a disappointment to learn that the cortege had turned down Washington-street, up Burnley-road, and through Huncoat. But it was doubtless all for the best. The floral tributes sent by people of all shades of thought showed how Mrs. Riley was respected and loved. A friend who went to see the flowers on the Sunday tells me she does not remember ever seeing such a collection of beautiful wreaths. White flowers predominated of course, but two or three of the wreaths were formed of roses, one, of dark red roses from Hapton House, being exquisite. The workpeople of Hapton Works sent a lovely wreath, and those from the Liberal Association and the Children's Society were conspicuous tokens.

October 11th

Mr. Will Bullough. I see, has sent £200 and Mrs. Bullough £20 to the Accrington Conservative bazaar fund. The bazaar did not reach the £5,000 aimed at, but our Conservative friends ought to be perfectly satisfied, the proceeds being nearer £4,000 than £3,000. That is a big sum of money to raise in these times. This, I trust, is the last bazaar in Accrington for many years to come. We can well spare them. They have but one redeeming feature, and that is the raising of money. If the saying one can have too much of a good thing is true at all, it is surely applicable to bazaars. Tradesmen have come to regard them as a nuisance, and some of them would not be sorry if they never heard the word bazaar again.

November 1st

Everybody seemed anxious on Monday to pay a tribute to the dead. That is not to be wondered at, for Mr. Arthur Appleby was so well know and so universally esteemed. A funeral procession of such length and so representative I have not seen before in Accrington district. The first portion of the cortege must have reached All Saints' Church ere the tail-end had left Mill House. From 40 to 50 private carriages, at I least 100 wreaths, and 700 or 800 people on foot—such a procession has certainly never been seen in Clayton-le-Moors, if in East Lancashire. Mrs. Appleby did not venture out of the house, but the four children, the nephews and nieces and Mr. Appleby's sisters went to the church. The family have my deepest sympathy.

* * *

Isn't it rather absurd to suggest that the bad weather we have had this summer is responsible for the poor attendance at our plunge baths! If the Corporation were only a little more eager to make the requisite improvements at the St James'-street establishment there would be no need to blame the weather, nor bewail a financial loss. That Accringtonians visit Blackburn and Burnley for their swimming exercises is not surprising considering the miserable facilities offered in Accrington at present.

November 22nd

The Choral Society's first concert of the season is on Wednesday, and the first Chamber concert on Friday evening. The Choral programme is mainly orchestral, and as 50 performers have been engaged from Halle's band the concert ought to be an unqualified success. If all goes off as expected it will be a feather in the cap of the Society's talented conductor, Mr. W. S. Walker. At the Chamber concert the Willy Hess String Quartet should also be a big attraction.

November 29th

Wednesday's Choral concert was undoubtedly one of the finest we have ever heard in our Town Hall. The most rosy expectations were fully realised. Halle's men were in fine form, and Mr. Walker filled the position of conductor with praiseworthy skill and care. The vocalist, Miss Muriel Foster, was all that could be desired. Possessed of a full, rounded contralto voice, which completely charmed her audience, she sang with due observance of technique and in excellent taste. Her best efforts, I thought, were "Where corals lie" and "The Swimmer" from a cycle of sea songs by Elgar. A burst of applause followed her last song, and the fair vocalist was re-called again and again, but she did not respond with another song.

* * *

As I sat at the Choral Concert on Wednesday I could not help thinking that it was a great pity the Town Hall Committee had not handed over the assembly room chairs for the Coronation bonfire on Moleside. The fire I remember was described as one of the biggest in Lancashire; if the Town Hall chairs had been added to the lumber the fire would have taken first place easily. But since the opportunity was lost, I would respectfully suggest that an auction sale is still available. Mr. Duckworth, I believe, is chairman of the Town Hall Committee. A happy idea isn't it?

December 6th

If the miserable weather we have had recently has done nothing else, it has certainly convinced many Accrington ladies that short walking skirts are preferable to long ones. Several ladies have already adopted short skirts for outdoor wear, and I am sure they look much neater than those one has to clutch with both hands; and assuredly to successfully navigate one's skirts clear of the mud during these grey damp days is a work of art — one in which unless appearances are very deceptive, few Accrington girls have attained to perfection.

December 20th

As this is the last Saturday publication of the "Observer" before Christmas, I hasten to express the hope that all my readers may have a good time during this week, and to wish them the old-time wish, "A merry Christmas." There seems every prospect of a wet Christmastide, but providing the misery is confined to the elements we'll not grumble.

1903

January 3rd

By their highly creditable performance of "Caste" at the Prince's on New Year's day, our amateurs have not only maintained but enhanced their reputation. The performances of the company in former years led to the anticipation that they would do justice to one of the best and most popular of Mr. T. W. Robertson's productions, and there was a large gathering, including many well-known townspeople, and the ministerial element was also conspicuous.

The cast of "Caste"

The dramatis persona was as follows:- Mr. Walter E. Kearns; Mr. Arnold H.Barnes; Mr. Fred J. Haywood; Mr. Will Kenyon; Mr. Bert Rushton; Miss Con. M. Kenyon; Miss Hilda W. Kenyon; Mrs. C. W. Crowther (Miss Maggie Crawshaw).

Miss Hilda Kenyon, as the daughter of the drunken "Eccles," established herself in the favour of the audience by her graceful impersonation of this most difficult part. To the various moods of lover, wife and widow she adapted herself with remarkable correctness. Her style and expression were charming, and her dialogue excellent throughout; indeed, it would be difficult to conceive a more finished "Esther."

"Polly", the part created by Miss Marie Wilton—now Mrs. Bancroft—had a clever representative in Mrs. C. W. Crowther, whose interpretation would compare favourably with many professionals. The inimitable humour and vivacity of the role were well maintained. Mrs. Crowther (then Miss Maggie Crawshaw) has often appeared in local performances, notably with the Amateurs in opera, and much was expected of her. The greatest compliment that can be paid her, then, is to say that she fully realised anticipations.

Miss Constance Kenyon made a prim Marquise de St. Maur. She retained the dignity of the proud mother, and caused not a little amusement by her frequent quotations from Froissart, aimed at her son, the Hon. George D'Alroy. The part of the Hon. GeorgeD'Alroy was ably portrayed by Mr. W. E. Kearns, who spoke his lines perfectly, and whose acting was as good as his speech. Mr. Arnold Barnes also gave a capital performance as "Captain Hawtree." Mr. Fred Haywood showed fine talent as drunken old " Eccles." Mr. Haywood, by the day, seems to be often cast in the part of an inebriated old man. His make-up is always excellent, and he is always entertaining. Mr. W. Kenyon, as " Sam Gerridge," added another to his long list of successes, and it would be almost safe to say that his excellent achievement in last year's operatic performance was eclipsed by his fine interpretation of the part of the gasfitter. As the prospective husband of "Polly," some amusing passages occurred between him and his "intended" in the third act. Although Mr. Ben Rushton as " Dixon " had little to say, and less to dot he acted his part very accurately.

The manner in which everyone acquitted themselves is a matter for congratulation, and especial praise is due to Mr. R. W. Kenyon, the promoter, and Mr H. Heap, the secretary. Mr. E. Whittaker's Orchestra, under the leadership of Mr. J. Hanson, rendered selections of music. The wigs and "make-ups" were supplied by Watkinson, Preston, and the military costumes by Birkenshaw, Liverpool. Mr. Fred Green arranged the scenery. Mr. J. B. Ormerod very kindly placed the theatre at the company's disposal.

The manner in which everyone acquitted themselves is a matter for congratulation, and especial praise is due to Mr. R. W. Kenyon, the promoter, and Mr H. Heap, the secretary. Mr. E. Whittaker's Orchestra, under the leadership of Mr. J. Hanson, rendered selections of music

January 10th

The invitations have been issued this week for the Gentlemen's Private Subscription Dance to be held in the Town Hall on Friday, the 30th of January. I hear that the arrangements are to be on a more elaborate scale than in former years, so those who have received invitations should consider themselves lucky, for if the enjoyment in any way surpasses that derived from the dance last year they are in for a good time. Of late years it has been voted quite one of the jolliest dances, and as there is a scarcity of both public and private dances in Accrington this season it will be hailed with more than usual pleasurable anticipation.

* * *

Seeing that I took no part in its production, I am again at liberty to congratulate the "Observer" staff upon Tuesday's Birthday Number.

Mrs. Dr. Nuttall's contribution, "A walk down the street," interested me very much. More than once have I referred in this column to the young people who spend night after night aimlessly traversing our main streets, apparently with no object in view save that of seeing and being seen. For hours the same batches of youths and girls stroll along, utterly regardless of the waste of valuable time. Mrs. Nuttall has evidently made a special study of those who frequent our public streets, and has made some startling revelations.

One or two extracts from Mrs. Nuttall's article will suffice to point out the deplorable state of affairs-.——

"Barely have we turned the corner ere we are jostled by a drunken man, who but narrowly escapes colliding with the tramcar in his unsteady passage across the street, and our ears are pained by language that smites us harder than the physical thrust. Close by stands a group of young people laughing and talking so loudly that we hope they do not hear the obscenity we quail beneath. And yet above the laughter rings a sickening jest. " 'A've been T.T. sin' th' Fair, but I'm saving up neaw for a bonny do at Christmas." This from the lips of an apparently respectable and certainly well-dressed young woman."

Mrs. Nuttall repeats the confession of a "bright, merry-faced wholesome looking young girl" over heard in the street—*"Oh! I reckon nothing of being tied to one young man, I like a change; change is always good."* Another extract:- *"One Sunday evening some months ago I walked behind a party of young people—three youths and two maidens—and as they preceded me along Blackburn-road I noticed how beautifully dressed the girls were and how gentlemanly the bearing of their knights' errant. Judge of my surprise when the whole party stopped at the lighted window of a tobacconist shop; the girls entered, and laughingly emerged therefrom a few minutes later each smoking a cigarette."*

I give these extracts in the hope that some fond mothers may see them, and may be led to inquire into the whereabouts of her own children in the evenings. Unless my judgment is at fault many of the girls and boys who take a delight in parading Blackburn-road do not spring from the lower classes, as is generally imagined.

* * *

It is a great pity one of the contributors didn't choose "Accrington Trams" for his subject. I'm sure with photographs to illustrate it the article might have been made quite interesting —certainly amusing. Mr. Bamber Baron, I see refers to our "great, big, ugly trams" in a mild way and supposes "a change will come ultimately." He suggests that our cars should be sold for greenhouses, refreshment rooms, offices, etc., and our lines electrified at once. Humph! It would be just as well if he tried to electrify the minds of those who have the business in hand, for they are evidently considering the matter still, and probably will continue to do so for some time yet.

* * *

Many difficulties will present themselves to those who endeavour to carry out the new Licensing Act, but if it only succeeds thoroughly in one respect, that of checking the cruelty which has been inflicted on the poor, helpless little creatures who have been at the mercy of drunken mothers in public houses and the public streets, it will rank as one of the finest measures ever passed.

January 17th

Each of our Mayors seems to signalise his term of office in his own particular way. Each, too, during his Mayoralty, manages to bring happiness and enjoyment to some section of the community. This year Alderman Broughton and his good lady have followed the example set last year of trying to bring happiness into lives where little sunshine falls. A thousand little bairns have romped and joked and made merry, and I am sure the Mayor's guests of previous years will be only too pleased that it has so happened.

I am selfish enough to regret that, seemingly, the pleasant succession of Mayoral receptions have been broken, especially in this quiet social season. But when I saw the almost riotous

Alderman Broughton

happiness of the Mayoress's guests both at Willow-street school and the Town Hall on Saturday my selfishness evaporated somewhat. The delight manifested by the children in the good things provided for them was a treat to see, and a reflected joy seemed to illumine the faces of those who waited upon them.

* * *

One wonders why, with such gentlemen in our town as Dr. Clayton and others, who appear to have the welfare of the rising generation at heart, such an evil-smelling building as that known as the baths in St. James'-street is allowed to remain in our midst. Why do not these gentlemen advocate new swimming baths and earn the everlasting gratitude of those who count swimming in a healthy atmosphere one of the finest exercises one could possibly have? Although everyone admits that the present establishment is a disgrace to the town, the general opinion—of the councillors—seems to be that nothing should be done to remove the stigma until the electricity works have become a paying concern, and the Corporation have got Blackburn-road property and the trams off their hands. Judging by the time expended in thought on the tram question, we shall not have the pleasure of seeing new baths for some time to come yet. I think if such admirable suggestions as the erection of new baths and the establishment of creches for the protection of infant life were acted upon at once instead of being allowed to grow old in thought, the disease of "tete montee" might be a little less prevalent amongst the councillors.

It is a pity some of the councillors' wives do not indulge in swimming exercises, as I'm sure, if they did, something would be done to alter the miserable facilities provided in Accrington.

January 24th

What a glorious day was Saturday! Dust and rust were gleefully rubbed from skates that for twelve months or more had not seen the light of day. Merry-faced were the groups of skaters who made the most of the brief spell of real winter's weather on the ice-bound ponds and lodges. The cricket field, too, afforded enjoyment for quite a crowd of people who, despite the cutting wind, declared that it was the finest day's sport they'd had for ages. There were many clever skaters on the field during the day, and many more who were apparently wearing skates for the first time, and who took the bumps and falls as part of the day's enjoyment, much to the amusement of the spectators.

January 31st

None who visited the Town Hall on Wednesday could doubt the popularity of the social and dance in aid of the Nursing Association. The good natured crowd in the assembly room spoke much for the steady perseverance of the ticket sellers, and the ladies who organised and carried out the affair so successfully are to be complimented. 'Twas perhaps as well the small tables in the room were dispensed with. Scarcely a square-foot of space was available in the Assembly room while the concert was in progress and I felt quite sorry for a large number of latecomers who were unable to obtain seats at all.

A few electric fans would have been welcomed when the dancing commenced. The heat became almost stifling. Many have expressed the wish that the Nursing Association will benefit annually by this enjoyable, if rather warm, entertainment.

February 7th

The general opinion of those who danced and made merry once again at the Gentlemen's Subscription Dance, was that Friday's gathering eclipsed all previous efforts. Perhaps the fact that it was held in the Town Hall accounted for the added enjoyment. Anyhow the alteration was a great improvement.

The room looked charming. Plants and mirrors were arranged skilfully on the ledges, and an array of palms and other tall plants lined the front of the platform, behind which were placed comfortable lounges and chairs, a soft carpet and two large electric lamps with yellow shades. Needless to say, this cosy retreat was much in demand during the evening. Mr. George Thornton's orchestra did justice to the dance music and appeared to derive almost as much enjoyment from the evening as the dancers. Mr. Thornton conducted with more than usual zest, and his good-tempered expression and joviality seemed quite contagious.

A correspondent furnishes descriptions of the dresses worn—from memory I fear. White was much in evidence and as usual looked very nice, but one of the most charming gowns was of rose-coloured silk, very simply made with elbow sleeves, and turned-down collar covered with insertion, a touch of velvet ribbon was introduced on the sleeve and a broad band of black velvet cunningly bowed at the left side of the corsage completed an appropriate toilette.

One young lady wore a cream cashmere, with a deep berthe of lovely lace, and elbow sleeves with frill. A brunette who wore blue flowers in her coiffure was neatly gowned in a tucked white glace silk, with tulle sleeves with white embroidered trimming. Another white silk suited a fair girl to perfection; a multiplicity of tiny V-shaped tucks on the skirt and bodice interspersed with rows of pretty cream insertion. Girlish and sweet was a white muslin worn by a young lady who evidently enjoyed to the full a rollicking polka; the skirt had frills and loops of green satin ribbon, with sash in a similar shade of green.

* * *

When I was much younger Accrington people always seemed to be boasting about their clean streets. I am sorry we can no longer lay claim to the description of a clean town. Of one thing I am sure. Taking our main roads as a standard, there is not a town in Lancashire in a worse condition than Accrington. The filth left by our trams——a compound of dust, oil, and water—is abominable. The road in front of the market has not been dry a single day this winter, and it never will be presentable so long as the water and dirt from the trams are deposited there without protest.

February 14th

Last night, in the Liberal club, Miss Bright and the pupil teachers gave their annual dance, which, as usual, proved a most enjoyable gathering.

February 21st

Last Saturday our Amateurs successfully maintained the high opinion formed of their performances earlier in the week. Many regretted that "The Mikado" was at an end, though no doubt those who took an active part in the proceedings would be glad enough that their work was over. They have worked hard and deserve all praise. On Saturday night, at all events, the public were lavish in their praise, and the curtain was rung down to the accompaniment of deafening applause.

* * *

The Gentlemen's Subscription Dance held in the Conservative Club last Friday was a very enjoyable function. The dancing went merrily all through, the guests numbering about two hundred and thirty. Refreshments were served on a long table at one end of the room near the orchestra; the music, as usual, being under the guidance of Mr. Geo. Thornton. Some of the ladies wore lovely gowns, many of them apparently quite fresh, owing no doubt to the scarcity of social functions in Accrington this season.

March 14th

Accrington folk showed their appreciation of the facilities offered them to hear the world- famed Sousa's band on Monday afternoon by flocking into our Town Hall in big crowds. Long before two o'clock people were waiting outside the market-side entrance of the hall heedless of the rain which was striving, in Accrington's best style, to damp their ardour as well as their clothes.

At last the doors opened, and the waiters on entering discovered a fair sprinkling of Accrington's aristocrats in command of the back seats. Naturally such a large brass band, would sound much better at the rear of the building, though why such profuse apologies were considered necessary to explain the presence of these people was rather puzzling to the usual occupants of the shilling seats who listened with wonder to the remarks made in high-pitched stage whispers, and marvelled—" You here?" "Yes, you see we're shilling people to-day. Of course, had it been a local affair or anything of that sort you know we should have been in the front seats," etc., etc. Obviously they had not pocketed all their vanity with the surplus shillings. Certainly frank and perchance more truthful was another remark overheard, "Well, it's no use shamming; I came here because it was a shilling."

In due course the members of the band and their energetic leader made their appearance. When the applause had subsided somewhat the orchestra struck up "Carneval Romaine." Then the crowd commenced to enjoy themselves. At least they appeared to be doing so. Personally I was rather disappointed, especially in the conductor, of whom I had read and heard so much. He was not half as entertaining as I had expected. Once or twice in "El Capitan" and '"Washington Post" there were signs of the vigour one associates with the name of Sousa, but nothing more. A little eccentric Sousa may be but he has taken infinite pains with his band, and has brought the members of it to a state of perfection in the art of playing such pieces as he selects. It was in the marches that they really scored.

* * *

Of course, hats—and some big ones, too— were worn by those who disregarded the fact that the people behind them had come to see Sousa and not their millinery. I was feeling most depressed by a couple of black ostrich feathers which had evidently weathered many a storm, but still stood upright and straight as sentinels in the hat just in front of me, when a woman from behind gently prodded the wearer with an umbrella, and the offending headgear was removed, much to the relief of everybody near.

March 21st

V ery creditable indeed was the production of the "Triple Bill" on Wednesday. A crowd of well-dressed people assembled in the New Church schoolroom quite early, and evidently enjoyed to the full the efforts of these young amateurs. "Ici on Parle Francais," a very humorous farcet was substituted for "Done on both sides." Everything went smoothly with the exception of a falling piece of scenery, which threatened to annihilate the excitable Frenchman. The audience, however, was a sympathetic one, and after a pause of but a minute's duration the farce proceeded.

"Jerry and a Sunbeam," a dialogue in one act, was in capable hands. Miss Constance M. Kenyon, as 'Mary Bellasis', was a decided success, and showed a complete comprehension of her part. both in face-play and stage-bearing she was good, and her self-possession throughout excellent. Very much at home also was Mr. Walter E. Kearns—"Jerry Corbet." His delivery was crisp and natural, and showed signs of careful study. In fact some of the epithets of the approved Sunday school type must have been practised pretty regularly to attain such perfection.

" Ici on Parle Francais" was boisterously funny, and elicited roars of laughter. Miss Hilda Kenyon had perhaps not sufficient scope as "Mrs. Spriggins," though she succeeded in a marked degree in impersonating the dignified descendant of the Fitz-Pentonvilles; Anna Maria (Miss Margaret Rendell) caused much laughter—her tie and ostrich feathers were a sight to behold. Miss Ruby Rendell made a quiet and unobtrusive "Angelina." Mr. Will Kenyon, of "Pooh-bah" renown, as "Mr. Spriggins," was also very good. In the garb of "Victor Dubois" Mr. Fred Haywood was easily recognisable. His manner and gestures were certainly much better than his French. Mr. Ben Rushton played the part of Major Regulus Rattan with necessary gusto, and Miss Constance Kenyon again shone as "Julia," his wife.

March 28th

W ith better principals Thursday's concert would have been among the best ever given by the Choral Society. The chorus was in splendid trim. Every member appeared bent on making the very best of Coleridge-Taylor's splendid work. Though it may seem unfair to criticise one who came as a substitute almost at a moment's notice, it must be said that Miss Blaney was not all we could have wished. The time-beating movements in which she indulged rather detracted from the wild solemnity of the death-bed scene of Minnehaha. "Spring has come", the opening solo in "Hiawatha's Departure," was far away her best effort. "From the brow of Hiawatha," etc., was lacking in power, and revealed a want of familiarity with the part.

The tenor, Mr. Herbert Grover, was off form, especially in "Onaway, awake, beloved," and I was not surprised to hear afterwards that he had been indisposed, and had to leave his sick room to fill his Accrington engagement.

A word about the chorus girls. Their general appearance would be much improved by uniformity of colouring in their attire. White always looks well, and there is no doubt that if they all adopted it the effect would be much prettier.

* * *

It has been very reasonably suggested that if men will continue to make a nuisance of themselves and cause the greatest inconvenience to ladies by going in and out of their seats between the acts at the theatres, they should be asked to sit apart in seats specially reserved for those who thus wish to fidget. One is weary of pointing out how grossly selfish and unmannerly it is for men to push, squeeze, and force their way several times during an evening's entertainment, past ladies whose dresses naturally suffer from the savage treatment to which they are subjected. Light materials are soiled, fragile nets and laces and trimmings are damaged, while their wearers are compelled either to continually rise to let a stream of men pass them, or else endure the discomfort, not to say pain, of being temporarily wedged between their seats and the passers-by. If women were to do the same thing, measures would be taken to abate the nuisance, and, as the chief patrons of the theatre, they ought surely to be entitled in their turn to consideration in this respect.

April 1st

Mr. Duckworth Holding, son of Mr. Grimshaw Holding, of Broadfield House, Oswaldtwistle, was married to Miss Hannah Crankshaw, daughter of the late Mr. Crankshaw, farmer and grocer, Green Haworth, at St. James's Church, on Wednesday, the Rev. Canon Rogers officiating. The bride wore a grey costume with hat to correspond. Miss Nellie Crankshaw, the bridesmaid, was attired in a crushed strawberry-coloured dress. The bride was given away by her brother, Mr. H. Crankshaw, and Mr. W. Holding was best man. The couple went to Llandudno to spend the honeymoon. The presents were numerous.

* * *

For the benefit of St. Paul's (Barnfield) Stall at the forthcoming Christ Church bazaar, an entertainment was given in St. Paul's Schoolroom on Wednesday evening. There was a good attendance. The artistes were the St. John's Black and White minstrels, the programme being contributed to by Misses R. Calvert, Hartley and Maudsley, Messrs. R. Calvert, G. Ashworth, junr., F. Pilling, G. W. Watson, R. T. Holgate, V. Grundy, F. Pilling, C. Ashworth, W. E. Bradshaw, F. Rigby, R. Calvert, and J. Whittaker, and Master G. Holgate.

May 9th

Truly we are having merry May weather — between the storms. The crowd waiting to see the laying of the foundation stones of the new Ambulance Drill Hall on Saturday did not regard the May weather very favourably. And the processionists certainly didn't look very merry. Saturday's collection must have suffered seriously by the heavy downpour of rain, and after Sunday's parade the ambulance men looked like the proverbial "drowned rats." One does not feel particularly generous with soaking garments and the water from a neighbour's umbrella trickling down one's neck. Lady Petre did not emerge from her carriage at all until the sky cleared—Sir G. Petre laid the first stone in her behalf. The procession, of course had its attractions for the multitude, but even the lively tunes played by the bands failed to dispel the gloom. How very different it would have been if only old "King Sol" had smiled bewitchingly on the scene! Doubtless the bazaar which is being promoted will go a long way towards raising the necessary £2,000 for the building. Sunday, too, was a disappointing day. Bright new gowns were laid aside in despair, and folks wended their way to the sermons past dripping house fronts and over innumerable puddles.

* * *

A stranger in the vicinity of the Accrington Town Hall on Wednesday evening, might well have paused and asked what was the matter. Everything was stir and hustle. Innumerable vehicles were conveying groups of children, and if one waited to see the conveyances deposit their human freight it was easily to perceive the children were attired for some more than ordinary function. People, too, were streaming to the hall in large processions, while there was a crowd of spectators eager to catch a glimpse of the little ones as they alighted. Had the stranger inquired he would have learnt that it was the May Festival of the Accrington Temperance Society and District Band of Hope Union, and that the ancient custom of crowning the May Queen was to be observed in the Town Hall. Entering the ante-room of that building what a scene of animation there is? The children who are to do homage to their Queen are disloading themselves of their sombre over-garments and displaying their gayer attire. Soon everything is in readiness for the coronation, and marching in procession to the assembly room above they take their places on the platform. It is a fascinating picture they present. Just fancy three hundred little maidens, arrayed in white from top to toe, their faces radiant with smiles, and their eyes sparkling with delight, seated in picturesque array, under the brilliant illumination of the electric light. Who could see and not admire? To hear them unitedly chant their praise of glorious May was a most exhilarating experience.

May 16th

It is regrettable that twenty-five lady members of our Mechanics' Institute should have resigned their membership this year. But this fact only points to the advisability of electing a ladies' committee to look after ladies' interests. The directors set aside a ladies' room a few years ago, but since then there has been no additional improvement made to that particular room. Several times in this column have I suggested games or a piano as pleasant additions likely to induce ladies to become members. Then afternoon tea is procurable in other institutes, why not in ours? If it can be obtained there is no notice up to that effect. Ladies have been nominated to the directorate in former years but never returned. An energetic ladies' committee I think could soon repair the damage done to the list of members, and might even find a means of wiping off the debt.

May 23rd

Summer at last—two whole days of it and fair promise of more to come. What a delightful change to be sure. (Hope it won't change before these lines appear in print.) It comes just in the nick of time, when the railway and steamboat companies are beguiling us with their list of Whitsuntide trips here, there and everywhere, and already the warmth and the sunshine begin to infect us with the holiday spirit. It wants but a week of Whitsuntide, and seeing that Whit-week this time fits in with the half-year end at Messrs. Howard and Bullough's works, the lucky employees at that great concern will be able to devote the full week to holidaying. At some of the local mills the rumour has been going round that, in view of the cotton crisis, they too would shut down for the whole week, but I do not find any confirmation of the story. The probabilities are that, except at Clayton-le-Moors, the mill holidays will be confined to Whit-Monday.

* * *

One sees with regret the number of notices of warning to individuals with a penchant for mischief. Not that these are unnecessary. I suppose it would be a state of affairs altogether too idealistic to have a park where every visitor is so alive to the public interest as to render warnings superfluous. At all events damage has been committed to no little extent, particularly at Milnshaw Park, where mischievous lads have robbed the nests of eggs and brood, and have also done considerable injury to the shrubs and flower beds. Notices are now posted threatening dire penalties on offenders when caught. An example by the magistrates would have wondrous effect upon those whose delight it is to play pranks with public property. Parents might do a good deal by exercising a restraining influence upon the young hopefuls who blossom in the parks after school hours.

May 30th

Every bullet has its billet, but it is not often, happily, that a stray leaden messenger seeks repose in a shop window. But that was what happened at a tradesman's establishment in Washington-street, Accrington, on Saturday afternoon. The shopkeeper's daughter was just reaching up to a cupboard near the window when there was a smash and a crash in the corner of the window nearest which she was standing, and an investigation resulted in the astonishing discovery that a bullet, evidently fired from a rifle, had caused the mischief. When picked up the bullet was still warm, so that there could be no question as to its being the culprit. Naturally the family, and especially the girl, who had escaped only by inches, were a good deal upset.

Now where, did that bullet come from? The likeliest explanation is that it was a stray shot that had ricocheted all the way from the Huncoat or Hapton rifle ranges. Some time ago, I am told, another window in the same district was shattered by a mysterious bullet in pretty much the same way. That there are such things as bullets getting very far wide of the mark, one only need take a walk over the footpath leading from the Coppice to the old road towards the Griffin's Head when firing is going on to discover. More than once when walking in that locality on a Saturday afternoon, have I been made apprehensively aware of the presence of the deadly missiles by the "buzzing" through the air, with the noise of a discharging rocket, of a misdirected or rebounding shot. If I happen to be in that direction when shooting is going on, it does not take long to climb over the stiles and resume the comforting shelter of the stone wall.

June 6th

What an ideal touch of summer has followed the winter of our discontent. A finer and sunnier Whit-week we have not had for years. Enfield Fair has flourished and disappeared for another twelve months. The cry of the cocoanut and brandy-snap vendors is silenced for the time being. No longer are the midnight slumbers of Claytonians disturbed by the whistle and music (?) of the merry-go-rounds. In short, Whalley-road has once more donned her garb of respectability, and the holidays are ended or will be to-night.

* * *

When is a holiday not a holiday? When it is a Bank Holiday. Anyone who has observed a Bank Holiday crowd must have noticed that it is not truly a festive crowd. Travelling in stuffy railway carriages packed with people journeying to a still more crowded holiday resort is not an ideal way of spending a holiday, nor is it one conducive to health and happiness. Indeed, the tired look on the faces of passengers who alighted at Accrington station after a dreary railway journey of several hours on Monday night was anything but healthy, and happiness was a feature altogether lacking. Holiday making in masses is a deplorable mistake, but there appears no remedy for the evil. Unfortunately the chief sufferers are the sober, hardworking and law-abiding citizens.

* * *

The state of the Accrington Choral Society's funds is deplorable. It is a question now of passing round the hat or having a bazaar to clear the debt, the latter being the more favoured project. I trust the amount will be forthcoming ere another season or the high standard attained musically by our society may suffer.

July 4th

Although it had been noised abroad that the marriage of Miss Tere Fox and Mr. Richard Wilding (Blackburn) was to be a very quiet affair, the Church of the Sacred Heart was Mr. Richard Wilding and Miss Tere Fox crowded on Wednesday afternoon long before the time fixed for the tying of the nuptial knot. A fair sprinkling of fashionably attired ladies were among the waiting crowd and a goodly number of babes in arms. The decorations of the sanctuary were much admired. Red

poppies showed up well against the white marguerites, and the palms looked refreshingly green.

The moment the bride appeared a march, "The silver trumpets," was played on the organ. The bridal gown was of ivory satin trimmed with beautiful Irish lace, the train being adorned with chiffon and orange blossom. She wore a veil of Honiton lace, surmounted by a coronet of orange blossom, and was altogether a dainty picture.

Mr. Richard Wilding and Miss Tere Fox

The shower bouquet she carried was composed of white heather, roses, and lilac. Master Alban Wilding, aged three years, undertook the duties of train-bearer, and sweet and kissable he looked in his little blue tunic. A very pretty touch at the conclusion of the service was the singing of "Ave Maria" by Mrs. Kilner, of Blackburn.

July 11th

The crowning of the Rose Queen on Saturday was a very pretty ceremony. Sir George Petre's kindness in throwing open the grounds of Dunkenhalgh was thoroughly appreciated. Rarely indeed has Dunkenhalgh welcomed such a crowd of people; The Queen, Miss Cissie Foster, in her trained dress with its wealth of flowers, and her maids of honour clad in white, looked charming. Their stately mien while Miss Marion Appleby placed the crown of roses on the young queen's head, was very quaint. Miss Kathleen Britcliffe, the retiring queen, attended by her retinue, also looked sweet.

July 18th

The Accrington branch of the N.S.P.C.C. are particularly unfortunate with their cricket matches. Last year, and again last Wednesday, rain interfered with the arrangements. There is no doubt that the wet weather on Wednesday prevented a big attendance on the cricket ground. Fortunately, however, those who had risked a wetting to watch our sturdy policemen play had a good time. The rain ceased during the match, and for a short time at any rate a burst of sunshine brightened up the scene. True, its stay was of short duration. The ladies' committee and the waitresses were kept very busy during the afternoon, attending to the wants of the guests.

Refreshments were eaten with evident relish, and the strawberries were pronounced excellent. It is expected that the Society will benefit to the amount of at least £40. May the weather next year be more propitious!

* * *

A correspondent writes:- *"Can anyone say when those wretched abominations, our baths, are likely to be improved or replaced? If the baths merit a quarter of the compliments (?) I heard showered on them by a party of young ladies the other day, the sooner they tumble into the Calder the better. Greasy, evil-smelling boards, conveniences with odour unbearable, water sable as to colour—these are but a few of the qualities the young swimmers attributed to our baths. If these young lady friends are anywhere near the mark, it is high time some of our councillors took the baths question up."*

July 25th

It is many years since a wedding on such a magnificent scale was witnessed in Accrington district as the one at St. John's Church, Baxenden, last Wednesday, when Miss Kearns was given away at the altar to Mr. Edward Hoyle. As anticipated, crowds of people gathered in front of the sacred edifice as the time of the ceremony approached. Only ticket-holders, however, were admitted. The chancel was very beautifully decorated with tall palms and ferns, the work of Miss Kearns and her friends. The service was choral throughout. To be the central figure of such an impressive ceremony must have been a trying ordeal. The graceful folds of the bridal gown of white crepe de chine, with satin train, were especially becoming to Miss Kearns's slim figure. The Maltese lace with which it was trimmed was very beautiful. She wore a wreath of orange blossoms and veil of Brussels lace. Her shower bouquet of orchids, heather and orange blossom was lovely. Wagner's Bridal March from "Lohengrin" was played on the organ as the bride walked up the aisle smiling winsomely. The three bridesmaids, Miss Mabel Kearns, Miss Christina Eadie and Miss Mildrid Riley were attired in cream voile dresses adorned with lace and deep collars. Their hats were of crinoline with lilac trimming, with bouquets of sweet peas.

The Misses Craven Hoyle and Mollie Tall acted as train-bearers. Their little white frocks and girlish hats of white chiffon looked very sweet. They carried sprays of lilac-coloured sweet peas. Another little maid [Miss Kathleen Galloway), the cushion-bearer, was also clad in white.

The mother of the bride (Mrs. Kearns) wore a gown of transparent black and white over green. Her toque was of black and white to match, with red roses and white osprey. She carried a shower bouquet of crimson roses. Mrs. Hoyle's (mother of the bridegroom) gown was of lovely white silk, with over dress of fine black lace, elaborately embroidered, with bonnet also of black and white. Showers of confetti descended on the happy pair as they left the church. A reception was held after the ceremony at Baxenden House, followed by luncheon served in a marquee specially erected for the occasion in the grounds. The bride and bridegroom are spending their honeymoon in Switzerland. The bride's travelling costume was of pale green with picture hat of red poppies.

* * *

The Accrington Moss-lane tennis players were successful in their match with Colne on Saturday, winning 21 sets to 11. The return match will take place on the Moss-lane ground sometime in August.

* * *

Wednesday was a red letter day in the lives of the poor children of Accrington, Oswaldtwistle, Rishton, and Clayton- Moors, many of whom on that day enjoyed their first glimpse of the sea and first sight of the golden sands which mark the confines of the mighty ocean. There are in Accrington district many people ever ready to assist those less fortunate than themselves, and a number of these, banded together at the Poor Children's Treat Committee, have during the past few weeks been busy collecting subscriptions to cover the cost of providing a day by the sea for those who could not provide it for themselves.

Their appeal has met with a hearty response, and Mr. Jabez Beckett, the treasurer, had about £100 at his disposal. Upon the shoulders of Messrs. J. Spencer, school attendance officer, and T. W. Lord, assistant overseer, fell the secretarial work, including such troublesome matters as railway arrangements and the big question of commissariat.

The total number of children who went on the trip was 880—Accrington 450, Church and Oswaldtwistle 325, Rishton 80, Clayton-le-Moors 25. Unfortunately rain was falling heavily when Wednesday morning broke, and the prospects were gloomy indeed. There was a fine interval while the children assembled, but just before they reached the railway station the rain came down heavily.

The Church and Oswaldtwistle contingent met at the Police Station, and were regaled with oranges. Headed by the Christian Institute Band, they marched to the station, but had not arrived there when the rain fell.

The Clayton section were conveyed by tram and the Rishtonians joined the train at Rishton. All was bustle and excitement at the railway stations, and the workers had rather an anxious time of it.

The train left Accrington at 8-25, and almost all the way the rain fell heavily. But notwithstanding it failed to damp the spirits of the children, who en route sang snatches of songs, and   munched the biscuits with which they had been provided, several of the children enjoying the wonderful experience of their first train ride.

Ere Lytham was reached the clouds lifted, and on arrival the sun gladdened the hearts of the visitors. The children were marched in procession to the beach, which could not have been better arranged for such a trip, there being acres of green sward, in addition to the extensive sands.

The manifold delights of the seaside were soon being tasted, clogs and stockings were speedily doffed, and paddling indulged in. Crabs, etc., were hunted, and the delight of one little fellow who captured a plaice was unbounded. Cricket bats and balls had been brought for the boys, and skipping ropes and balls for the girls, whilst Mr. R. Hargreaves had provided ice cream in abundance for all. Then there were the donkeys, Messrs. T. E. Higham and J. T. Rothwell, of Lytham, having placed quadrupeds at the disposal of the trippers. The sun shone undimmed, and the change from the town to the seaside must have been a great treat to the children.

Just before twelve the whistle sounded and the children gathered on the green in 11 companies of 25, and were fed by the attendants. The menu consisted of a substantial potted meat sandwich, a four ounce bun, and coffee. Then the Mayor and Mayoress, who were present, gave each an orange, after which the children were soon again exploring the wonders of the sea-shore.

It would be too much to expect that the day should pass off entirely without mishap, and one girl got an unexpected ducking, as did a boy who chivalrously went out to her assistance. Four hours of it, and then again came feeding time, the food being buttered teacake, a three ounce bun, and tea. The catering was done by Mr. Riley, of St. Annes. The food was brought in baskets on a lurry, and the hot tea in farmers' milk kits. A company of pierrots entertained the company, and then after another hour on the beach, the time arrived for return. They were marched in procession, and, headed by the band from Oswaldtwistle, paraded to Lytham Station, which was left at 7-20 p.m., Accrington being reached just before nine o'clock. A few of the children had managed to lose articles of attire, some a stocking, some a cap, but, thanks to the efficient arrangements, there were no serious mishaps, and all the children arrived home safely, the better for their outing.

August 29th

The holiday season is at its height at present, and all those who can possibly afford it are out of town revelling in the pleasures of seaside or country resorts. Serges and light woollen materials are in demand for travelling gowns, while they come in very usefully on the many dull and even cold afternoons which an English summer is never without. These toilettes are of the loose bolero and pleated skirt description for the most part, for this fashion has fulfilled the continued vogue foretold for it by the chroniclers of fashion, and is not only worn now but will continue to be seen on into early winter in, of course, heavier materials. Many of these costumes are trimmed with braidings of all kinds, which become more popular each month, and are certainly much more beautiful than the heavy cloth braids and their jet and gimp fringes which were fashionable in our mothers' youth, and which they are supposed to closely imitate. I wonder with what astonishment our grandmothers would view the fascinating varieties of silk, chenille, velvet, and tinsel cordings and braidings which are to-day to be purchased for the same or even lesser prices than were paid by them for coarse and inartistic work.

September 26th

Mrs. Nuttall (Avenue-parade) writes: *"Dear 'Stella,'—Earlier in the year you very kindly drew attention to my little effort to awaken thought amongst readers of the "Observer and Times" respecting the growing evil of street peregrination by the young people of our town. The interest evinced by your remarks on that occasion encourages me to seek to enlist your sympathy concerning a conference of women workers to be held in Oak-street Congregational School on Tuesday, October 6th. This conference is under the auspices of the Lancashire County Union of the National British Women's Temperance Association, and will be addressed by women of culture and refinement who are earnestly engaged in combating social evils, especially the twin evils of intemperance and impurity. Many of these are women who have literally given themselves to the unspeakable difficulties and disappointments of rescue work, women who assuredly share Christ's agony and load of sin-bearing. The Countess of Carlisle had hoped to be present—she is our national president now, having recently succeeded Lady Henry Somerset—but ill-health has necessitated her cancelling all such engagements for the near future. I will send you a programme of these meetings in due course. My object in writing before arrangements are completed is to ask if you will please kindly name the fact that such meetings are impending—for, interested as your readers undoubtedly are in matters artistic and sartorial, yet there are certainly those amongst them who recognise and reach after beauty and adornment of another kind."*

October 3rd

Ihave been asked to say a good word for the Literary and Philosophical Society. With pleasure. I attended several of its lectures at the Mechanics' Institution last winter, and I was convinced they were deserving of far better audiences than ever assembled. It is to be hoped there will be considerable improvement during the coming winter or Mr. Hartley Herald, the secretary, will feel even more discouraged than at the end of last session, when the members had to seriously discuss whether the society ought to be allowed to lapse. The opening lecture is on Monday evening, when Mr. Henry Neville, senior member of the China Commercial Mission, is to speak on "The China man at home."

October 10th

Friends of our local Amateurs would be pleased to see the announcement of the caste for "Iolanthe " in Tuesday's " Observer and Times." With the exception of the Fairy Queen, all the principal parts were allotted at Monday night's rehearsal. The selection on the part of the committee I am sure will give satisfaction. Two new hands appear in the list of principals—Mr. Ben Bury and Mr. Tom Noble. It seems almost paradoxical to refer to Mr. Bury as a "new hand." but this I believe will be his first appearance in light opera. He is, of course, well known in the concert room, where he is an ever acceptable artist, and he should prove a decided acquisition. Mr. Tom Noble has been in the opera chorus two or three years, but has not before had the opportunity of taking a leading part.

* * *

It is interesting to learn that the "tram" question was discussed at the monthly meeting of the Town Council. Whether discussion will be the limit of the efforts made to end these street ornaments remains to be seen.

The question of new public baths is, I fear, but a minor consideration with the members of the Council. The fact that many Accrington ladies and gentlemen visit adjoining towns for their swimming exercises is no credit to the town.

October 17th

Notwithstanding the hour's delay caused by the failure of the electric lights, the Hippodrome, a new structure erected on Ellison's Tenement, was crowded on Monday night, when the first programme of the season was successfully carried through. Long before seven o'clock, the time announced for the opening of the first "show," an enormous crowd had gathered in front of the corrugated iron building; but the doors remained closed. People speculated as to the cause. At last it was noised around; the electric light had failed, and that the performance would not commence until about eight o'clock. Although the evening turn did not go with the smoothness of an old established place of entertainment the audience throughout were most appreciative. The programme was made up of half-a-score of turns. The

The Hippodrome Theatre, opened in 1903 and later destroyed by fire

biggest attraction, of course, was Miss Ella and her troupe of lions, which kept the audience spell-bound. Her lions are well trained and appear to be under much better control than many performing animals of a less ferocious nature.

The cinematograph show was one of the most interesting features, and certainly claimed the full applause of the audience. Next came Grant and Allen, a couple of laughter-provoking merrions, and among the other artistes were George Neno, W.

L. Verren, Alf. Bishop, Miss Maud Beaumont (whose singing was marred by the loud orchestra), Mons. Gusto (an exceedingly clever cyclist), Miss Lillie Turner, and Miss Lilla Lassa.

Although the interior of the Hippodrome is still in an unfinished state, one's impressions were favourable. At one end of the building a large stage has been erected for the variety artistes, and, of course, there is the usual ring for equestrian and other performances.

In introducing Miss Ella, Mr. Sylvester, the manager, expressed his regret that inconvenience had been caused by the delay in opening, but he wished the audience to understand that the fault was not on the side of the management, but lay entirely in the light. He promised that everything should be in order for to-night's performances, and that the advertised shows—two every evening—would be given. We are requested to state that the failure of the electric light was not due to any shortcoming at the electricity works.

* * *

In a fortnight the municipal elections will be upon us. I wonder will any aspiring councillor take up the question of new baths? Now is the time for the disgusted ones—and do they not include everyone who has visited the baths this summer?—to make their feelings known. At the last Council meeting the Borough Surveyor reported upon the bad condition of portions of the main woodwork of the baths. Assuredly it is high time took the matter up seriously.

October 24th

The little folk at Hargreaves-street deserve all praise for their clever interpretation of "The Three Bears." Twice this week, on Wednesday and Thursday, these very youthful amateurs entertained a school well filled with people. When one considers that some of them have not yet seen five summers, one marvels at their intelligent grasp of the play. No doubt they owed much to the tuition of the Misses A. Heap and M. Rendell, though the two instructresses must have found the teaching of such bright pupils not altogether unalloyed with pleasure.

Phyllis Cronshaw's acting as the Queen Gundreda was splendidly done. To pose as a veritable virago with advanced views is no easy task. She assumed the manners and bearing of this grande dame with no little skill, and her supercillious stare and use of the lorgnette spoke much for her keen appreciation of the character. Her singing, too, was tuneful and sweet.

Godred, the King of Man, was impersonated by Master H. Cunliffe. His "Calm yourself, my dear!" never failed to elicit roars of mirth from the audience. A perfectly sweet Princess Golden Locks was Miss Kathleen Kenyon, in her white frock with blue sash and blue bows. Her actions while singing "My dear little dolly," in a childish treble, quite charmed everybody. Master Wilson Cunliffe seemed to thoroughly enjoy the part of Jack Frost. He had a great deal to say. It was surprising that a little fellow could remember so much. The dancing of Merlin, the Wizard

(Nellie Livesey) was very graceful. The imps attendant on her contributed no little to the enjoyment of the performances. Their round, chubby faces were a delight to behold, and judging by their knowing smiles they had as much fun out of the play as anybody. Marjory Cunliffe represented Santa Claus very well indeed. Douglas Haywood, Dolly Bainbridge, and Alan Cronshaw made three jolly bears. The little bear won all hearts by the pathetic droop of his head and his plaintive cry, "But she broke my chair." The second act, "The forest in a snow storm" formed a pretty picture with the fairies clad in cotton wool and the enormous snowball. The proceeds were added to the bazaar fund.

November 7th

Although the 5th of November does not appear to create so much excitement as formerly, the youthful element of the population of Accrington at all events had a good time on Thursday. The bang of Chinese crackers, and the whiz of fireworks as they wended their sparkling flight through the darkness were thoroughly enjoyed by the youngsters, while the flames from numerous bonfires were visible above the housetops.

* * *

To read that the general health of the community is unusually good this autumn despite the fact that the air is laden with damp, and the streets perpetually running water, provokes a feeling of aggravation, instead of one of gratitude, that we have not had all the ills that flesh is heir to as an outcome of the disastrous weather. For it does seem like encouraging the clerk of the weather in his pranks when everyone positively thrives on deluges of rain.

November 14th

General lamentation followed the efforts of the Fire Brigade last Friday. Shortly after eleven o'clock a party returning from the Conservative Club noticed flames issuing from the Corporation baths in St. James-street. The Fire Brigade were promptly summoned, and were quickly on the scene. For once in a way the firemen were too early in the field, and the establishment known as the Public Baths was rescued from a fitting and not untimely end. True, most of the private baths were destroyed, but much to the regret of everybody concerned the plunge bath, for so long the despair of Accrington swimmers, was little more than scorched by the flames. It would take some time to burn the sodden boards surrounding the plunge bath. This perhaps is one reason why the devout hopes of the spectators, expressed without any hesitancy, were not more fully realised. Surely the Baths Committee will not attempt to patch up such a wreck! Several of the councillors elected recently advocate new baths. Now is the time to use their influence in the matter.

* * *

I am not a politician, and do not care two straws whether our Mayor is a Tory or a Radical so long as he is really interested in the welfare of the town—in the uplifting of the masses, in trying to elevate the thoughts and the tastes of the people, in making their homes happier and their surroundings pleasanter. I am, if you like, a Socialist in so far as the word means the people's amelioration, the people's good.

The Mayor of a town is chosen as the chief citizen, the elect of the people personified in the Town Council. And as a progressive citizen I desire to enter my protest against the snub— the studied insult the Conservative members of the Town Council gave our new Mayor on his

John Duckworth was elected Mayor in 1903

election on Monday. The Mayor, once elected, is entitled to the hearty co-operation of the whole of the Council and the exhibition of bad manners on the part of the Conservative members of the Council does not augur well for a peaceful and prosperous year. I am glad to learn that the action of the Conservative councillors does not meet with the approbation of my Conservative friends—and I think that among personal acquaintances and correspondents people who have Conservative leanings predominate, that is among those who trouble themselves about politics at all.

* * *

This winter promises to be rather busy in Accrington. Socially, at all events, the season will not be dull. One Chamber concert has already been held, and two others are to follow. On Monday there is the banquet to the retiring Mayor, Alderman Broughton. Ladies are never invited to these functions — why, I don't know.

November 21st

The dismal daily deluge and the ridiculous behaviour of irresponsible sunspots have made us keenly appreciative of this week's spell of fine weather. Fogs have been a little too frequent perhaps, but the suggestion of frost in the air has added zest to all outdoor pursuits. Golf has had many votaries, and cyclists have brought out their machines in high glee.

* * *

Talking of golf reminds me that very few ladies in Accrington have taken up this healthy exercise. There are only twenty, I believe, enrolled as members of the Accrington Golf Club. If ladies only knew the beneficial results of a round on the heights and the enjoyment of the game, I am sure many, more would be eager to join. Unfortunately I cannot speak in such glowing terms of the facilities offered for ladies at the club house. In fact, the comfort of the fair sex does not seem to have been considered at all.

* * *

Alderman Broughton's reminiscences on the subject of Avenue-parade and the Coppice were very interesting. It is to be regretted that the magnificent trees which grew on the Coppice in the old days were ever cut down. There seems no reason why this pretty bit of nature's handiwork should not have been left standing, and, of course, one can only suspect why the plantation was cut down. The avenue leading up to Accrington House was very different from the Avenue- parade of to-day—an avenue in name only. The ex-Mayor's suggestion to replant the trees in Avenue-parade and on the Coppice is worthy the consideration of the Corporation of Accrington. The Coppice, planted with trees and furnished with walks, rustic benches, and shrubberies, with kiosks or shelters similar to those now being built on the promenade at Blackpool at intervals, would be an ideal spot, a place wherein the people of Accrington might seek recreation away from the madding crowd and noisy trams.

* * *

The seventh annual Charity Ball, perhaps the most fashionable of all the season's functions in Accrington, was held in the Cannon-street assembly-room last night where the capacious ball-room provided a scene of unusual brilliance. The charming music discoursed by Mr. George Thornton's band, augmented as it was by several special instrumentalists, the picturesque dresses admired by everyone, the splendidly upholstered chairs and couches, the elegantly framed mirrors situated at either end of the room, the evergreens, suitably arranged at intervals, and the radiant electric light piercing every corner—these were the features of a beautiful display. What a contrast it formed to the condition of affairs outside, where the drizzling rain made things as gloomy and as miserable as could be. Rain has been associated with this event for one or two seasons now, and last night probably interfered with the attendance, which was only about 100.

November 28th

On the whole Wednesday's Choral Concert was voted a success. There is no doubt that miscellaneous concerts appeal to the majority of concert-goers, and none of the artistes on Wednesday had anything to complain of in the way of encores. At the commencement the chorus appeared to lack confidence, but later there was nothing to grumble at. Principals and chorus seemed to enter wholly into the spirit of the 91st Psalm, and rendered this little gem of Handel's with skill. "Autumn," by Brahms, was one of the sweetest part songs of the evening. Although Miss Mary Spencer may almost be termed a local artiste, as she hails from Haslingden, this I believe was her first appearance at these concerts. With such remarkable talent close at hand the Choral Society need never lack a solo pianist.

December 5th

Mr. Barlow, I am sure, numbers among my readers many friends who sympathise with him in his sad bereavement. In "The Little Owd Chap's" hunting articles that have appeared from time to time in the "Observer" references have frequently been made to his "t'other half." After fifty years of married life the parting must be all the keener, though 75 years is a long span for a woman in this life of stress and bustle and Mr. Barlow will be thankful that she was spared so long.

December 12th

After this week's brilliant achievement, and with the remembrance of the equally successful production of "Mikado," I am beginning to think that our Amateurs are capable of performing anything in the operatic line—grand opera or comic. Some people never tire of saying truisms—that "Iolanthe" is not so popular as "Mikado," and so on. But there can be no gainsaying the fact that "Iolanthe" has drawn bigger crowds than any previous opera. That may be due to the opera or to an ever-increasing appreciation on the part of the public. The point is of little moment; the unparalleled success of the week's work is what I am anxious to urge. Monday was admittedly the best "first night" and the performance has gone one better every evening.

December 19th

Saturday brought to a close a splendid week's work. Tributes in the form of chocolate boxes and flowers were presented to the artistes during the week, and on Saturday lovely bouquets were handed to the principal ladies bearing Mr. Bridge's card. Pink roses, maidenhair fern, showers of smilax composed the bouquets of "Phyllis," "Iolanthe," and the "Fairy Queen" while a bouquet of chrysanthemums was given to each of the principal fairies.

It has been suggested that as the opera has taken place so early this year, our Amateurs should organise a concert to be held in the Town Hall sometime in February. From "Les Cloches" to "Iolanthe"—ten operas in all is a far cry.

December 26th

Before the "Observer" is printed again, Christmas will have come and gone. So I take the opportunity of wishing my readers a Merry Christmas! Pessimists would have us believe that Christmas is "out of date," but, judging by the vast numbers emerging from the shops with arms full of queer-looking packages this week, I am inclined to believe that the festive season is more popular than ever before. Postmen have already experienced a big difference in the bundles of letters, cards and parcels they have had to deliver. From a weather point of view snow and ice seem very far away. But even though the weather fails, the kindliness and cheery good-fellowship which we always associate with Christmas' will no doubt be sufficient guarantee for a happy time.

1904

January 2nd

Once again I am asked to warn my readers to be chary about taking goods from people who come hawking at their doors. All kinds of diseases are spread by the foolish practice of purchasing laces, tape, buttons, etc., from the filthier kind of tramp, while the hawker with the polished manner is often a fraud. Several young ladies have acquainted me with their grievances on the subject. Not long ago a lady, to all outward appearances a reduced gentlewoman, visited several homes in the town, and asked for the lady of the house, giving in each case the correct name, an easy matter when one has a directory at hand. Her business was to get orders for the "Life of Queen Victoria" at 2s. per volume. She was not above strategy either. Failing a direct order, which in many cases was not forthcoming, she meekly asked for the address to be written on a scrap of paper so that she might forward a copy of the book on approval. Those who were not quick enough to see through the ruse had unintentionally signed an order form. Very soon a traveller appeared with the book, and ladies, on seeing their signature, were obliged to pay.

My advice is, go to the tradespeople of Accrington to make your purchases rather than allow any stray traveller to dupe you. There are, of course, honest hawkers, but—well, you know that a tradesman who has been in the town for years is not here today and gone tomorrow. It may seem a silly way of putting it, but if I carry the point home, that is all I want.

* * *

In Observ(er)ations a few days ago I noticed a communication from a lady correspondent suggesting that the application of a hosepipe would remove the dirt from our streets. I have lived in Accrington many years, and I cannot recall a Christmas when the footpaths were so difficult to negotiate. They have been thick with mud and quite as slippery as during a spell of snow and frost. In Blackburn the streets (and footpaths) were cleansed last week by the aid of the hosepipe. There is, I believe, more water in the local reservoirs than has been known for years. Why couldn't more of it be used for washing our footpaths and cleansing our sewers?

January 16th

Mrs. Bunting has consented to become the local lady president of the Society for the Prevention of Cruelty to Children, a position which the late Mrs. J. E. Riley, of Arden Hall, filled so admirably. Many other institutions besides the N.S.P.C.C. have been poorer by the loss of Mrs. Riley, who was such a power in promoting charitable functions.

* * *

At the Annual Meeting of the Moss Lane Tennis Club, held recently, it was decided to re-open the courts for the season on May 1st—sun spots permitting. My correspondent tells me that the meeting, though not over-crowded, accomplished the business of the evening with praiseworthy dispatch, and the representative members soon dispersed, after electing Miss E. Lill as tea secretary for the coming season, and re-appointing Mr. T. Kenyon as secretary. Mr. Kenyon must have felt the work in connection with the club but a light task, after the many pretty speeches delivered in appreciation of his services, while Miss May Entwisle, who so ably fulfilled the appointment of tea secretary last year, was awarded the thanks of all the members, extended in the usual courteous fashion.

January 23rd

Two well-known ladies, both closely identified with the New Church will be carried to their last resting place at Accrington cemetery this morning.

Mr. E. J. Riley, head of the firm of billiard table makers, sustained a sad blow on Thursday evening by the death of his wife, which took place at Sprinfield, Whalley-road, after a protracted illness. Mrs. Riley, who was 43 years of age, had a large circle of friends by whom her demise is much lamented. She was prominently connected with the New Church, Abbey-street, and was at one time a member of the choir. She was also a member of the Choral Society, and had been, connected with the tennis club since its formation. The remains will be interred at Accrington Cemetery at noon to-day. Four members of the tennis club will Act as bearers.

Mrs. Saul, widow of the late Mr. Saul, died at her residence, Cobham-street, on Wednesday morning, aged 69 years. Mrs. Saul was the only daughter of the late Mr. Robert Holt, and leaves two sons. She was & regular worshipper at the New Jerusalem Church, and in her young days a teacher at the Sunday School.

To the members of the Saul family and to Mr. E. J. Riley and those who weep with them, I desire to convey my deepest sympathy, and I think may venture also to extend to them an expression of deep regret in the name of my readers.

January 30th

It is with pleasure I give this week photographs of four Great Harwood children whose attendance at Sunday school is something out of the ordinary. To attend school for thirteen years without once being late is the splendid record of Miss Alice Hallsworth. Even when visiting in the summertime at the seaside she has regularly attended Sunday school, thus gaining her mark. Only two years behind is her sister Clara, who has also attended the Congregational school for 11 years, while her brothers, James and Archibald, attendances number respectively nine and seven years. Surely a remarkable incident in the religious world!

The Hallsworth children

February 6th

It reminded one of old times to see Mr. and Mrs. John Hargreaves at a bazaar in Accrington. Although it is to be regretted that they are no longer residents in Accrington it was fitting they should open the bazaar on Wednesday. Christ Church owes much to the Hargreaves family, and it is satisfactory to know that the "younger end" have not lost all interest in the church in which their fathers took such an active part.

* * *

Many ladies will be grateful to Mr. Langham for his reference at the Council meeting to the vile habit of spitting on the pavements. Unfortunately nothing can be done to remedy the evil, unless the expectorators themselves are made to realise the injury they do. The health of the community is in danger, while the damage done to ladies' gowns is by no means a small item. I have observed that the lower classes are not wholly responsible for the sickening appearance of our pavements. To spit at all has always seemed to me quite unnecessary, but if men will be guilty of this offensive practice, why can't they "operate" where the remains are not likely to contaminate, or meet the eye of persons of more cleanly habits?

* * *

It was good to see the faces of the old folks on Saturday. One of the guests, John Green, had reached the age of 96 years, while the oldest woman was aged 93. Who says Accrington, with all its rain, is not a healthy town? Is there not a touch of pathos in the fact that one old man of 74 is obliged to go out to work at five in the morning and keep at it till six o'clock at night?

February 20th

Little children do much nowadays in the way of entertaining. On Friday and Saturday the young folks at St. Peter's performed the charming operetta, "Snow White and the Seven Dwarfs." Very sweet looked Miss Daisy Wilkinson as "Snow White," and her attendants, who also wore pure white frocks, were equally nice. The singing was tasteful, and their actions gave evidence of careful training.

On Saturday, and again on Tuesday, those clever little performers whose portraits appeared in Tuesday's "Observer" repeated "Britannia" to crowded and appreciative audiences in the Town Hall. The performances reflected credit upon the coach and the little ones alike. No doubt their success in this direction will lead the Education Committee and the Women's Guild to further efforts.

February 27th

If a lady correspondent's note re the Gentlemen's Private Subscription dance be correct, last Friday's affair was one of the jolliest yet held - a fact which makes me regret more than ever I that I was unable to attend. "Outside the rain came down in one pitiless, never-ceasing deluge; inside all was mirth and laughter." "The decorations," she tells me, "though not on the lavish scale of last year, were very nice. Utilised as a sort of lounge where one could rest and watch the seemingly tireless energy of the dancers below, the platform, with its screens and basket chairs was a charming retreat. Refreshments, as before, were supplied in the ante room just beneath the platform, Mr. Thornton's orchestra occupying an impromptu platform at the far end of the room. The floor, by the way, was not in perfect condition. The M.C.'s and stewards worked really hard and wallflowers were quite unknown. Some of the gowns worn were very pretty, and you will be surprised to learn that a gentleman observed them to such good effect that he was able to give me a full description. Here are a few, for which I am indebted:—"A very effective gown was worn by a striking girl, of some sort of cream stuff with orange coloured satin, draped across the decolletege and round the waist. Her hair was nicely arranged, and she appeared to be having a good time. Another lady had on a pure white crepe de chine, with short train and frilly sleeves, admired because it looked so very I sweet and clean. 'Chic' seems to be the most appropriate adjective for a white gown with deep collar of white lace, interthreaded with tiny pink and blue chiffon roses, and a highly dressed coiffure with a pink rose nestling at the right hand side. Very smart was a black dress with fichu and frills, the skirt trimmed with medallions of cream lace. A tall girl wore grey cashmere, rucked and unrelieved by any trimming. Stylish was a black, with black and white frills and garland of white flowers and green leaves. Green of a peculiar shade, prettily inserted with wide cream lace, looked well. Joining hands while Auld Lang Syne was sung; then out into the wet drizzle away from the sparkle, wit, & beauty, we wended our way homeward in the wee small hours of the morning."

March 5th

The Parks' Committee, I am sure, will have no difficulty in finding ladies and gentlemen willing to offer prizes for the plant-growing competition among the school children of Accrington. In other towns children have produced splendid results in similar competitions, but even if some fine specimens are not forthcoming, it is something to have given the young an interest in the cultivation of plants, and will lead to a wider knowledge of flowers and plants in the future. In May the plants will be distributed, and each scholar will be expected to attend to his or her plant at home. When large enough the plant will have to be repotted and finally brought to an exhibition at which the plants will be shown and prizes given for the best specimens. About thirty or forty children from each school in the borough will be allowed to compete. It is essentially a step in the right direction, and I trust will bring forth excellent results.

March 12th

Although the "Spectre's 'Bride" is not generally known, the majority of the large crowd assembled in the Town Hall on Wednesday appeared to thoroughly enjoy Dvorak's cantata. Hearing the work for the first time some were disappointed, but it is essentially one of those masterpieces which improve on closer acquaintance. Late arrivals and early departures detracted considerably from the enjoyment of the music Some people have an unhappy knack of entering the hall when the overture is being played and seem utterly oblivious to the cold displeasure of the people they inconvenience in passing to their seats and the glance of disapproval from a pair of black eyes on the platform. Why will people be so persistently unkind? This, however, is not so bad as an entrance while a plaintive solo is engaging the attention of an audience. How anyone could mar such a beautiful soul-stirring composition as the first soprano solo in "The Spectre's Bride" by marching to their seats passes comprehension.

* * *

A correspondent writes:- "*I have no desire to criticise the arrangements at our Choral concerts, but should like to make a few friendly suggestions which, if carried out, would add to the comfort and pleasure of the concerts. The doors might be kept closed at all events while the music is in progress, with benefit to those who do not care to have their enjoyment disturbed by late arrivals. Programme boys might also retire, or at least cease from parading the aisles when once the concert has commenced. The piano cover is not a thing of beauty, and its removal would certainly improve the appearance of the platform. Either a special train or a different time arrangement would enable the bandsmen to retire without the stampede which is now a most disagreeable feature of our concerts. The last item on the programme naturally suffers. "Tannhauser" " rushed " is not a pleasant finale to an otherwise successful concert. Another noticeable item is the demeanour of the bandsmen. There is not the same decorum amongst them as when Richter or Risegari is at the helm.*"

March 19th

Spring really did come last week. Was it not delightful to be out? Thursday and Friday were glorious days. Last Tuesday, too, was calm and summer-like. There was no March gale. To realise to the full the delights of such a day one needed to be among the trees, flowers, and green fields. As soon as my tasks were ended I shut up the "copy" book, wiped the pen, pumped up my old bicycle, and sped away to the country. The trees and hedges were swelling with the warmth, and the earth as one passed along had a delightfully sweet fresh smell. The birds seemed as if they could not carol loudly enough to show their appreciation of the sunshine; larks were singing gaily in the blue sky, and ever and anon one heard the beautiful warbling of a thrush, a little wren perched on a hedge chirped, while a couple of bright chaffinches rolled playfully in the grass as I passed by. Pendle, Whalley Nab, and dear old Kemple End, transformed by the sun, were magnificent to behold, the road over Waddington Fell gleamed white in the distance, while the turrets of Stonyhurst glistened in the sunlight. It was indeed a charming scene! We are now past the middle of the month, and have had no March gales yet, so evidently he will have to go out like a raging lion, but even so we shall have several nice Spring days to look back to, when his tameness was a delight.

* * *

Music lovers spent an enjoyable time last night listening to the ever-welcome Brodsky quartette. It is only at our Chamber Concerts that we in Accrington have the opportunity of hearing this quartette. Brahms pianoforte quintet in F minor, with Mr. Max Myer at the piano, was an exceptional treat for Accringtonians.

The Brodsky Quartet

* * *

I regret that the Literary and Philosophical Society is to be disbanded. It seems a great pity that such an organisation should he dissolved. Although of late the attendance has been considerably diminished, there are many who still take an interest in the debates. Perhaps some energetic person will come forth and help to revive the society next session.

April 2nd

Easter weather, as a topic of the moment, has this week provided a not unwelcome variant to such questions as "When will Parliament dissolve?" or "How much will the rates go up this year?" For just now the holidays are uppermost in the minds of most of us, and the question is:- What is the weather to be? Is it to make or mar our Easter jaunt? "Unsettled" is the verdict of the experts, but weather prophecy was ever an uncertain game, and perhaps the experts will be wrong—at least, I hope so. Sunday's sample is just about my ideal of what the Eastertide ought to be.

* * *

Wednesday morning with its snowstorm was not very encouraging though, was it? Just when the snow was lying thickest about the streets, a sloppy, chilly mixture, I had a ring over the telephone from a Blackpool friend. "Beautiful morning," he cheerfully observed. "Oh, well, yes," said I, "if you're partial to snow at Easter." "To what? Snow! Why, there's been no snow in Blackpool. It's a bright, breezy morning here; perfectly fine!" "Aye," was my final comment, "and then we wonder why folk go down to the seaside to live!" I only mention this just to show you that it doesn't at all follow that they're having the same variety of weather thirty miles away as we're having in Accrington.

* * *

As a general thing industrial concerns in Accrington and district will cease work for Friday and Saturday, though I hear of one or two mills that will be closed for a longer period—too long to please the employees. Time was when hardly anybody thought of "going off" at Easter, but nowadays there is a very considerable exodus to the seaside, and a very appreciable change it is, if only the weather, always an uncertain quantity in early Spring, lends its benediction to the proceedings. The railway companies, I note from their programmes, are catering for holiday makers in a very ample way.

April 16th

It was decided at the Council meeting on Monday to spend £50 in patching up the "remains" of the plunge bath. Isn't it false economy to attempt anything short of a complete reconstruction of such a place? It is quite evident that members of the committee are not interested in swimming. Nor do they seem much concerned about the health of the rising generation, who, with their teachers, pay daily visits to the baths in the summer-time. Where, oh where, are those worthy councillors with their tales now that they have been elected? One hears no great agitation from those who professed, on paper, a few months ago that they would do all in their power to obtain new baths. Last year people had to visit adjacent towns to indulge in their swimming exercises in properly ventilated buildings and magnificent plunge baths, and there is no reason why they shouldn't go this year. It seems a pity that the little ones should suffer. Why not build a structure that would be a credit to the town, with Turkish, plunge, and private baths complete, instead of wasting money trying to redeem a disreputable place that is beyond redemption ?

* * *

The appointment of a female inspector who would visit the poorer houses in the district and give instruction to mothers who cannot attend properly to their off spring has for some time been under consideration. I am inclined to the belief that town councils think in centuries. Meanwhile this crying need is apparent to the densest, and the infant mortality list increases by leaps and bounds. A thoroughly efficient lady inspector is what we want. Then why don't we get her without wasting time in "thinking" the subject threadbare? Wouldn't a lady councillor also be a blessing?

April 23rd

Two letters received from correspondents command first attention. They refer to subjects of interest not to members of the fair sex only, but to the community at large. One of the communications deals with the question of Accrington's public baths; the other with our trams. It is perhaps well that I should at the outset explain that I have received other letters on the baths question, but a few extracts from the epistle before me may be given as typical of the rest, for not one of my correspondents dissents from the comments "Scribbler" and I ventured to make last week.

"An Old Swimmer," who took part in the opening of the plunge bath, competing for the first captaincy in fact, wishes to support the protest against tinkering with the present baths. They were, he points out, built by the late Mr. Eli Higham as a commercial venture. In their early days—that was before the wood began to rot and before the place got so filthy—the plunge bath was immensely popular. The water, obtained from Messrs. George Hargreaves and Co.'s pit, was so clear that the smallest object could be seen at the deep end of the bath. Threepenny pieces were easily discerned, and my correspondent says he has picked up from 15 to 20 small objects in one dive. It was a pleasure to visit the place in those days, and almost every morning the plunge bath was the rendezvous of the leading trade and professional men of the town. But in time the wooden building —only regarded from the outset as a temporary structure—began to decay, as all wooden erections do when in constant contact with water. The marvel is that Mr. Higham's baths stood so long. "*In no other town of the size of Accrington,*" says my correspondent, "*would a wooden structure have been tolerated. It has done good service and ought to have given place to modern baths years ago. But even now, when partially destroyed by fire, our local senators are afraid to supply one of Accrington's greatest needs. The insurance money, if I am rightly informed, amounts to a substantial sum, and there is no excuse for further tinkering with the baths. If November were near at hand not a single candidate who favoured the 'patching-up policy' would have a chance of election. I agree with you, dear 'Stella,' that our baths have long been a disgrace to the town, and that it is a reproach to Accrington that her sons and daughters have to go to other boroughs in the neighbourhood for a swim in a bath with decent surroundings.*"

* * *

My other correspondent relates the experiences of a tram ride to Rawtenstall, or rather to Haslingden, for though she had booked through to Rawtenstall she deemed it prudent to leave the car at Haslingden and complete the journey on foot. The car, she says, rocked and plunged, reeled, and did almost everything but come asunder.

The oscillation was so great that my fair correspondent left the car with a "tearing headache" and took good care to make the return journey by train. From a financial standpoint the Tramway Co. seem to be very short-sighted. True, the lease has not very long to run, but how many hundreds of passengers do they lose in consequence of the "fearful oscillation" spoken of by my contributor? At Haslingden she complained to a friend of the miserable journey she had had. "Oh, we never use the cars now," was the reply; "we go by train even though the double journey involves the descent of and climb up Jacob's ladder."

Personally I think even our ungainly looking trams are better than none at all, especially in rough weather. But something could surely be done for the comfort of the passengers. Take, for example, the conductors. They are a body of men who command my sympathy, for they have long hours to work for little pay, and plenty of humbug to stand. I wouldn't be a tram conductor for four times the money they earn, even if I were eligible for the post. (A lady conductor would be a decided novelty.) Our tram guards have many unpleasant duties. At the end of every journey they have to help in the reversing of the engines, and it falls to their lot to handle the dirty pins which connect engine and car, with the result that their hands become filthy. Again, I say, I don't blame the conductors. But it is rather hard on the passengers to have to rub against conductors whose hands are greasy and whose coats are often dripping wet. One day I saw a lady enter a car with a new fawn jacket. The conductor assisted her from the step into the car by placing his hand on her shoulder. His intentions were good, no doubt, but the results were disastrous. Four lovely finger marks were

The newly formed Church Battery Band

left upon the jacket which had to be sent to the cleaners.

And how many dresses have been soiled by the conductors and inspectors forcing their way through the narrow cars? On one occasion a lady with a charming pale heliotrope dress was returning from a social function and jumped into the car to escape a shower of rain. She regretted afterwards that she had not braved the storm. Her dress would no doubt have got wet, but would have escaped that awful streak of dirt which she looked at in amazement after contact with the conductor's soaking-wet overcoat.

Sunday was a glorious day for the Church Battery of the 3rd L.R.G.A.'s church parade. Many people watched the procession on its way to Church Kirk, and not a few enjoyed the strains from the new band, as the instrumentalists played all the way to church. It was rather a novel idea to have the band accompanying the hymns during the service, and no doubt added zest to the singing at the old church.

May 7th

"Rose of Persia" is the happy choice of the Opera Committee for our next amateur production in December. Although not exactly a popular opera, it has many admirers. To those who have studied its bright libretto, varied characters, and pleasing numbers it appeals as a thing of extreme beauty. The music is of Sullivan's best, and Basil Hood was author of the "book." Written after the Gilbert and Sullivan quarrel, the opera was first produced at the Savoy in November, '99, but had not so long a run as some of the previous Savoy operas.

"Rose of Persia" is by no means an easy opera to attempt, but Accrington amateurs were ever ambitious, and they never yet met with failure. No doubt there is plenty of material in the Society to supply the characters needed.

* * *

Oak Hill Park is looking particularly nice just now. On Sunday crowds of people flocked there to enjoy the sweet Spring air and show their new gowns. Many looked with admiration at the beds of vari-coloured tulips and crocuses, and the trees bursting their buds under the influence of the May sunshine, but far more interest was shown in Mary Ann's new dress and Jane's millinery. Wasn't there a delightful parade of new finery? Some of it, I fear, would be very different after the showers of rain, which, regardless of all things new, descended mercilessly.

The men or boys who cut away the labels from seats specially reserved for ladies and appropriate the forms for the whole afternoon deserve punishment. They don't possess consciences or manners, or they would vacate the forms when so many of the weaker sex are obliged to stand or walk about.

* * *

Those who have worked so hard to make the May Festival a success must have been gratified by the appreciation shown by the audience on Wednesday night. The Town Hall was well worth a visit if only to see the bright, happy faces of the children, who made a pretty picture, the effect being intensified by the electric light. Mothers and friends of the children were present of course, and it was amusing to see how eagerly the eyes of the little ones scanned the hall in search of their own particular friends. A new and very pleasing feature was the procession round the room, in which the principal performers took part. Of course, the chief event of the evening was the crowning of the May Queen, and both "Her Majesty" and the retiring Queen carried themselves with a grace and dignity worthy their high position. If one item was more appreciated than another it was the flag song, representative of England, Scotland, Ireland, and Wales, and one little girl amused the audience vastly by the earnest, energetic way in which she went through her part. Altogether the entertainment was a great success.

May 14th

Master W M Hartley Higham, the little son of Mr J. S Higham J.P, C.C., who on Saturday laid the children's stone at the Lancashire and Cheshire Band of Hope Union's new headquarters in Manchester.

May 28th

Here is a "Society " par that will no doubt interest my readers:—" Mrs. Hartmann [of Church] intends selling her Berkeley Square beautiful house, as since she has done up the White Lodge and taken to living there more, she has taken such an immense liking to the place that she does not care in the same way for being much in town. Every Saturday to Monday Mrs. Hartmann goes down to her delightful home in Richmond Park, and there she invariably has lots of her smart friends down for Sunday, where she entertains them either to tea or dinner. The White Lodge, too, is a favourite drive from London of the Royal family, both the King and Queen frequently

Master W M Hartley Higham

motoring down there on a Saturday or Sunday afternoon, and remaining to dine with Mrs. Hartmann and her house-party."

* * *

Talking of the Steiner family reminds me that the Comte de Jaucourt has taken the Grange at Wilpshire, the former residence of Mrs. Edgar Appleby.

* * *

Bad trade may have accounted for diminished bookings from Accrington station this Whitsuntide, but the number of people who cycled, walked, drove, and motored through Whalley on Whit-Monday, led one to believe that after all "trade" was in a flourishing condition. Sawley, Gisburn, Mytton, Hodder, Clitheroe, and surrounding villages were simply overrun with holiday makers. Never before I think has the exodus into the country been so great as this year.

June 4th

A member of the Parks Committee informs me that every third seat in the Park is reserved for ladies, but there is difficulty in keeping the plates on the seats— due, no doubt, to the mischief-loving proclivities of the male sex, who I notice have no scruples about appropriating the forms with or without plates. A charge of a penny each occupant of certain seats might ensure their being properly reserved.

* * *

Next Saturday at noon General Baden-Powell is expected to arrive at Accrington Station. At 2.30 a procession of military and semi-military men will form in Avenue Parade and march to the Drill Hall. It was decided at the General Purposes Committee meeting on Monday to suitably decorate the town in honour of Baden-Powell's visit, and present him with an address of welcome. Won't there be some excitement amongst the schoolchildren next week? Baden- Powell and his exploits will be the subject of conversation for some time to come. The tradesmen have made special display of bunting and flags. One or two of the windows look bright and gay in honour of the great soldier's visit.

June 18th

Wednesday was by no means a perfect day for a garden sale. A forbidding morning gave place to an alluring burst of sunshine for a short time in the

Broak Oak House, the home of the McAlpine's

early afternoon. The favours of the Clerk to the Weather were, however, of short duration, and the proceedings at Broad Oak suffered in. consequence. Happily Mrs. Macalpine had arranged for the erection of a marquee in the grounds. This temporary structure afforded shelter for a large number of guests when the rain resumed its unwelcome attentions. Inside the tent goods were arranged temptingly on stalls, with several ladies in attendance. Judging by the apparent earnestness of the stallholders and the obvious willingness of ladies to purchase, the sale itself suffered very little financially. Afternoon tea was dispensed by a bevy of charming young ladies in summerlike costumes, white gowns predominating. Small tables arranged on the green, covered with dainty tea-cloths, were speedily removed when the rain came to the shelter of huge spreading elms, whose branches for a time proved rain-proof. The fact that, despite the inclemency of the weather, every guest partook of tea and cake speaks much for the heroic efforts of the waitresses.

From my perch in one of the tents I viewed with admiration the clever navigation of trays by young maidens who, despite new gowns and smart millinery, braved the showers. The Military Band played selections in the vicinity of the large tent. To hear the enlivening strains and mark the contrast ,'twixt the dripping trees, soaking grass, damp clothes, and instruments glistening with rain-drops, was not without charm. The beautiful grounds of Broad Oak are admirably suited for a garden party. Well-kept lawns, magnificent trees, shaded walks, and pretty flowers are all there. The greenhouses were thrown open for the enjoyment of the visitors. The house itself, with its broad windows and fine stonework was the object of much admiration. In truth, had the sun but shone for a little while longer, the garden sale, in aid of the British and Foreign Bible Society, would have been one of the pleasantest functions held in our district for some time.

* * *

From early morning till late at night our town wore a festive air quite unusual for Accrington, on Saturday. Never before, I fancy, have the streets been so crowded as they were that day. Thousands and thousands of people came from far and near. "B.-P." received a welcome he is likely to treasure in his memory for some time to come.

The opening of the Ambulance Drill Hall. The procession forms up outside the Town Hall

His stay was short, but during the time he was in the town everybody who cared saw and admired Baden-Powell, and one lady, I believe, succeeded in procuring his autograph. His bronzed face, tall stature and Commanding bearing were the admiration of the ladies, one of whom was heard to say, "Isn't he a darling?" He had absolutely "no side," and his movements were graceful. All this I had heard beforehand, but I was surprised to find that the Hero of Mafeking is a good platform speaker as well as a sterling soldier. His Town Hall speech was, remarkably well delivered. Not at all prosy, his short, well-finished sentences were heard in every part of the building. He never had to pause for words, his language was good, and his sentiments excellent. It is not often that in speech, appearance and manners a hero comes up to expectation. "B.-P." is the exception.

The street collections were not nearly so large as one would have expected from such vast crowds. This was the only flaw in the day's programme. And the collectors were not free from blame. They seemed anxious to cover too much ground—to keep up with the procession. I have heard people say they were never asked to give and never saw the collecting boxes. It would be a pity if any person who was really wishful to give had not the chance of doing so. Supt. Ogden or any of the officers will be ready to hold out both hands for contributions, be they ever so small.

It is satisfactory to learn that the day passed off without accident. With such crowds mishaps easily occur, and we may consider ourselves fortunate that no calamity happened. While the people were orderly in the main, one had not far to seek to find the seamy side later in the day. It is lamentable that men, and even women, cannot take part in such festivities without descending to a plane of animalism revolting to anyone with the least sense of refinement. Rowdyism was inevitable with such a crowd, but to see youth and, in some cases beauty, defiled by contact with people who had imbibed too freely was indeed pitiable.

June 25th

Heartiest congratulations to Miss Mary Ashworth, who last week succeeded in obtaining the coveted post of headmistress at Coal Clough Infants' School, Burnley. As there were a large number of applications for the post, credit is reflected on the abilities of Miss Ashworth, who for many years was a teacher at Willow-street School.

* * *

Has PC Carr drawn your shillings for the Police Cricket Match on July 13th? Maybe the zealous ticket-seller does not like to stop the fair sex to the extent he button-holes the gents, and for that reason I suggest that when you meet Carr you reverse the order by asking him for a ticket. The cause is excellent, but money is rather scarce. Let us all try to help the Children's Society. The tea is worth the money charged for the afternoon's entertainment.

July 2nd

Congratulations to Mr. and Mrs. Joseph Broughton, who were married at the New Church on Wednesday. The Rev. J. R. Rendell performed the ceremony, assisted by the Rev. J. Moffat Logan. Not many people attended the wedding, as it was desired to keep the affair quiet. The bride (Miss Riley) looked sweetly pretty in her gown of soft white crepe-de-chine with insertion trimming. A large white picture hat was very becoming, and her shower bouquet was composed of choice white flowers, the inevitable orange blossom being worn in the form of a spray. Miss Ethel Riley and Miss Fanny Broughton also looked well in their gowns of pale blue, trimmed with silk insertion. They wore very nice black picture hats and carried bouquets of yellow iris. "Happy is the bride that the sun shines on" is an old saying, and there was no lack of sunshine on Wednesday. A more perfect day could not have been. The honeymoon is being spent at Oban, in Scotland.

* * *

Heartiest congratulations to the Accrington Dramatic Society. They did splendidly on Monday. Imagine the energy necessary for such a performance on such a night. It was dreadfully hot, even for those who had only to view the performance and laugh at its humorous touches. What must it have been to act the parts? Surely they deserve the St. John medal for heroism.

I was astonished to see such a "full house." Every seat appeared to be occupied, and lots of people stood during the performance. A compliment to the performers, surely, in such heat. Although I have previously seen our amateurs perform "A Pair of 'Spectacles," I enjoyed Monday night's performance as well, if not better, than on the former occasion.

Many were pleased when Mr. R. W. Kenyon and Mr. H. Heap received their curtain call. These two work silently but well, and only those who are behind the scenes know just how much the success of the performance is due to these admirable secretaries.

* * *

A correspondent writes me:—"In Burnley on Tuesday strawberries—and real beauties, too—were selling at 2d. per pound. In Accrington the same day they were 6d. How do you account for it?" Sorry I can't solve the riddle.

July 9th

Mr. Carnegie's offer of £7,500 for a free library has quite taken Accrington by storm. Negotiations have been going on for some time, and at last Mr. Carnegie has cast his gaze with some effect on Accrington's need. There is some doubt as to which site will be suitable for the new structure, but surely with an example of such munificence before them some lady or gentleman will proffer the requisite land. My one regret—and I am sure many will echo that lament—is that

Mr. Carnegie isn't interested in the construction of public baths. How nice it would
be to have a combined structure.

* * *

The sun managed to shine on the children on Saturday at Dunkenhalgh. What a
charming picture they made in their white frocks, and floral decorations, with the
background of stately elms. The procession was made up of serious and comical
elements very diverting to the crowd, who appeared to be intensely interested in
every phase of the entertainment. The retiring of last year's Rose Queen (Miss Cissie
Foster) and the crowning of Saturday's Queen (Miss Lizzie Pickup) were, of course,
the chief events of the afternoon. Both girls and their attendants went through the
ceremony with pretty grace, the girls looking charming in their white frocks with
regal trains, and pretty flowers.

July 16th

The storm of Tuesday cleared the atmosphere beautifully for the Police cricket
match for the Children's Society on Wednesday. It is so long since the teams
have met for their annual match in really good weather that the officials were
despairing of ever hitting on a lucky date. Of Wednesday there was nothing to
complain as far as weather and cricket were concerned, but the waitresses, I fancy,
would find it rather too hot for comfort. The pavilion stand was packed with people.
It was, I believe, the largest gathering ever seen at this hardy annual. No doubt the
financial results are satisfactory. The young ladies who perform the duties of
waitresses get their meed of praise, but the ladies who "cut up" and preside over the
tea urn, by far the hardest work, are to many invisible. Mrs. Home for several years
has smiled a welcome on all and sundry. Mrs. Haworth has dispensed tea for as long
as I can remember these matches. Then that ready organiser of charitable movements
and steady worker, Mrs. Cronshaw, does her share at the tea table. Mrs. Carter, too,
works with right good will. There are many more, including Mrs. W. Sharples, Mrs.
G. Whittaker, and others to whom the N.S.P.C.C. are indebted.

July 23rd

At All Saints' Church, on Thursday afternoon, in the presence of a large assembly,
the marriage took place of Mr. W. F. C. Schaefer, of Rishton, a member of the
East Lancashire Soap Company's office staff, Clayton-le-Moors, and Miss Ellen
(Nellie) Broughton, only daughter of Mr. Broughton, postmaster, Clayton-le-Moors.
The event was a pretty one, and aroused considerable interest. The service was
conducted by Canon Johnson. Mr. A. Storey officiated at the organ, and rendered the
Bridal March from "Lohengrin" and Mendelssohn's "Wedding March." The bride,
who was given away by her father, was attended by two bridesmaids, Miss Hettie
Harrison, Oswaldtwistle, and Miss E. K. Whittaker, Whalley-road, Accrington. She
was prettily attired in cream voile adorned with ecru insertion, and wore a cream
picture hat with ostrich feathers. Her shower bouquet was composed of lilies and

white roses. Both bridesmaids wore grey voile and picture hats, Miss Harrison's being white and Miss Whittaker's black. Each carried bouquets of sweet peas. The duties of best man were carried out by Mr. Jack Schaefer, brother of the bridegroom. After the ceremony the guests drove to Higher Hodder, where the wedding repast was served, and yesterday the newly-married couple proceeded to Blackpool, where the honeymoon is being spent.

LIST OF PRESENTS

Bride to bridegroom, gold ring. Bridegroom to bride, pearl and ruby brooch.
Mr. Broughton, cheque.
Mrs. Broughton, household linen.
Mr. and Mrs. Schaefer, cheque.
Mr. Jack Schaefer, picture.
Mr. Arthur Schaefer, barometer.
Mr. and Mrs. Thompson, gas bracket and globe.
Mr. and Mrs. T. Riley, linen tablecloth.
Mr. D. Riley, set of brushes.
Directors, East Lancashire Soap Company, walnut sideboard.
Workmen, East Lancashire Soap Company, butter cooler and Ewbank sweeper.
Mr. and the Misses Broughton, bed linen.
Mr. and Mrs. Hyde, letter rack and dessert spoons.
Mr. and Mrs- T. Lovell, oak tea tray and d'oyley.
Nellie and Edme, copper plant pots.
Mr. and Mrs. Drummond, linen tablecloth.
Misses H. S. Harrison, sideboard cover and bamboo table.
Mr. and Mrs. Sumner, curtains.
Mr. and Mrs. Bradshaw, brass paper rack.
Mr. and Mrs. Holmes, Great Harwood, rug.
Mr. and Mrs. Frankland, Great Harwood, blankets.
Mrs. Pickup, quilt.
Mr. and Mrs. W. Pickup, rug.
Mr. Harry Taylor, hand-painted placques.
Mr. and Mrs. Kennedy, copper crumb tray and brush.
Miss Noble, linen tablecloth.
The Misses Heys and Houghton, vases and d'oyleys.
Mr. and Mrs. Wolstenholme, Chenille tablecloth.
Mrs. Hall, set of vases.
Miss Rhoda Hargreaves, silver fruit dish.
The Misses Hargreaves, silver and cut-glass salts.
Mr. and Mrs. Harrison, Rishton, linen tablecloth.
Mr. Pugh, dressing bag outfit.
Mr. H. Hindle ruby salts.
Mr. and Mrs. Thornton, tea service.
Mr. and Mrs. Duckworth, linen tablecloth.
Miss Duckworth, toilet covers.
Mr. and Mrs. Kenyon, knives and forks and dessert spoons.
Mrs. Walmsley, salts, teapot, and jug.
Mrs. Sharples, quilt.
Mr. and Mrs. J. Edwards, fire brasses.
Mr. D. Hacking, silver cruet.
Mr. and Mrs. Tennant. Burnley, salver.
Mr. and Mrs. Cottam, Rishton, tablecloth.
Mr. and Mrs. Joseph Horrocks. linen tablecloth,
Mr. and Mrs. Braithwaite, Rishton, flower stand.

The Misses Braithwaite, clock.

July 30th

Mrs. Bunting, the new Lady President of the Accrington Branch of the N.SP.C.C., invited her colleagues and the committee and collectors to a garden party at Quarry Hill on Thursday. The weather had been threatening, but the afternoon was fine, and the charming grounds of Quarry Hill, with their well-stocked greenhouses, looking at their best, were much enjoyed by a company numbering perhaps fifty. Afternoon tea was served in the grounds, Mrs. and Miss Bunting having the assistance of a large number of young ladies. Mr. George Thornton's band played selections of music, and every guest was made to feel at home; indeed the little garden party was a most delightful affair all through.

* * *

A pretty wedding. So everybody declared. It was the marriage of Mr. Will Kenyon to Miss Lizzie Lill, at Cannon-street Baptist Chapel on Wednesday noon. Members of well-known local families, the wedding had aroused considerable interest, and the ceremony was watched by a large congregation. Still a young gentleman, the bridegroom has been before the public for quite a long period. As one of the principals in our local Amateur Operatic Society, Mr. Kenyon has played many parts and I know that every member of our local amateur societies will join with me in wishing "much happiness" to him and to his comely bride.

The dresses of the bride and bridesmaids and some of the guests were the work of Miss M. Coward, Whalley-road, and were much admired.

August 6th

The Pot Fair opens on Monday. It is not an institution which commends itself to me, indeed if I had my way there would be no "pot fair" on our market ground. But I suppose we are not all of the same way of thinking, and hundreds will revel among the pots daily and enjoy their "cheap bargains". Here and there no doubt a good line may be picked up, but in buying pots at more or less exciting "sales" it is necessary to be cautious or the buyer may herself be sold" A word to the wise is sufficient.

August 13th

Up to the time of writing holiday weather, of the right kind has been—well, better than the I average Accrington Fair weather. Saturday was enough to damp the ardour of any holiday maker. It may have been jolly at the seaside lounging in some comfortable nook watching the hats and impedimenta of passers-by blown into the water; to be on the sea itself, however, I found a very different matter. I defy anyone who is having a bad dose of mal-de-mer and wet through with spray to look or feel "jolly." The only comfort of Saturday was the knowledge that almost everybody going across to the island, was as bad as one's self. At Fleetwood I scorned the receptacle proffered by the Stewardess in my cabin, but before the boat had reached Douglas I was hugging that tin as my only means of salvation. It was a terrible passage! The lashing of the waves on the rocks round Douglas Head was a grand sight—to those who had energy left to see it. The white foam rose and fell against the dark background of cliffs with splendid effect. Unfortunately most of my fellow travellers were too intent on reaching terra-firma once more to enjoy the picture presented by the merciless waves. One little boy walking up the pier was heard to remark, "We'll never go on the sea no more, will we mamma?" Sunday and Monday were fine, the storm having cleared the atmosphere considerably.

* * *

To stand night after night listening to the "Going, going, gone!" of the auctioneers at the Pot Fair must be a trying ordeal. Judging by the reappearance of ladies every night one is led to believe that love of bargains makes them oblivious to fatigue. Some of them seem to positively enjoy the excitement which the loud-voiced vendor arouses amongst his listeners. Others stand meekly by listening to the vendors' open and by no means gentle criticism of a too wary housewife near who has her own ideas of the value of crockery and refuses to be "sold." There may be some satisfaction in getting a bargain, but it is scarcely elevating to listen to vulgar taunts voiced in doubtful language.

August 20th

To many people the advertisement hoarding is the only familiar picture gallery. It adds colour and brightness to otherwise drab streets. As an incentive for children to master the mystery of spelling it is unequalled, and the art which it instils is very often better than that of some picture shows with more pretensions and less utility. Unfortunately it has its weak points. The Haslingden educational authority has passed a resolution calling on the Town Council to veto the placarding of pictures of murders and crime as theatre advertisements. Such advertisements are invariably crude and an insult to eye and understanding alike. They familiarise the public, especially the juvenile public, with the idea of vice and crime far more than can the most maligned of "penny-dreadfuls". Therefore it will be well for the youth of Haslingden if the Town Council adopts the by-law suggested by the Educational Committee.

* * *

In the course of his journey by motor car from St. Just to Aberdeen, General Booth will pass through a considerable section of Lancashire, including Accrington. August 23rd, is the date fixed for his arrival in Accrington. As it is his first visit to the town, this particular Tuesday will be a record day for the Salvationists in this district. The Mayor and members of the Town Council will welcome him at the Town Hall entrance, after which he will address a meeting in the assembly-room on "The lesson of my life." The Rev. Canon Rogers will entertain the chief of the Salvation Army at the Vicarage. Three other motor cars, containing members of this staff and pressmen, will accompany the General's car. The Accrington Salvation Army band will proceed in front of the car, playing selections, from the bottom of Manchester-road to the Town Hall. If the General's musical taste but equals his zeal for the cause from the bottom of Manchester-road to the Town Hall will be the most memorable part of his route.

* * *

I am glad to hear that the two brothers at the Smallpox Hospital are well on the road to convalescence. No fresh cases have been reported, so that the temporary isolation has proved satisfactory to all concerned.

* * *

Bishop Thornton's idea of teaching boys to swim with their clothes on is one that will commend itself to all sensible people. Many men able to swim well enough without garments have lost their lives when cast into the water fully dressed. The Vicar and his son are having the boys from their schools taught to swim with clothes on, an admirable method which ought to be copied by everybody. If only we had decent public baths in Accrington some clergyman might follow the Bishop's good example for the benefit of our young boys. The present establishment is not inviting. I can imagine the enthusiasm of anyone evaporating before the many odoured atmosphere which is perceptible even at the entrance to our baths.

* * *

Accrington Market Ground has once again resumed its normal state. Crying vendors, the sound of falling pots, the sight of straw and rubbish—all have disappeared for another twelve months. Auctioneers voted this a bad year, so it is hoped they will try some more prosperous town another time. I fancy, though, despite lament, they found plenty of ladies willing to be gulled. Thank goodness peace and quiet have been restored to our town by their departure. Fairs always seem to bring a number of undesirable people into our midst.

August 27th

People from adjacent towns flocked into Accrington on Tuesday to see and welcome the hero of the hour, General Booth. The occasion was unique, and aroused considerable interest outside the ranks of the Salvationists. It is only a few weeks since Accrington had the privilege of greeting another famous General. What a striking difference 'twixt the two though. Every movement of Major-General Baden-Powell's betokened strength, vigour, and splendid training, and his face seemed to bring the hot glare of the African sun across one's vision. Slighter in build and much older—for he has passed the allotted span of years—General Booth is a different type of man. Tall and thin, with a long flowing beard and hair as white as snow, the Salvationist leader looked very feeble when compared with the younger General, and yet one could not fail to admire his straight figure, his bright eyes, his smiling face. Pale and careworn he looked as he stepped upon the platform of the Town Hall assembly room supported by one of his trusted lieutenants. His manner and his speech revealed a man of nervous, temperament, very highly strung.

General Booth had by his side two of Accrington's Grand Old Men, both of whom have gone grey in the service of the Master. It was indeed inspiriting to see three such veterans as General Booth, the Rev. Charles Williams, and Canon Rogers, whose combined ages represent 225 years or more. Mr. Williams is the General's senior by three or four years, but he retains the vigour and energy of a man of forty, and could probably give the Salvationist chief one half the distance in a five mile race. He too is a veritable globe trotter, though his mission has not been among the submerged tenth like the General's. Mr. Williams must have felt gratified at the hearty reception accorded him after his long trip.

Canon Rogers, too, had a cordial greeting. He is a man of a stamp altogether different from the two veterans by his side. He works in his own quiet way, but his heart is as big as the General's; he is equally solicitous for the weak and the lowly. It was not at all surprising to learn that he had readily consented to entertain the great Salvationist during his brief stay in the town.

Doesn't an hour and seventeen minutes seem an incredibly long time for a man so old and apparently so feeble as General Booth to address a big audience? Though his speech could scarcely be called eloquent it was earnest, was not lacking in vigour, and had many touches of humour. Here is one of his happy illustrations as near as I can remember. A woman in the lowest depths of degradation was discovered one day in the gutter helplessly drunk. Asked whether she would be taken to the police station or the Salvation Army shelter she was understood to choose the latter. Awaking next morning she inquired abruptly where she was. The attendant tried to assure her that she would take no harm as she was in the Salvation Army barracks. "For God's sake, get me out of this," she exclaimed, "or my reputation will be gone."

A wonderful organisation is the Salvation Army. Take the present motor-car mission as an example. Every detail is arranged with the utmost care; nothing is left to chance. The programme is carried out with clock-like regularity. It was announced that the General would arrive in Accrington at three o'clock, and he was there to the minute. "What time do you leave?" a friend asked one of the staff. "At six-thirty sharp!" was the reply, and at 6 30 they were off. And so it has been all through the tour. Six motor cars are employed in conveying the General and his staff from town to town, and the procession down Abbey-street and Blackburn-road was awaited with great interest. General Booth must have got a. rather bad impression of Lancashire weather. Almost every day while he was in the County Palatine King Sol was not over kind—not nearly so generous as our own King Edward has been to the originator of "Blood and fire."

* * *

It is not my intention to dwell upon the awful tragedy which has this week blotted Accrington's fair name. But I must express indignation at the heinous offence committed in our midst. That a woman should live a useful and peaceful life for well nigh four score years, and then to meet her end at the hand, of an assassin, and in a town like Accrington, too, is indeed very lamentable. Mrs. Westwell had done nothing to warrant such a termination of a long existence, and a woman who has lived so long might surely have been allowed to end her days in peace. The miscreant or miscreants will, I trust, meet with speedy justice. If he, or they were left to the mercy of the good operatives for whom Mrs.Westwell has for years provided early-morning tea, he or they would meet their deserts. This is the fourth foul tragedy in Accrington within a quarter of a century. True

Murder victim Mrs Westwell

the record is not a very black one, especially when we takes into account the fact that in two of the four cases the perpetrators of the crime were afterwards certified to be insane, but the number is far too great. I trust many years will elapse before it is the duty of local chroniclers to record such a dastardly outrage as that perpetrated in Hyndburn-road during Wednesday night.

September 3rd

A more charming day than Saturday for a garden party could not be wished for. The beautiful grounds of Bank House looked at their best with the sun shining so lavishly upon them. Ambulance workers and guests seemed equally delighted that for once King Sol had decided to smile on their efforts. Mrs. S. Briggs- Bury was graciousness itself to all her guests inviting many of them to partake of tea indoors.
Cosy seats were arranged along the walks and the lawn for the benefit of the visitors. Here the more sedate could be comfortable watching the endeavours of ladies to run with "eggs on spoons." The tug of war between the ladies, needle threading race for both sexes, sack race and half-mile race provoked much mirth. Very interesting, too, was the course of drills the Ambulance men performed.
Music by the Military Band was another attraction. Garden parties of this description are a decided acquisition.

* * *

Accrington seems all at once to be attaining an undesirable notoriety. The cruel murder of an old woman last week and the supposed murder of a baby this week are scarcely happenings of which a town may be proud. To put a newly- born babe in a drain is a type of cruelty which even the most hardened would shrink from. Surely the perpetrators of such a foul deed will not go undiscovered.

* * *

Some 700 plants were distributed amongst school children in Accrington at the end of April. Fuchsias and geraniums chiefly were given to be cultivated by the children. To-day the plants will be on view in the Town Hall, together with a collection of blooms from nurseries in the district. So there will be a good show. Successful competitors will be awarded prizes. Won't the excitement of children have been intense this week? Should this system bear the desired fruit Accrington will be a pleasanter place by and by. For if only every patch of garden were properly cultivated how very different would look our streets.

September 10th

Excitement grew intense on the outskirts of the crowd formed in Church-street on Monday night. To nothing less than a murder, terrible accident, or street brawl would the uninitiated attribute the large gathering. Sympathetic questions were asked about the supposed injured person, while many in imagination heard the clatter, clatter of the fire engine steeds. Conjectures of passers-by, however, were all wide of the mark. Several curious creatures elbowed their way through the pack of people to ascertain the cause of all the commotion. What was their astonishment to find on reaching the scene that it was but the result of goods arranged and ticketed for a shilling sale on the morrow.

On Tuesday one would have thought some celebrity had arrived in the town. At an early hour people formed in line, awaiting the opening, of the shop doors. I leave my readers to imagine the confusion which ensued. Sardines in tins would be comfortable by comparison with such bargain hunters. Women went to the windows, and clutched what had taken their particular fancy; more than one in the excitement of the moment tied the articles round their necks, lest others should covet and carry off the prize. Poor shop assistants! What an unenviable time they'd have! To study human nature at such a time spells ruin to the idealist. Entering the doors was difficult, but to get out again was, I hear, well nigh impossible. Isn't it surprising what some people will do when there is a chance of getting anything cheap?

September 17th

Gorgeous is the only adjective which adequately describes last Saturday's fete at Oak Hill. As soon as dusk descended the park was transformed into a veritable fairy garden by thousands of Pain's illuminated fairy lamps. To the left of the bandstand was represented a Chinese pagoda — a blaze of Chinese lanterns of every colour. Round the bandstand itself, where the Military Band performed in their very best style, was brilliantly lighted with patent lamps. Above the pond and reflected in the dark water was an effective glittering crown with E. R. blazoned on either side. The museum from ground to roof was a mass of bright illuminations.

But magnificent though these arrangements were, the pyrotechnic display was even grander. Rockets soared to the sky with telling effect descending in showers of golden rain, and there were prismatic torrents, nests of silver snakes, shooting stars, jewelled headed cobras, etc. Perhaps the most magnificent device was the blazing sun effect with chequered designs flanked by a terrace of smaller suns, and great silver clouds. Arranged on the incline by the cannon the trees around this rose coloured light and' groups of people standing near were silhouetted against what appeared like a unique sunset. Niagara was depicted on a set piece of flaming lights. The floral fan, too, was a clever invention, while the revolving fountains charmed the spectators. Interesting, too, was the naval combat at Port Arthur. A bouquet of coloured rockets and serial guns was a fitting finale to such an exhibition.

Subsequent investigations proved that there was no serious damage done to any part of the Park. One assumes from this that the enormous crowd gathered to see the fireworks was a conscientious one, and quite appreciated the trust reposed in them. The Corporation, I believe, received £25 for the use of the Park from the Company, so as there are no ill effects there seems no reason why this should not be a precedent for other displays.

* * *

Is it not rather a reflection on our Baths Committee that the contingent of ladies from our town who visit Rosegrove baths has been so great this summer? On this subject a correspondent writes: —"There are so many regular lady attenders from Accrington that the baths manager has asked them to compete for prizes offered at a forthcoming ladies gala." The baths manager there is evidently an enterprising man. I have seen the baths at Rose-grove, though, and when one compares the lofty building, marble fittings, and huge plunge bath filled with deliciously clean-looking water with the miserable facilities afforded at the St. James'-street establishment, one ceases to wonder why these ladies prefer to take their swimming exercises out of town. Another item worth noticing is the price of admission. Threepence is the regular charge for ladies at Rose-grove, while at Accrington 6d is the usual fee, I believe.

* * *

Altham Harvest Festival always brings crowds of people from adjoining towns and villages. Sunday was no exception to the rule, as the quaint old church was crowded to the doors at every service. In the evening especially the church was much too small to admit all the visitors anxious to hear the Vicar's sermon and see the decorations inside the edifice. Every available seat was utilised, while many stood in the porch, and a number of late arrivals heard the service seated on tombstones by the church door. The interior of the building was decorated with fruit, vegetables, corn, and flowers; the chancel and pulpit being prettily adorned with pink and white asters. The singing was tuneful, and in the hearty, natural style only heard in village churches nowadays. "Thanks, giving" was the theme of an excellent sermon preached by the

Rev. W. H. Green at the evening service. As usual, the Vicar experienced no difficulty in bringing each phase of his sermon clearly before every member of his congregation. Possessed of a fine voice and a remarkable gift of expression, he lacks not the distinct manner of delivery so necessary to a successful speaker. The bulk of his sermon was audible to those outside the building. I trust the offertories for the day were in keeping with the large attendance.

September 24th

Now that the "cast" is chosen there is no need for delay with rehearsals. So say the Accrington Amateur Operatic Society, and they have entered on this season's difficult work with their usual zest and determination. "Rose of Persia" affords plenty of scope for a large number of artistes, and I see by the list that several who have been relegated to the chorus in former years have now been offered a chance to distinguish themselves. Mr. Will Kenyon and Mr. C. P. Critchley one naturally expects to see at the top of the list after their manifold successes. The former takes the character of "Sultan" while "Hassan" has been allotted to the latter. "Yussuf," the storyteller, who has some excellent songs to sing, is a fitting character for the gentleman who acquitted himself so well as a noble Lord last year—Mr. Ben Bury. "Soldier of the Guard" is being undertaken by Mr. Tom Dobson. The other gentleman of lordly fame, Mr. Tom Noble, has at least one magnificent song, "When Islam first arose," as "Abdallah," Mrs. Bellingham (Miss Nellie Pickup) has been chosen to impersonate the modest and sweet "Sultana." The three slaves, "Scent of Lilies" "Hearts Desire," and "Honey of life" are in the hands of Miss A. Slater, Miss S. Crossley, and Miss Nuttall. "Dancing Sunbeam," "Hassan's" first wife, is the part given to Miss Thornton, while "Blush of Morning," his twenty-fifth wife, will be taken by Miss Jackson. "Oasis in the Desert," "Moon upon the Waters," "Song of Nightingales," and "Whisper of the West Wind," Hassan's wives, will be impersonated by Miss Hargreaves, Miss Eglin, Miss Berry, and Miss Wilcocks. A lengthy "cast" assuredly!

October 1st

The Rev. Jesse Hatten must have felt gratified, on Saturday when the Christian Endeavourers of Barnes-street presented him with a purse containing £20, a token of their esteem and appreciation of his unflagging zeal in Christian work. It is always a satisfaction to know that one's efforts are appreciated, and Mr. Hatten's face when he received the gift showed how surprised and pleased he felt at the solid acknowledgment of his services.

October 22nd

Isn't it surprising in these hard times, when everybody is crying poverty, how much money can be raised by bazaars and sales of work? The total proceeds from Oak-street sale of work amounted to something over £400. There must be many clever ladies connected with. Oak-street, for on each of the four days the opening ceremony was performed by members of our sex, while other ladies filled the chair and graced the platform. In every case the ladies showed themselves capable, and if the speeches did not positively scintillate with brilliancy, they at any rate had the saving grace of brevity. After all there is nothing so depressing as long-drawn out speeches at affairs of this kind. I was at a bazaar not long ago where the speakers claimed attention for nearly two hours by a flood of eloquence which, though admirable enough, well nigh defeated the object in view by taking up time which should have been devoted to buying and selling.

* * *

On Saturday, the last day of the sale, Mrs. Jardine performed the office of opener to the bazaar, while Mrs. Higham, of Highfield, presided. Mrs. Higham discharged her duty in a few well-chosen phrases, expressing amongst other things a wish that the sewing meetings, which had been such an enjoyable feature of the sale of work, should be continued during the winter months. For a first attempt at speech-making Mrs. Jardine acquitted herself remarkably well, and no doubt will be called upon at some future time to perform a similar ceremony. She spoke of the pleasure her connection with Oak-street and its bazaars afforded her. Especially did she dwell on the pleasure and profit to be gained by attendance at the sewing classes.

* * *

There seems no reason why such a delightful plan of having ladies as platform speakers should not be more common at our bazaars. The work of sewing and preparing for these functions devolves largely upon the womenkind, and the glory of oratory would, if nothing else, relieve the monotony. Their appearance, too, on these occasions is always so much prettier than that of mere men.

* * *

I was glad to read on Tuesday that the improvements at Accrington Station booking office are nearly completed. Accommodation for the public we are told has been doubled, and there are now four booking places. This will be a relief to the good people who travel on busy days, providing, of course, there is a man to attend to each booking place, and not one pair of hands expected to hand tickets to a long stream of people impatient at the delay occasioned by this silly method.

* * *

The young people of Cannon-street Chapel, I understand, have started a crusade against the idlers who throng our streets on Sunday nights, regardless alike of the Sabbath and the means of keeping it holy. By speech and song these young folk entertain the people and invite them to meetings illustrated by lantern slides in the school. The Salvation Army seems to have been the only organisation formed to cope with this sort of thing in the past. It is a worthy cause. May it meet with success.

October 29th

What really pleasant affairs the Women's Liberal Association "At Homes" are. On Wednesday and again on Thursday these energetic lady workers received large gatherings of people, entertaining them liberally with music and social chatter during the evenings.

* * *

On Tuesday the Burnley Choral Union had the Halle Orchestra down for their first concert this season. As usual, the Mechanics' Institute was well filled with musicians, for if anything Burnley people are more musical than Accringtonians. With Dr. Hans Richter as leader the concert was a huge success. It is a great pity two such big events as Kubelik's concert and the visit of the Halle Orchestra should occur within a fortnight of each other, as one of them naturally suffers financially. The musical contingent from Accrington was not proof against such extravagance on the part of Burnley, taking advantage freely of both concerts. Who shall say they were not wise, for since concerts at Manchester are barred owing to poor train service, there are very few chances of such musical treats.

* * *

It will be deplorable if the strike threatened by some of Bullough's workmen comes to pass. In the merits of the dispute I have no business to enter, but surely there is a more amicable and sensible way of settling such grievances than by striking. For everyone knows what strikes portend. With winter approaching it would seem foolhardy to cast away one's daily bread for the sake of differences. My heart bleeds for the poor women and children who at such times pay in starvation and poverty for the fool hardiness of their elders. Lamentable indeed would such a state of things prove when with a little more tact and moderation on the part of employers, and a trifle more of prudence and toleration shown by workpeople such a regrettable contretemps might be avoided. I sincerely hope for the sake of the women and children that the dispute will be settled amicably and a catastrophe averted.

* * *

Finishing touches are being put to goods intended for the forthcoming Ambulance bazaar in November. Time seems all too short to admit of completion for numerous delicious creations intended to grace the stalls. Heaps of garments have been turned out by sewing classes alone, and individual ladies are engaged in producing daintily-embroidered goods and fancy work as quickly as their busy fingers can work. What a huge bazaar it promises to be, after all this exertion on the part of our sex!

* * *

If November is to be taken as a criterion of social events for the winter, this season will be by no means a dull one. On November 2nd Robt. Cunliffe's orchestra are giving their annual concert in the Town Hall. The first of this season's Chamber concerts is arranged for the 4th of November. Ambulance bazaar will occupy days from the 7th to the 14th of the month. Ladies' subscription dance will in all

Accrington's popular and successful Robert Cunliffe Orchestra

probability take place towards the latter end of the month. The first Choral concert will be late in November, while December 2nd is the date fixed for Enfield Cricket Club dance—always a jolly affair. Then there is our amateur production, "Rose of Persia," early in December, to say nothing of professional theatrical companies' visits to the theatres during the winter months, and numerous socials and musical evenings always available at this time of year. Then there are private whist drives, always an enjoyable feature of December. Was there ever a gayer winter prophesied for Accringtonians socially ?

November 5th

That was a touching sight at Altham Church on Sunday. The grief of the congregation at Mr. Green's removal was manifested in various, ways during the farewell service, many weeping audibly. The Vicar's voice, too, was not free from that harshness which betokens keen sentiment when he referred to his long connection with Altham. As usual he preached with fine eloquence, in that refined mode of address which has so endeared him to the hearts of others besides his parishioners. Keen regret is felt through the district at his departure, though one cannot help realising that in Leeds he will have more scope for his talents.

* * *

Wednesday evening testified that the concerts of the Robert Cunliffe Orchestra are growing in popularity. Wagner, Brahms, Paggi, Haydn and Weber were represented in the programme, indicating a desire on the part of band and officials' to attain a high standard. Sullivan was the only English composer to find a place in the list, and as I sat during the interval the thought occurred to me that the orchestra might, on some future occasion, give us a Sullivan night. It would be an agreeable change, I think, and ought not to be a difficult task, though, strange to relate, "Patience" was the most indifferently executed piece at Wednesday's concert.

Brahm's Hungarian Dances were, to my mind, the most polished items of the programme. Tannhaueer seemed to lag, though the cornet solo "Star of Eve," was clearly and well played. In the Austrian Hymn, the variations were perhaps a little too conspicuous, the melody at times being lost. "Le Carnaval de Vendee" found most favour with the audience, whether because of the difficult six-eight time or the result attained 'twere difficult to say.

In spite of some defects, I have no hesitation in saying that the Cunliffe Orchestra has made wonderful improvement during the last couple of years. I hope they will remain loyal to the organisation, and if they make as much advancement during the two or three seasons coming, as they have done in the past, they will indeed be a credit to the town.

* * *

To-day is the 5th of November. May I suggest to the Town Hall Committee that they have a huge bonfire? They have plenty of materials in the assembly-room chairs, the destruction of which would call forth, a chorus of approbation from all concert goers.

* * *

Even at the risk of being accused of repetition, I must again offer a protest against the use of immense hats in the concert room. Picture hats are pretty in the street or in the park, but in the theatre or in the concert room they are a positive nuisance. One or two worn on Wednesday evening were the size of umbrellas, almost, and a friend tells me that she only got one or two glimpses of the singer by looking under the hats in front of her.

* * *

Another suggestion, and this time for concert and entertainment promoters. It is that the time of the concert should appear on the tickets. Circulars and advertisements of entertainments invariably get lost before the time, but the tickets are generally to be found, and if the time were named on the tickets it would save a lot of trouble.

November 12th

Accrington is too poor to build decent swimming baths. Yet Blackburn, which a few years back was considered far behind our own town in point of enterprise, is erecting a magnificent structure for the use of the population in the Daisyfield district. In addition to the ordinary slipper and plunge baths, Turkish and Russian baths are being provided in this building. Blackburn too already possesses much larger and nicer bathing establishments than we can boast of. It is left for such a "go ahead" town as ours to provide councillors who deem swimming unnecessary and cleanliness out of date. A fairy tale about a property owner who couldn't let his houses because of the baths he had built in them is being used as a clinching argument that baths are not wanted by the ordinary working man. Even so, what right have these brilliant theorists to take away from little children the love of cleanliness which is the mainspring of health ? Doctors in the town are agitating for baths, on the plea that disease and ill-health, are inevitable without them. What is the expense of baths when compared with the fevers and other diseases prevalent among those who have no means of washing themselves? Bah! such short- sighted policy on the part of our councillors makes one sick.

* * *

A meeting of members and subscribers of the Accrington Choral Society was called recently. The object was a bazaar to clear off the debt of £140 incurred by the society in past years, and to start a reserve fund. With the Ambulance bazaar close at hand, and other sales of work in progress, it is not surprising that a large contingent of expected lady enthusiasts did not turn up at the meeting. Perhaps another gathering will be called at a more propitious time. Some folks think a bazaar beneath the dignity of so old a musical organisation as our Choral union, but there seems no other way of raising the desired money, and it is clearly time such benefactors as Mr. R. Broughton and others who have proffered financial help were relieved.

* * *

What is really wanted is some form of entertainment with which Accrington people are not satiated. The proceeds from such an entertainment would go far towards buying materials for the proposed bazaar. Would it not be well to ask some of the town councillors their opinion on the subject ? It seems a pity so much brilliancy and so many inspired ideas of which our councillors are capable should be wasted on a mere scheme of slipper baths for the people.

* * *

Rain descended incessantly on Wednesday, but not even the vilest weather could deter patrons from attending the Ambulance bazaar, which must be pronounced a huge success. It was the most crowded opening day known in bazaar-land for some time. Never, I think, have I been present at a bazaar where it was so difficult to reach the stalls. To late-comers nothing was visible but a turbulent sea of ladies' hats. The Marquis of Breadalbane is gifted with a flow of eloquence which rendered the opening ceremony most interesting. Festoons and plants and fair ladies adorned the platform. Screened from view were tiny tables for tea, where a bevy of fair maidens in geisha costumes attended gracefully to the hungry ones. Many elaborate and pretty confections were worn by stallholders, and I am afraid much dainty and perishable finery was completely ruined in the confusion which ensued when the bazaar was declared open. I had intended giving a list of the beautiful gowns I saw, but ere I had recognised the wearer of some pretty costume she had vanished in the crowd.

November 19th

Bright, lovely weather favoured Mayoral Sunday. A large number of people gathered to see the Mayor and his attendants on their journey to and from church. And truly the processionists made a brave show. Scarlet uniforms were a pleasant contrast to the sombre garb of the civilians. It must have been a proud morning for Alderman Rawson, for in addition to the array of public men and officials who grace this annual assembly, a contingent of young ladies from the new Mayor's Sunday school class honoured their teacher by joining the procession. It was quite an innovation.

Alderman Rawson,
Mayor of Accrington 1904/5

* * *

There is no reason why ladies should not help to beautify these public affairs by their presence. "Scribbler" suggested on Tuesday that councillors, magistrates, etc., should be invited next year to bring their wives along with them when they accompany the Mayor to church, but he spoiled the suggestion by the sordid remark, "What would become of the Sunday dinner?" It does seem rather a pity that the maxim "Feed the brutes" must be strictly adhered to all the year round. One must get tired of continually ministering to the hearts of the Lords of Creation" through their appetites. I don't wonder "Scribbler" blushes for his sex when so large a number of them apparently live to eat.

* * *

"Nothing succeeds like success." Considerably over £2,000 has been realised by the huge bazaar in aid of the Ambulance Drill Hall. No wonder Choralites are anxious to promote a similar venture to clear the Society's debts, for a grander institution for raising money was never established. Never, I believe, has there been a bazaar certainly not for many years, in Accrington where policemen were required to keep people outside the doors, owing to the crush inside.

November 26th

In some things Accrington is far behind other towns, as instance the poor provision for swimming and wretched trams. A lady who had occasion to visit Blackburn on Tuesday evening was surprised to find not a trace of Monday's downfall of snow except on the house-tops and in the church-yards. Here and there was a touch of frost, but, nothing more. On returning to Accrington she was disgusted to see trodden snow in abundance both, on the roadway and on the footpaths. Indeed some of the main roads did not appear to have been touched. My friend noticed it all the more because at Blackburn she felt so dreadfully out of place in her snow shoes. Since we hear so much of the unemployed, it seems very strange that the Corporation cannot enlist the services of a few hundreds, instead of relying on a handful of men. Should the frost continue, we may expect the inevitable cinders, which make our footpaths filthy, and blacken all our carpets. It is quite time Accrington forsook some of its village ways.

* * *

In one respect I am glad to see we are improving. The illumination thrown from the electric light standards on Bull Bridge is a wonderful step in advance of the farthing candle-light, obtained from the old gas lamps. The traffic over Bull Bridge is enormous. It is a short cut from the Station and Blackburn-road into Whalley-road and on to Clayton-le-Moors, and is one of the busiest thoroughfares in the town. To those who are unacquainted with the locality this may seem somewhat of an exaggeration, but any who doubt the accuracy of the statement need only spend an hour on or near the bridge which spans our filthy river, and they will be satisfied. Let us hope, now that the thoroughfare has been adequately lighted, the dangerous bend at the corner of Croft-street will be speedily removed. It is one of Accrington's death traps.

December 3rd

Well done, ladies. The dance was a huge success. I have never seen the Conservative Club look nicer than it did last Friday. Around the room were mirrors and draperies, and some delightfully comfortable chairs and lounges; the platform being almost obscured by refreshing green palms and other plants. Behind the green array, Mr. Geo. Thornton's orchestra discoursed sweet music for dancing. One corner of the room near the platform was utilised for refreshments, a table being erected for the purpose on which were placed all manner of dainties. The floor was in perfect condition, and as is customary "when youth and pleasure meet to chase the glowing hours with flying feet," all went merrily. A most unusual but very amusing feature of the dance was the scarcity of young ladies. Gentlemen passed hither and thither among the fair ones unable to procure sufficient dances to fill up the blanks on their programmes. It is much nicer when such is the case however, and we girls had a splendid time in consequence. As it is practically the first of this season's balls, a few notes I made on some of the gowns will not come amiss.

A very pretty cream voile with palest blue flower pattern had for its trimming festoons of pink chiffon roses around the skirt and cream lace yoke, the corsage being finished with frill upon frill of softest chiffon. One of this year's brides looked charming in a gown of soft creamy material with skirt gauged below the hips and folds at the hem; the bodice had medallions of lace and a deep pointed collar beneath the yoke. A couple of terra-cotta chrysanthemums arranged in the coiffure added the desirable note of colour.

Very sweet was a pale green dress with broad horizontal tucks and gaugings on the skirt, the bodice made with fichu of accordian-pleated chiffon surmounted by Paris embroidery and large poufed sleeves; a broad directoire belt completed a very becoming "toute ensemble."

A young debutante wore a simple but sweet frock of white crepe-de-chine; the pointed collar was adorned with cream insertion, the short skirt had alternate rows of tucks and pretty lace insertion, with pure white satin belt and streamers at the waist.

* * *

Wednesday's Choral Concert passed off fairly well, although some of the artistes were not up to Choral standard. Miss Blanche Mackie possesses a well-trained soprano voice, but lacks the "weight" necessary for a successful interpretation of such songs as Weber's "Ocean, thou mighty monster." There is much sweetness in the tone of her voice, and no doubt in a few years—she is very young—will acquire the strength and power necessary for such efforts. The delightful cuckoo notes in the song she sang as an encore were much more suited to her voice. "The Rosary," too, was very sweetly sung. The tenor, Mr. H. Beaumont, was disappointing at first, but improved as the evening advanced. "I'll sing thee songs of Araby" was tastefully interpreted, and the Irish ditty which followed was as pleasing as it was funny— scarcely the type of song one would expect at a Choral concert though. A ponderous style is Mr. A. Tucker's. Technique was manifest in his songs, but zest was denied them, they lacked light and shade throughout. "The Diver" was "his best song. The 'cello solos were the features of the evening. Mr. W. H. Squire introduced a depth of expression into them which quite charmed everyone. "Te Cygne" was beautiful. I could have listened to its repetition the whole evening. The favourite "Melodie," Rubinstein, too, was well done, showing a keen insight into the composer's love of delicate harmony. "Papillons" (Popper), though so different in style, was equally charming.

The chorus singing was good, in "Jesu, Priceless Treasure" (Bach) exceptionally so. In the "Spinning Chorus" for female voices, and the "Spanish Serenade," the chorus acquitted themselves with credit. One or two harsh voices in the choir were clearly never intended for Choral work; they become most obtrusive in "piano" passages. The male element, too, is rather lacking. There were under a dozen tenors, and not twenty basses. This surely is not the best muster of which Accrington is capable? Mr. Forbes as accompanist was excellent, his ability being most marked in "Jesu, Priceless Treasure."

* * *

Though I may be accused of repetition, I cannot let the rudeness of early departures from the concert pass without comment. Such thoughtlessness on the part of a portion of the audience must be very disconcerting to Mr. Walker or any other conductor.

December 10th

It is nearly twenty years now since I first began to take an active interest in newspaper work. During those twenty years' intercourse with newspapers of every description I have never come across a scheme which has roused the excitement and interest of readers to such a degree as the offer of free seats for the "Rose of Persia." Over 7,000 coupons, I understand, were delivered at the "Observer" office, and a considerable portion of the staff for the greater part of three days did nothing but open envelopes the whole day through. Excitement must be intense amongst those seven thousand "couponists." and I trust many of my readers will be amongst the lucky one hundred and fifty; for the Editor, I understand, set the crown on his previous act of generosity by securing, for his readers fifty additional tickets. There will, of course, be many disappointments.

* * *

Still another effort was put forth last night, in aid of the Ambulance Drill Hall. A Cafe Chantant in the Liberal Club, promoted by Mr. Frank Rowland, aided by Mrs. Peltzer, besides adding to the funds of the cause provided much enjoyment. "Browne" was a delightful play, well done. Dancing and songs introduced during the evening provided pleasant variety.

* * *

The Hockey Dance has been arranged for Friday, the 30th of December. It is becoming quite a hardy annual, and always most enjoyable to friends, as well as to votaries of the delightful game of hockey.

December 17th

So much has been written about our Amateurs that it seems almost superfluous to say more. But I cannot let such a, production as the "Rose of Persia" pass without some comment. With Monday's performance I was disappointed, but since then the opera has gone exceedingly well. The cues on Monday were not taken quickly, resulting in one or two rather awkward pauses, but on the whole it was, for a first night, excellent.

Although not a popular opera our Amateurs have done much to make the "Rose of Persia" acceptable. Only in a first-class company do we find voices, speaking generally, so good as we have listened to at the Prince's Theatre this week. The acting, too, has been natural, and the chorus seems to gain in volume every year,

Would, it be possible to find a comical character in light opera in which Mr. "Charlie" Critchley couldn't shine? "Koko," "Lord Chancellor," and now "Hassan," not to mention a host of others, and in all he has pleased everybody.

Mrs. Bellingham takes the part of "Sultana" with her usual vivacity. Of all the characters she has portrayed in past years there is not, I think, one more suited to her style.

Mr. Will Kenyon is a dignified "Sultan" and, as usual acts very well. There is not much scope for his ever-present sense of humour, but he makes the most of his opportunities.

Mr. Ben Bury "Yusuff, the storyteller" could not be improved. His voice is his strong forte, though his acting, especially in the love scene with "Heart's Desire," is capital.

Miss Sally Crossley gives a refined representation of "Heart's Desire," winning all hearts, in the first act by her girlish demeanour in her short blue frock with its border of gold trimming, jaunty coat, and small crown.

It is fair to assume, perhaps, that the lack of demonstration on the part of the audience in the early part of the week was due to the fact that they were not familiar with the opera. They know it better now, and are able to appreciate its tuneful numbers. The attendances during the week have been very satisfactory, filling the theatre to the doors.

December 24th

Saturday's performance of the "Rose of Persia" was a brilliant "wind-up" to a successful week. Despite the fact that many professed not to care overmuch for the opera itself, the theatre was literally packed with people. The "house" had sufficiently thawed during the week to admit of rapturous applause, and the audience "enthused" to their heart's content. Who shall say our Amateurs were not gratified thereby? Six beautiful bouquets bearing Mr. J. W. Bridge's card were presented to the principal ladies during the evening. Mrs. Bellingham, Miss S. Crossley, and Miss Florence Thornton each received a lovely shower bouquet of tea roses, smilax, and maidenhair fern. Equally pretty were the bouquets of terracotta and yellow chrysanthemums given to Miss Jackson, Miss Slater, and Miss Nutall.

* * *

That was a sad ceremony at Whalley Parish Church on Monday when the body of Miss May Alexandra Appleby, only daughter of the late Mr. Edgar Appleby, of Wilpshire, who had died at school in London, was lowered to its last resting place. She was born sixteen years ago about the time the then Prince and Princess of Wales laid the foundation stone of the Black-burn Technical School, and as her father was at the time Mayor of Blackburn, she became the god-daughter of the Princess, receiving from her godmother a silver christening cup.

* * *

All doubts as to the close proximity of Christmas are dispelled by the ever-increasing weight of our letter bags. Many people prefer to have their greetings delivered before Christmas day, but for those who don't, the system of posting cards several days before, and having them delivered as usual on Christmas morning, is excellent. Everybody is shopping just now except the children, who with wide-eyed wonder gaze at the gay trappings of mirth displayed in the shop-windows, and the numerous toys which in due course will find their way into the inevitable Santa Claus stockings.

To-morrow is Christmas day, so I take this opportunity of wishing all my readers a Happy Christmas!

* * *

On Wednesday a number of unmarried ladies of Accrington gave a Spinsters' Ball in the Conservative Club. The room was beautifully decorated with flowers and palms. Along one side of the rooms were little supper tables, with vases of flowers, and screens round. The anteroom was furnished a la drawing-room, and the corridor arranged the same way. Mr. Thornton's band played from 8.50 until two o'clock. There were about 150 people present, and the evening was voted a great success.

December 31st

Christmas Day, with its interesting cards of greeting and fascinating parcels has come and gone once again. The clerk of the weather office did not arise to the occasion as one expected. Was ever Christmas Day so murky and dismal out of doors? With my Inverness buttoned cosily up to my ears I ventured out into the blackness, but not for long. Feeling chocky and miserable with the damp sticking to my hair I trudged on, until encountering the ruddy glow in a house close by I paused. Silhouetted against the firelight, ensconced in comfortable-looking arm chair, with feet extended to the warm blaze, engrossed in what appeared to be an absorbing novel, was a human figure. It all looked so inviting and "Christmassy" that in great haste I retraced my steps and spent the rest of the day toasting myself before a generous fire, and the foggy atmosphere knew me no more.

* * *

There is always a pleasurable excitement connected with the coming of the New Year. It is fraught with charming possibilities. Pangs of regret at the passing of 1904 are not very keen; it has been but a shabby-genteel sort of year. We, have been threatened with a general election, war with a great European Power, and have at last realised the inefficiency of an army which is one of the bravest but most expensive in the world. Still, 1904 has not been lacking in individual pleasures for the multitude. A more sunny summer, with its attendant social functions we have not had in Accrington for some time. But the feeling of exultation connected with the opening of a brand new account book will not be suppressed.

* * *

There is a shadowy prospect of a new bathing establishment being erected in our midst, and then there is always a possibility —very faint, but still a possibility—of Accrington's gaze descending with surprise and rapture some day on new tram cars. If 1905 but brings these two desirable projects to fruition it won't be a bad sort of year after all. The baths may come; for the new tramway system I fear we shall have to wait a while.   .

* * *

Those who in the kindness of their hearts gave of their musical gifts to the sufferers in our hospital this Christmas-time have done much to alleviate the pain and loneliness of patients who, deprived of their home life by physical ailments, must have otherwise felt the hours of this festive season drag heavily. The wards, with their wealth of holly, mistletoe, dainty pink shades and mottoes inscribed in letters on a background of white cottonwool looked very pretty indeed. There was something very pathetic in the scenes while the concerts were in progress. The faces of patients, many of them showing signs of the intense pain they must have endured, lying on their white pillows visibly lightened as the artistes gave of their best. St. Peter's choir boys delighted the invalids greatly. "Father Christmas" with his little gifts was evidently an exciting innovation. Mr. Rowland must have felt gratified by the pleasure his "get-up" gave. The kindly faces of the nurses beneath their snowy caps were beaming good-naturedly, doctors smiled benignantly on the proceedings, several taking active parts as vocalists, while the interest in anything which concerned their patients was keenly manifested in the sympathetic faces of Miss Carpenter, the matron, and her able assistants.

1905

January 7th

What a pity "Jedbury Junior" was performed on a Saturday. Especially was it unfortunate the date fixed was the last Saturday in the old year, one of the very busiest days for shopkeepers. There is no doubt the absence of tradespeople made a great difference in the receipts, but of course our Amateurs were obliged to take the theatre when it was available.

The play itself had the charm of novelty, but can scarcely be compared with some former works chosen by our Amateurs, especially "A Pair of Spectacles." None can deny, however, that the performers came through the ordeal with flying colours. Miss Constance Kenyon as "Dora" was excellent. Her enunciation was good and her appearance very refreshing throughout. Miss Kenyon's stage-bearing is very graceful, and at all times she is self-possessed, showing a familiarity with stagecraft. "Mrs. Glibb" was in the capable hands of Miss Margaret Rendell. She affected the society drawl and manner admirably, and quashed her "worse-half" in fine style. Miss Hilda Peltzer gave a modest interpretation of "Nellie." At times her voice was not quite strong enough to reach all parts of the theatre.

I do not like to grumble about anything pertaining to Saturday's performance, but I cannot leave it without offering a suggestion to the management of the theatre. A folding door at the top of the steps would go a long way towards putting an end to the abominable draughts people in the circle complain so loudly of, and two doors would effect an absolute remedy.

* * *

Judging by the number of times we have been treated to the strains of "Fine old English gentleman," the coffers of local bandsmen must this week be in flourishing condition. Eight times in one afternoon I heard the air repeated. I began to wish the "old gentleman" had died in infancy. When there are so many "fine" gentlemen living only a few yards apart, wouldn't it be as well to substitute, say, "Jolly good fellow" or some other musical treasure? New recruits, too, in the musical world seem to have been much in evidence this Christmas time. One band especially reminded one of a village orchestra. It was unique. After the first few bars the air was indistinguishable. The cornet struggled, sometimes hitting the correct notes but oftener missing them, the trombonist blew a mighty blast, generally at the wrong moment, two bars behind, several bandsmen were doing their utmost to keep going, one or two wavered uncertainly between a whole octave of notes, while others becoming breathless ceased blowing their instruments with a despairing wail; the conductor, oblivious that his post was a mere sinecure, smiled serenely. Rain descended copiously on the struggling musicians, and many a naughty word, too, I'm afraid. I don't know how that particular band concluded their repertoire — before the finale I'd jammed on my hat and fled away, anywhere out of sound of discordant notes and despairing wail of brass.

January 14th

On a clear, frosty day, when the ground is hard, a "paper chase" is fine sport, but on such a day as Saturday one needed to be very enthusiastic indeed to squeeze much enjoyment out of that old game beloved of school-boys. Nevertheless a party about thirty in number braved soaking wet grass, puddles, mud, and other discomforts on Saturday afternoon for the joys of the chase. A bevy of young ladies armed with, bags of confetti, and looking almost as energetic as hares, started for Whalley. Fifteen minutes grace was permitted, then the "hounds"— members of the sterner sex—followed in hot pursuit. The route taken was over Whinney Hill, past Hard Farm, via the canal towing path—(oh, the horrors of that muddy path)—out at Hyndburn Bridge, thence over Whalley Nab into the village of Whalley. Ascending hills at a brisk walk and running headlong downhill the girls managed to get a good start, despite the clinging mud and splashings of dirty water. Nothing was seen of the "hounds" until the Nab was nearly traversed, when the "hares" descried them close on their heels at the foot of the hill. (It has been said, but tell it not in Gath, that the hounds had a rest and a smoke en route, and made up for lost time by taking a "short cut," but that is, or rather was, by the way). Then it was the chase waxed fast and furious. "Hares" darted forward at renewed speed one or two being trapped. Several evaded their pursuers and contrived to out-distance them reaching Whalley in advance a few minutes. To see the faces as each one dashed into the Assembly-room was a sight, I can assure you. Dishevelled appearance, cheeks glowing, in some cases to a deep purple tint, with the vigour of the chase—it was a comical picture. Later, tea was served to the hungry "hunters" and their "quarry," followed by a dance and drive home.

* * *

Heartiest congratulations to Miss Ruth Walton Kenyon, who has passed the Licentiate of the Royal Academy of Music, and is now entitled to use the letters L.R.A.M. More than once, at places of entertainment, she has charmed by the grace and beauty of her piano playing. Congratulations are due, I believe, in another direction, but that is more or less a private matter.

* * *

After much talk the Baths Committee have decided to spend £100 in "patching up" (sic) the St. James'-street bathing establishment. Handsome, isn't it? Makes one want to rave about the beauties of economy. It is comforting to learn that a baths' manager in a town not more than five miles away from Accrington is arranging special facilities for the summer for those of the ladies from our town who desire to indulge in swimming, without the risk of typhoid or other disease. That arrangement solves one difficulty, only it seems a reflection on our town to be compelled to take advantage of other people's swimming baths. What a pity a Marie Corelli does not dwell in Accrington to convince our councillors and others that cleanliness is next to godliness.

* * *

The Mayor's tea party on Saturday was a big event for the poor children of Accrington. It was a thoughtful way of celebrating Alderman Rawson's birthday, and one which, when he saw the pinched faces around him made happy for a time by his generosity, I am sure he would not regret. It is always a pleasure to give freely to the little ones; their delight is such a genuine thing. Stories related in such a way as to be appreciated by the juvenile mind were part of the entertainment, and not the least enjoyable part either from the child's point of view.

January 21st

Another excellent programme is provided at the Accrington Hippodrome this week. A big turn, in which great interest centres, is presented by Miss Annie Hartley, who, with her colleague, Augustine, performed some marvellous barrel jumping feats, and after each trick manipulated the barrels in a way which surprised the audience. Rice, Rose, Davis and the "Half" gave a smart burlesque scene, and Flemine, the one-legged acrobat, was one of the surprises of the night. Henri Bekker also performed some clever juggling tricks. Among the rest of the artistes are A. Walton, descriptive vocalist; Flo Atkins, lady concertinist; G. Scott, vocal comedian; and Connor and Traynor, comedians and boxers.

* * *

After such a chilly blast Monday's downfall of snow was scarcely surprising. The country, clothed in a garb of untrodden white, presented an entrancing sight, but snowdrifts and the persistency with which the snow penetrated even the tiniest crevices in windows and doors of our domains was scarcely voted so picturesque, and was by no means welcome.

I must compliment those who are responsible for the roads on the dexterity and rapidity with which the snow was got rid of on Tuesday.

January 28th

The winter of discontent has not been confined to Britain or the British, judging by the injured, almost plaintive tone of letters from friends in the South. To have journeyed to the Riviera with a phalanx of boxes containing numerous dainty creations, only to find climatic conditions almost as bad as in England must be distressing. From Menton I gather that the frost has almost ruined some of the beautiful gardens out there. Nevertheless one feels a spark of something akin to envy when one sees the departure of lucky ones bound for the sunny South with its violets, mimosa and turquoise blue sea.

* * *

Members of Moss-lane Tennis Club held their annual meeting on Monday. It was decided to re-open the courts on the first Saturday in May, providing the weather be propitious. Financial results for the past year appear to have been satisfactory, as the club finds itself with a balance in hand of £30. Mr. Langham is secretary for the coming season, and Miss Elsie Kenyon has undertaken the duties of tea-secretary.

* * *

Blackpool Promenade will be a fine sight by Easter if, as expected, the new sea wall is sufficiently complete to admit of a double line of trams running along the entire length of the Promenade. It has taken nearly three years to build the wall from south to north, but as the foundations have now been joined there is every hope of its completion by Whitsuntide if not earlier.

* * *

Have you ever played "progressive pit"? Until recently, when on a visit to Southport, I was in happy ignorance of the game. I had a vague idea it was some sort of a round game played with cards, but that was all. "Pit" sounds simple enough, doesn't it? Days have elapsed since that evening party, and I am still hoarse. My hostess assured me the game was absurdly easy, so nothing loth I took my place at one of the tables. dealt the cards very swiftly, and almost before I had scanned mine the "pit" was declared open, and the buying and selling began. Oh, the babel that ensued! Ladies became excited and almost screamed in their eagerness to dispose of their unnecessary cards, while gentlemen cried their goods in loud tones, grabbing others in exchange. I have but a confused idea what happened after that until cried "corner," and then for a moment the row ceased, followed by questions such as "Had you barley?" "Oh, who had 'oats'?" "Great Scott! I only wanted one to complete a corner in 'wheat'. Who had that one?" Then the game was resumed, and with brief pauses the roar continued. Now it rose, now it fell, now it remained almost at a set level, and ever resembled a thundering wave of clangour. It all seems like a dream even now. If this up-to-date nightmare resembles the Wheat Pit, as it is supposed, I am sorry for the poor men who have to do the buying and selling. It must be horrible. Why, the roar was so great at times that neighbours turned out to see what had happened. And yet I'm eagerly watching the post-bag in the hope of receiving another invitation to "pit" soon. Though noisy, there is something fascinating in that latest mania.

* * *

The family of the late Mr. Eli Heyworth, J.P., cotton manufacturer and ex-mayor of Blackburn, have this week communicated with the trustees of the Peel Foundation, offering to provide two scholarships of £50 each, tenable for three years at a university, in his memory. The offer represents £3,000, and has been accepted with thanks.

* * *

One is glad to learn that there is a decrease in the proportion of blind children. At the annual meeting of the Accrington and District Blind Society, it was stated that the Society's latest departure had been the attempt to have each day school visited. When put to the test, 650 children were found to have defective sight. Over a hundred cases demanded immediate attention, many of them requiring the services of a skilled eye surgeon. It is a most deplorable state of affairs. May the good work of the Society continue.

February 4th

The trio of Accrington musicians must have felt, flattered by the reception given them on Wednesday evening. One expected a fairly large gathering, for there is always a section of the community who take a keen interest in the doings of local musicians, but such a response from the public surprised even the most sanguine. It was a great compliment. Every available seat was pressed into service, and the result was a "house worth playing to." There was no lukewarm applause either, though many of the items on the programme must have been a degree above the understanding of the majority. The programme was, if anything, a trifle too long, especially with the encores added. Even the most enthusiastic get tired of sitting on those terrible chairs too long. The interval was hailed with delight by those who, for a brief space, could vacate their seats and stretch their aching limbs. Those who didn't avail themselves, of the opportunity were foolish indeed, for the results of such endurance, I have found by experience, are acutely painful. When will our Town Hall Committee come to the rescue of a long-suffering public?

* * *

Miss K. A. Whittaker, whose soprano voice charms by its sweetness, sang exceedingly well. She wore a girlish-looking gown of white with a deep gathered flounce on the skirt, and a berthe of pretty lace, a similar frill of lace adorned the elbow sleeves; her sash of black was a contrast to the whiteness of her gown. "When Celia sings" (Moir) was far away her most pleasing contribution.

Of the quality of Mr. Bridge Peters's rich baritone voice there are no two opinions. With such a voice he ought to go far in the musical profession. Nor does he lack the confidence necessary for success, and his

Mr. Bridge Peters,
BARITONE.

enunciation is clear. His songs were of a high standard, too high, perhaps, for most people, as one young fellow was heard to remark: "Bridge is in fine form to-night, but I wish he'd sing something we could appreciate." "She alone charmeth my sadness" (Gounod) was exceedingly well interpreted, giving evidence of careful training and much study. "Don Juan's serenade", (Tschaikowsky) was perhaps his most finished effort, though too late in the evening to gain, the encore it deserved. Here, too, Miss Ruth Kenyon's accompanying was well done.

* * *

The violinist, Mr. Arthur Catterall, was in good form, playing with a power of expression. "Dance of the Elves" (Popper) was delightful while both movements in Greig's "Sonata in F" (piano and violin) were remarkable. He has a splendid touch, and plays with ease and certainty. The piano portions lacked nothing either, in the hands of Mr. Forbes.

* * *

Mr. Willy Lehmann's performance was the best I have yet heard from him. He brought out the notes from his 'cello splendidly. Under the touch of a master hand the 'cello, is always inspiring, so rich and dulcet are its tones. "Kol Nidrei" (Bruch) was excellently rendered, eliciting well-deserved rounds of applause. Popper's "Hungarian Rhapsody" was also keenly appreciated. After one particularly difficult passage the audience interrupted with loud applause, and for some time Mr. Lehmann was unable to "rhapsodise" further.

Many besides children will be glad to learn that the firm who gave the pyrotechnic display in the park have offered to give other displays, one in July and another in September, subject to the approval of the committee. I see no reason why, as there was no damage done, the park should not be given over for this form of enjoyment on two Saturday nights. The Corporation, of course, might secure better terms than on the first visit.

February 11th

Haven't the comparatively warm and spring-like days this week been welcome? Tuesday especially was a glorious day, quite the clearest and balmiest we have had this year. I never remember revelling so much in the sunshine before. To be on the summit of a hill and breathe the delicious freshness in the air, bask in the lavish sunshine, and dream of a few weeks hence when the trees will have donned their new spring costumes of freshest green, is by no means an employment devoid of pleasure.

* * *

Pleasurable and profitable proved Thursday evening for those who spent it with the Young Men's Fraternal Society at Willow- street. The audiences, not confined to the Baptist denomination by any means, are generally large, and Thursday night's gathering quite filled the large room. Ludwig van 'Beethoven, the grandest musical genius of the 19th century, was the subject of a comprehensive paper, compiled and read by Mr. James B. Macalpine. At times his delivery was just a trifle rapid. Several humorous touches in the paper helped to brighten the sad and disappointing features of the great musician's life. The vocalists, Mr. J. Hanson and Mr. B. Peters, contributed several songs.

* * *

Nothing definite has been done, I see, with regard to the acceptance of the offer made on behalf of Mr. W. Peel of a portion of Hillock Farm to the Corporation to be converted into a park. Next month, perhaps, when the great ones have inspected the Coppice, we shall have a favourable report. It is a good site for a park, and no doubt any little difficulties with regard to the privileges of golfers and others will be speedily overcome should the committee consider the offer a desirable one.

* * *

The bazaar in aid of the Park Congregational Sunday School, P.S.A. and P.W.E. has had a great interest for many this week. Judging by the large numbers of people in the Town Hall on Wednesday, the opening day was a success. One bazaar is very much like another, however, and they all seem to have for their motto the old formula, "To sell and be sold." The decorations, in the form of a Japanese village, were something out of the ordinary and very effective. May the proceeds more than realise expectations.

* * *

It was pleasant to see the "old folks" enjoying themselves once again on Saturday. One thousand is rather a stiff number to supply with tea, but it was managed somehow, and the old people enjoyed themselves immensely. To have 209 over seventy years of age is a record for the annual gathering, and one of which Accrington is no doubt proud, even if its birth rate has diminished rapidly of recent years.

February 18th

Should the plans of the new Library drawn by Mr. Newton, the Borough Engineer, meet with Mr. Carnegie's approval, we shall add another imposing structure to our limited number of public buildings in Accrington. And if the building be on such a scale as the design illustrated in Tuesday's issue represents, it will be an addition worth having. Judging by the picture, our future library will be a magnificent edifice. What a pity Mr. Carnegie only deals in libraries! A swimming establishment now on a similar scale would be delightful.

* * *

If it wasn't for the disagreeable thought of having to sit for hours on those uncomfortable chairs in our Town Hall, I should be living in pleasant anticipation of next Wednesday's orchestral concert. For I hear the Robert Cunliffe Orchestra have a splendid programme arranged. Perhaps it is better to have good music and poor seats, though, than good seats and poor music. Nothing like an optimistic view.

* * *

Although it was announced that Miss Appleby's wedding was to be a very quiet affair, owing to the recent death of her cousin, crowds of people gathered in and around All Saints' Church, Clayton-le-Moors, long before the time of the nuptials. Each side of the awning from the gate to the church porch was lined with people standing three deep, groups of people gathered outside the gates, while folk jostled one another to get into the sacred edifice. Selections of music were played on the organ before the bride appeared, while those who had gained admittance marvelled at the beautiful decorations in the church. Stately palms were arranged in dignified array, pink roses, lillies, daffodils, and other choice white blooms shed their fragrance on the surrounding atmosphere. Tastefully arranged was the chancel with its wealth of flowers, the communion table also being prettily set off by other blooms. Excitement grew intense as the clock neared the half-hour, but scarcely had the chimes ceased when the bride, leaning on the arm of her brother, walked up the aisle. Up to the time of wedding the weather had not been quite as nice as one would have wished, but the sun shone unmistakably on the bride, and the clouds disappeared, leaving a peerless blue in the heavens before Captain Fairclough and his wife left the church.

The conventional phrase, "the honeymoon is being spent at so-and-so," will hardly apply in this case, as after the ceremony Captain and Mrs. Fairclough started for London, the first stage of a bridal tour which it is understood will extend over a year. From London they proceed to the Riviera, and a brief stay there will be succeeded by a spell of globe-trotting, which will take in portions of every continent.

February 25th

It was pleasing to note on Wednesday that one or two additional lady violinists had become members of the Cunliffe Orchestra. There is no reason why members of our sex should not help to swell the ranks of a musical organisation which is steadily rising both in numbers and musical progress. When one thinks of the commencement of this society and its subsequent development, one feels proud of our local talent and the way it has adapted itself. Who, listening to the orchestra long before it rose to the dignity of a Town Hall performance, would have guessed that someday the same players would attempt a programme such as last Wednesday's? I don't mean to infer that the instrumentalists are perfect by any means, but only to draw attention to the rapidity and certainty of their progress.

March 4th

It is regrettable that the Victoria Cottage Hospital report for 1904 shows such a falling off in the income on revenue account. To bad trade is attributed the decrease in workmen's subscriptions. There have been so many concerts and entertainments promoted this winter for various other charities that a decrease from that source too, is not surprising. Really, I think there never was such a winter for entertainments. What with one thing and another, people are becoming positively satiated with pleasures, and not a little tired of purchasing tickets for any and every kind of charity entertainment. Still, a deserving institution such as our Hospital, which is doing such excellent work in our midst, should not be allowed to languish for lack of funds.

* * *

With the sentiments expressed in Mr. Duckworth's letter, re new baths, in Tuesday's issue, I agree. More than once I have referred to the inadvisability of trying to patch up the St. James's-street building. Older people have long since transferred their swimming exercises to the more sanitary buildings of adjacent towns, but it is the poor children from the schools who in all innocence risk diseases from the bad smells. I also think "there is grave responsibility on those who permit school children to use the baths."

* * *

The decision of the Darwen Parks Committee to abolish Sunday music in the Darwen parks is no doubt admirable from the point of view taken by some people. I am glad, though, the same weighty decision has not appealed to our Parks Committee, for, as "Scribbler" says, there is much, enjoyment afforded by this innocent amusement, and there are always the hills for those who prefer rest and quiet. The Darwen committee stated that "music interferes with the right use of a park." Why? What is the right use of a park?

* * *

March, though it may bring in its train cold east winds, is very welcome. For is it not the month when new fashions become more than suggestions, and sale bargains, which have presented such dejected sights in our shop windows for weeks past, give place to new spring goods? Shopping in Accrington has been robbed of all its attractions for many weeks, owing to the display of old and sometimes dirty stock. It will be quite a relief to see something fresh and new.

March 11th

Judging by the list of artistes whose services have been secured by our Choral Society, next Wednesday's concert will be above the average. The chosen, works are "Stabat Mater" (Rossini) and Mendelsohn's "Hymn of praise." The principals are Miss Gleeson White (soprano), Miss Annie Worsley (contralto), Mr. Webster Millar (tenor), and Mr. Fowler Burton (bass).

* * *

The Conservative ball was not very successful in point of numbers, though no doubt the postponement of the dance accounted for the decrease. It seems a great pity, though, for at one time it was one of the big social events of the winter season. The assembly room is so large that anything under a hundred dancers barely fill the place comfortably and there is nothing more depressing than a sparsely attended function of this description. However, better luck next time, I hope.

March 18th

Once again the Choral Society deserve all praise. Wednesday's concert was voted generally a success. Barring one or two imperfections it was fit to rank with any of the previous successes in the musical line. A little more light and shade in the chorus work would have been an improvement, but on the whole the chorus singing was exceptionally well done. In "Hymn of Praise" especially the chorus excelled. The principals, excepting Mr Fowler Burton, were in good voice. He, unfortunately, was not up to his usual concert form. In the chorus and recitative "Eia Mater", he was decidedly flat. He began on a false note, and was afterwards, apparently, unable to recover himself. Anyhow, it was a most disappointing rendering of one of the prettiest portions of "Stabat Mater", quite obscuring any beauty there might have been in the chorus part. His delivery of "Pro Peccato" was good. Miss Annie Worsley, the second soprano, sang exceedingly well, although apparently very young.

Miss Gleeson White quite won all hearts by her charming personality and bell like voice. I could have listened with pleasure all night to Miss White's melodious and withal powerful voice.

The tenor, Mr. Webster Millar, also sang well. Some of his top notes were not quite so peerless as one would desire, still he has a voice considerably above the average concert tenor and uses it remarkably well.

* * *

I regret to see the number of tenors has not increased since the last concert. It is not a muster of which Accrington ought to be proud.

* * *

There are still people who leave the concert room regardless of all else, save their own, very often noisy, exit.

March 25th

The Cafe Chantant in the Liberal Club last night proved most enjoyable. Quite a number of talented local artistes rendered valuable assistance in making the evening pass pleasantly. Dancing was the last item on a very good programme and, needless to say, was much appreciated by the youthful portion of the assemblage.

* * *

"Sunday" at the Prince's Theatre is well worth a visit. Tragedy is so closely intermingled with wholesome and spontaneous humour that one is irresistibly moved from laughter to tears and vice versa with astonishing rapidity. One doesn't feel proud of the disgusting behaviour on the part of a few of the "gods" one night this week. Even if a play is a shade above the average educational level of some people there is absolutely no need to expose such deplorable ignorance.

April 1st

Merrie England, I venture to predict, will be among the most successful works our Amateurs have undertaken. The "book" is not so amusing as some of Gilbert's, but the opera teems with sparkling music.

* * *

A friend writes about a wretched tram ride she experienced on Sunday evening from the Manchester-road district to Blackburn-road. "Would you believe it? There were no fewer than sixteen people with standing room only inside that car, while half a dozen more shared the conductor's footboard at the rear." I can quite believe my correspondent when she says "The experience was most distressing." But surely there is a by-law prohibiting over-crowding and, if so, whatever are the police doling not to enforce it, and thus do away with the scandalous crowding together? Our cars at the best are not exactly inviting. With so many passengers, that ride must have proved decidedly uncomfortable. The atmosphere, too, was stifling, and when, my correspondent eventually managed to extricate herself from the mass of struggling humanity, she was as limp as a rag. Could not the Tram Company run cars oftener to avoid such disagreeable menagerie-like crowding?

* * *

A crowded Exchange Hall awaited the appearance of Madame Clara Butt at Blackburn on Wednesday. A world-famed songstress, she easily maintains her unrivalled popularity, and Blackburn concert goers gave her a perfect ovation. She was recalled three or four times after each song, but did not respond to the deafening cheers till the last song, "Abide with me," which had been substituted for "Promise of Life". Madame Clara Butt loses none of her power. She is a woman of immense stature. She sings with more pathos, and modulates her voice to a much greater degree than when last I heard her, now several years ago. She still retains her clear enunciation, and in this respect sets an example others would do well to follow.

* * *

It was hard to realise at the meeting of Socialists in the Town Hall on Tuesday that Lady Warwick, who less than a year ago was being congratulated on the birth of a second daughter, was a grandmother. The burden of her speech was the feeding of poor children and secular education. Her views, as expressed on Wednesday, are not one whit different, from those held by all progressives, and might appropriately have been delivered on a Liberal platform. One could not help admiring her zest and energy for the cause of the children, even though not agreeing with the Socialistic movement.

April 8th

One feels inclined to put a brake on the months, so rapidly do they seem to come and go. Not long ago we were exclaiming, "Here is March," and now April, with its showers and sunshine, is on the eve of its second week. Saturday and Sunday were two choice examples of the moods of this varied month. Rain, rain, rain, in ceaseless rotation on the window panes was the music of Saturday afternoon at any rate. But Sunday, with its lavish sunshine and balmy atmosphere gained in splendour by contrast. The hills stood out clearly against the blue of a summer-like sky, flecked here and there with white, while the gorgeous sunlight transformed all nature into loveliness. To watch the ever-changing light on the slopes of dear old Pendle on such a day was well worth a tramp from Accrington. Some enthusiasts voted the top of Waddington Fell the finest centre from which, to view the lovely countryside, while others gloried in the panoramic display afforded from Kemble End. Whalley Nab had its votaries, and some people were content with Moleside for their point of vantage, and basked in the sunshine while the birds carolled overhead, and nature in a thousand different ways unfolded its alluring promise of a radiant summer.

* * *

How men can waste the hours of such a day as Sunday in country public-houses, and when they emerge hopelessly intoxicated, making the night hideous by their drunken shouts and maudlin jests, is beyond comprehension. Conveyance after conveyance laden with these specimens of humanity are, alas, very common any fine Sunday in Whalley and the adjacent villages.

April 22nd

Fortunately Easter weather, though tempered by showers, was quite good enough for holiday making, and crowds of people availed themselves of the sunshine to have a really good time. Many people object to going far from home at Easter-time as the weather is so variable, but it is an easy matter to seek temporary shelter during an April shower, and truly last week-end the showers were of short duration, and the sun emerged triumphant after a lapse of a few minutes. It is advisable to take a few days' holiday, as the change of environment—if it is only two miles distant—alters the tone of subsequent return to dull routine, and is certainly refreshing, no matter how short the stay may be.

May 6th

The most absorbing local topic of the week has been the smallpox epidemic. It is not a savoury subject nor is it a topic with which I am conversant, but even to the uninitiated the diverse opinions of local doctors as to what is and what is not smallpox are surprising. The matter is too serious for laymen—and laywomen—to pretend to settle, but in face of such a serious epidemic there ought to be but one aim, and that to stamp out the disease. The efficacy of vaccination, or otherwise, is not in question at the moment. How can we prevent the disease spreading is the question of the hour. A smallpox epidemic is a costly business. I should not be surprised to learn that Accrington's smallpox bill of the spring of this year will run to four figures.

* * *

That was a very sad tragedy at Rishton on Sunday evening, when a woman from Harwood attempted to take her son's life as well as her own. It was fortunate that the little fellow clung so tenaciously to life and managed to crawl out of the canal unharmed, beyond a thorough wetting. The mother, poor woman, succeeded in taking her own life.

* * *

Outsiders who know not the value of rare orchids have marvelled at the high prices given for some of the stock at Bank House this week. By the rarity and beauty of her specimens the late Mrs. Briggs-Bury made Accrington an orchid centre noted throughout the orchid world. The conservatory at Bank House is an orchid fancier's dream, and to those who do not understand the worth of this delicate flower the dainty colouring and beauty of the specimens appeal as rare floral gems.

May 13th

The testimonial presented to Mr. James Townson on Monday was a fitting tribute to his good work in the cause of the blind. Thirty years is a long time to have taken an active interest in such a cause, and the prevention of complete blindness to numerous poor school .children, who otherwise would not have had either the means or the opportunity of preserving their sight, by the timely aid of the blind society, is a far better testimonial than any devised by subscribers or promoters.

* * *

Oak Hill Park was a beautiful sight on Sunday. Crowds of people, apparently in their new finery, strolled across the green or loitered by the band stand enjoying to the full the balmy atmosphere combined with the strains of instrumental music. Tulips in variegated splendour adorned the flower beds, pansies and other modest spring flowers joined the walks on either side, and the fresh green of the trees supplied an attractive background. Birds vied with each other in their full-throated melodies, and the rooks in the rookery as evening drew nigh held a noisy concert all to themselves. It was an ideal day for enjoying nature in a quiet, lazy way.

* * *

Members of the Golf Club held their spring meeting on Saturday, and judging by the prizes competed for and won it was a fine day's sport for the gentlemen. When I read of anything in connection with golf I always regret that more members of my own sex are not enrolled on the list of players. It is such an invigorating game and so beneficial to health. True, the facilities for lady members is very poor indeed up at the club-house, but keen sportswomen are able to overcome small difficulties of that kind.

May 20th

What a glorious touch of summer has followed the winter of our discontent. This week has been simply delightful; lavish sunshine tempered by a gentle breeze, and a sky of blue that would do credit to the Riviera. Though a trifle hot, the weather has been ideal for rambles through the country. One day I pumped up my old bicycle and sped away Hodder-wards and was amply repaid for my ride. On every hand the trees are wearing their first spring suits of green, and the dust has not yet robbed them of their pristine freshness; the grassy banks and meadows are idyllic in their velvety greenness. To lounge on the banks of the Hodder listening to the song of the birds and the wish-wash of the water as it formed a miniature waterfall over the stones, with on either side prolific sycamores, beeches, birches, and other trees casting graceful shadows in the water, I voted time well spent, and it was not till eventide, after a thoroughly lazy but charming day, that I returned homewards. As I rode along the country lanes to the accompaniment of the evensong of the birds, the lights changed and deepened and faded away, giving place to other colours until at last that tender rosy tint so dear to those who watch the sky at the hour of sunset, held everything in a passing splendour. In this mystic light the graceful silver birches at the foot of Whalley brow stood out like so much delicate tracery, and one realised why the silver birch had been named the lady of the forest.

* * *

A recent visit to the Accrington public baths has but served to confirm my opinion that, despite the lavish sum the committee decided to spend in patching up the establishment, the place is still unfit for anyone who has any regard for his or her health. It is my firm belief that the unsavoury aroma, which is the strongest feature of the plunge bath's surroundings would penetrate a dozen coats of paint and nothing but reconstruction will avail.

* * *

Writing of automobiles reminds me of Mr. Robert Crossley's non-stop run of 585 miles in the Scotch motor trials last week. In another part of the paper a detailed account of the trials is given; suffice it for me to congratulate the member of the Automobile Club on his successful run.

Mr Robert Crossley and his 30-40 H.P Belsize

May 27th

There has never been a more enjoyable reception than that given by our Mayor and Mayoress on Thursday afternoon in the Town Hall. Everybody admired the capital arrangement of the room. An impromptu platform erected on the Blackburn-road side whereon were seated the Mayor (Alderman Rawson) in his robes, the Mayoress wearing her chain, proved an excellent position for the artistes. Although not over-crowded the room was well-filled, the majority being of mine own sex, though there was a fair sprinkling of the masculine element. An excellent musical programme, interspersed with brief speeches, was provided. I was just a little disappointed in Miss England's address, which was not so eloquent as on the occasion when I had the pleasure of hearing her at Haslingden. Miss England at her best is one of the most able lady-speakers I have heard. Tea was dispensed by a bevy of young ladies, wearing sprays presented by the Mayor, with praiseworthy grace and dispatch. It was altogether a most enjoyable social function.

June 10th

The meet of the North-East Lancashire Automobile Club at Whitecroft House, Haslingden, last Saturday, proved a most enjoyable social function. Arrangements were admirably carried out from beginning to end. A most cordial welcome was accorded to all the guests by the host and hostess, Mr. and Mrs. E. A. Riley, and everybody spent a very pleasant afternoon.

Though not extensive the grounds of Whitecroft House overlook a view of Holcombe and the surrounding country, which is very fine indeed. A marquee had been erected at the far end of the tennis lawn, where refreshments were served, while from the lawn in front of the house a string band discoursed sweet music. Invitations had not been restricted to members off the Automobile club, with the result that there was a large and fashionable gathering, including many prominent Haslingden people. Over

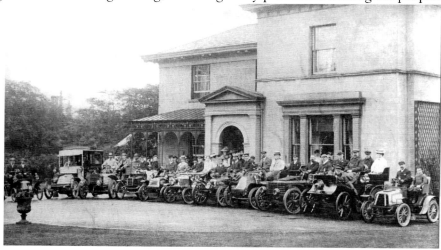

An early gathering of the East Lancashire Automobile Club prior to the introduction of number plates in 1904.

twenty motors of various types were arranged in a field just outside the grounds, where photographs were taken of cars and occupants.

June 17th

A most undesirable feature of present-day holidays is the motor traffic. No longer is it safe to meditate dreamily along country lanes, for, alas, such dreams are suddenly dispelled by the hoot of a motor horn.

What visions of wrecked cars, and injured humanity the very sound of that horn conjures up in the minds of the gentle wayfarer, who, standing at one side to give the motor-fiend a clear run in his diabolical machine, is completely enveloped in a cloud of dust, and almost stifled by petrol effluvia.

June 24th

The members of our police force—or some of them—look really smart in their new uniforms. The South African sombreros are quite becoming, and must be much more comfortable and cooler than the close-fitting helmets. I often wondered,

Members of the Accrington Borough Police Force wearing their South African style bush hats in 1905.

on hot summer days, how the poor policemen managed to endure the heat inevitable when wearing such headgear.

* * *

Rain did not appear to deter people from attending the sermons on Sunday. At Oak-street and Cannon-street large congregations assembled for the anniversary services throughout the day. Collections were large at both places, amounting to £160 at Cannon-street and £100 at Oak-street. Music which plays so large a part in church services nowadays, was quite a feature of Sunday's anniversaries. And justly so too, for "Some to church repair, Not for the doctrine, but the music there."

July 1st

As expected, the turn-up at Wednesday's cricket match was a large one. The Gentlemen were in good form, and, despite the sturdy efforts of members of the Force, their score was soon passed leaving the Gentlemen easy victors. Mr. Moore's splendid exhibition at the wicket was well worth seeing. Mr. Critchley and the Chief (Mr. Sinclair), so long associated with this fixture, were again to be seen on the field, taking the duties of umpires with their usual joviality.

Mrs. Horne, Mrs. W. Sharples, Mrs. Arthur Wilson, Mrs. Cronshaw, Mrs. G. Pickup, Mrs. Bardsley, Mrs. Harvey, Mrs. Carter, and several other ladies who yearly give their services for the children's cause, were, also in evidence. To say they were assisted by a bevy of fair maids would scarcely suffice for the willing helpers who carried tea round. It wasn't their fault that, owing to numbers, they often seemed to get in one another's way. This did not deter them, however, from satisfying the wants of the people. Little fellows tugged at the dresses of the waitresses, displaying their tickets and clamouring for tea, and adults all appeared to require tea exactly at one time. A great drawback, too, was the scarcity of crockery. Waitresses besieged the four women employed in washing and drying pots in the ante-room, "cup" being their one cry. It is expected the proceeds from the. match will realise nearly £50, which is being handed over to the local branch of the N.S.P.C.C.

July 8th

Luckily the weather on Saturday was bright enough not to mar the pretty effect of the Co-op. procession. Thousands of little children paraded the streets of Accrington to the accompaniment of music from three bands. Morris dancing and an interesting dumb bell display were some of the main features of the parade, while a number of girls prettily dressed in white carried flowers, several more holding the streamers of two elaborate banners. It was a most picturesque affair.

July 15th

Arrangements are being made for a garden party at Quarry Hill in aid off the N.S.P.C.C. Mrs. Bunting, the lady president, has very generously placed her grounds at the disposal of the guests of the Society, and, needless to add, will make a charming hostess.

* * *

To-day (Saturday) there will be an attractive display of fireworks at Oak Hill Park, if it be but as nice as the last pyrotechnic display given by the same firm, the Park will be well worth a visit.

* * *

A correspondent writes me that the Trades Council were much impressed by the clever address Miss Pankhurst, on "Woman's Suffrage," gave in the Mechanics' Institute. Miss Pankhurst is essentially one of the women who, if Woman's Suffrage comes in our time, would take a prominent part and place in the political world. A daughter of the late Dr. Pankhurst, of Manchester, barrister and social reformer, and of Mrs. Pankhurst, an equally strenuous worker in the field of politics, Miss Pankhurst in many ways proves herself a true child. She has herself gained the law degree of the University of London, and had the temerity (?) to claim admission as barrister. The powers that be, with true man-like chivalry, refused absolutely such request. Miss Pankhurst, however, keeps working hard, and I hope someday her plea will be granted. Women are everywhere to-day admitted to the medical profession. Then why not the legal?

July 22nd

On Saturday the decorations were very pretty and fairylike at Oak Hill Park, but not nearly, I thought, so gorgeous as on the last occasion the firm visited Accrington. At the Park gates was a blaze of splendour, and the walks were lined on either side with Pain's fairy lamps, some of them twined round the trunks of massive trees: but that effective glittering crown, and letters above the pond were absent, while there were no signs of that splendid lighted pagoda, illustrated by blazing Chinese lanterns. However, the pyrotechnic display itself was no doubt on as grand a scale as before, though of course the charm of originality was gone and the fireworks not quite so awe-inspiring as on a first acquaintance. The sum realised—£200— proves beyond a doubt that a very large number of people appreciated the display.

* * *

Sunday's concert at Oak Hill Park proved a rare musical treat. If anything the singing sounded more beautiful than last year. Large crowds of people availed themselves of the chance to hear some really good music in ideal surroundings. Everybody within easy reach of the stand thoroughly enjoyed the afternoon's programme, while even those at a distance had the pleasure of hearing the lovely melody, though words were not distinguishable. The Mayor was sufficiently recovered to take part in the proceedings, and I was glad to see, though he still wears his arm in a sling, that he looked remarkably well. The proceeds, including, the collection (£41 14s.), were £70.

July 29th

All who took part in the crowning of the (Rose Queen ceremony at Clayton-le-Moors were disappointed in the weather. An event that has been so much talked about by children and their elders for weeks past ought to have had the privilege of disporting its many attractions on a fine day. Better luck next time! Miss Foster, the Rose Queen, went through her duties with pretty grace, and her attendants looked sweet in their white frocks and floral adornments, while the retiring Queen, Miss Pickup, and her retinue were also graceful and self-possessed. Mrs. Arthur Wilson performed the coronation ceremony. The fete was well worth the sixpence charged for admission, and as it has been established for four years it is to be hoped will continue one of the summer events at Clayton-le - Moors.

* * *

To have one of the very best days of the summer was the happy lot of the picnic party which started from Accrington, comfortably ensconced in motor cars, last Thursday. Mr. Tom Higham had invited members of the Electricity and sundry other committees and chief officials to a motor car ride through the Ribble valley. Everything went splendidly, and the motorists, after a delightful spin through beautiful country, were entertained at Mr. Higham's country residence at Chadswell.

August 5th

Members of the North-East Lancashire Automobile Club and friends spent a delightful afternoon at Billinge Scarr, Blackburn, on Saturday. Luckily the weather, which had been unpleasantly wet in the morning brightened into a fine afternoon. Marquees, were erected in the beautiful grounds, where delicacies in most tempting variety abounded; a regimental band provided a musical element to the proceedings, and everything possible was done for the comfort of the guests. Despite the early morning rain, a large company turned up. Mrs. Birtwistle and her charming daughter must have been quite fatigued when the reception was ended. Both ladies and gentlemen were interested in the splendid garage, for Mr. Birtwistle possesses a wonderful array of cars.

* * *

Canon Rogers on Monday ended his 36 years' service as vicar of St. James's, Accrington. Many people regret the close of his ministry, but when a man has passed the allotted span of years—be is now 73—and has led such a strenuous life, it is surely, time to rest. Canon Rogers will be greatly missed, both in public and private life. I sincerely hope the years of his retirement, which he intends to spend at Preston, will be peaceful and happy.

* * *

The long anticipated holidays have come at last! What a time the children will have—those who are lucky enough to know the joys of a week or two at some seaside resort. There is nothing more interesting than to watch the little ones with buckets and spades building their tiny castle on the shore. Other great attractions are the troupes of pierrots. What laughter they evoke by the witticisms and funny stories, to say nothing of the Punch and Judy shows and ventriloquists and other entertainers on the sands. I hope my readers will enjoy themselves and have a good time. A holiday in the summer time, besides providing a relaxation from humdrum routine, should be used in such a way that reserve energy may be built up to draw upon during the winter months.

August 12th

Truly Accrington Fair weather! It is disappointing after toiling through the excessive heat of the summer months that are over, to experience such provoking rain and leaden skies just when the majority of people take their holidays. It is

Accrington Pot Fair in 1905

such a short time for many, and to think they haven't the chance of sunning themselves lazily on their favourite stretch of beach owing to this tearful behaviour of the skies!

Fortunately the wretched weather was but local. Much better conditions have prevailed at the sea-side—at Blackpool and Douglas, Morecambe and Llandudno and elsewhere—but in Accrington district rain has fallen every day, with scarcely an hour's sunshine.

August 19th

Building operations have been commenced immediately below, and close to the grounds, of the Victoria Hospital. I hear the Hospital authorities had the first offer of the land, but they could not see their way to plunge into deeper obligations. For the time being the hospital land appears ample, but it is astonishing how, as the district grows, the ground will be gradually covered by hospital extensions, and it seems a pity the committee did not feel justified in snapping up the land. I fear that as years roll on they will be blamed for not doing so.

* * *

I had heard so much about the "tin-box brigade" as "Scribbler" dubs them that I thought I would spend a short time at the railway station on Saturday evening witnessing the return of holiday makers. I confess I was astonished. I never saw such crowds. Trunks and boxes there were of every hue and shape and size. It was with the utmost difficulty porters coped with the work and kept the platforms anything like clear. Especially was this true of No. 4 platform, where the trains from Blackpool and Southport, Morecambe and Liverpool, arrived. Cabbies had a rich harvest, but many trippers had to carry their own boxes, or engage boys to do so. In some cases funds would not run to a cab, and others preferred to walk home after being "boxed up" in a railway carriage for hours.

* * *

Although some of the trains were too long for the platforms, every compartment seemed crowded with passengers, and tales of long and tedious journeys from Blackpool were on almost everybody's lips. Certainly many of the passengers looked haggard and weary. As one old lady put it, "We've had a grand time at Blackpool, but that railway journey has taken it all out of us." I fear there is much truth in the remark.

September 9th

Congratulations to Mr. and Mrs. (Miss Flo. Bell) Cope, who were married on Wednesday at Altham Church. I understand the ceremony was a quiet one, very few outside the two families talking part.

* * *

Second in interest only to weddings has been the Church-street shilling sale. In fact the sale seems to have been more popular with the womenfolk. The sound of the word "bargain" seems to act like magic on some people. On Tuesday, I am told, women assembled at six o'clock in the morning in order to be in time for the opening of the shop doors, fixed for ten o'clock. This will seem incredible to the more prosaic ones, but I am assured that it is quite true. One can understand people waiting hours to see some great personage who has won his way to fame by daring deeds of valour or other notables, great in their own particular spheres, but to rise at break of day merely on bargain-hunting intent seems-well, rather foolish. Several coldblooded specimens of the opposite sex have found enjoyment this week in watching the police keep the bargain-hunting crowds in order, and seeing fainting women carried from the shop, and others, in more or less exhausted stages, emerging triumphant from a seething mass of humanity, hugging the coveted "bargain." In their eagerness to obtain goods they had marked for their own special purchase, women all but tore one another's hair, so a member of the sterner sex assures me. Poor, poor shop assistants! What a wretched time they'd have during that chaotic onslaught. They have my sympathy.

* * *

Members of the Moss Lane Tennis Club, and their recent successes at the Conishead Tournament, call for special congratulation. They contrived to win no fewer than eight prizes. Especially praiseworthy was the triumph of Mr. J. T. Kenyon, jun., and

Miss May Entwisle, who, in addition to carrying off the first prize in the mixed doubles handicap, won a third prize in the open mixed doubles.

September 16th

A pity that Saturday should be such a wretched day. Besides being the last day of the cricket season, there were several other local events utterly spoiled by rain. No wonder in such downpour cricket was absolutely tabooed. Yet, according to "Scribbler's" notes on Tuesday there were crowds of people at the football match clamouring for a continuation of the play, though rivulets were streaming from hats and umbrellas, while the players, with scarcely any protection from wind or rain, were splashing through miniature lakes, muddy in hue, chasing the glistening ball. Doesn't it seem exciting? Well, well, all the better for the doctors, if people will run such risks to see a football match, but it seems a pity wives and mothers should have the trouble of nursing invalids who have been so foolhardy. To see these enthusiasts returning from a football orgy of this kind is enough to make the gods smile. Faces blue with cold, hands dug deep into pockets of coats soaked through and through with rain, and hats shedding streams of water down their necks, with boots completely soaked and ruined; shivering with cold from head to foot, these pitiable-looking objects with slouching gait retrace their steps homeward. What wonder if their wives have doubts as to their sanity?

* * *

A correspondent writes:- "*It has been suggested by several lady members of the Mechanics' how nice it would be, now that the library is no longer available, if suitable games were provided in the ladies' room to help out the very inadequate supply of books there.*"
More than once I have commented on the very poor facilities offered for ladies at the Institution, and ladies are perfectly justified in considering themselves rather indifferently treated in that respect. My correspondent goes on to say that several ladies held a solemn conclave recently, deciding if nothing more attractive were forthcoming they might as well resign membership. It seems a pity to do that, as the lady members, I believe, are already limited in numbers. Why not get up a deputation to the directors, asking for such things as are desired? If accommodation is to be given ladies in another part of the building when the present ladies' room shall be given over to the new Library, such a deputation is almost certain to have the desired result. In the meantime cards or games might be supplied, though how they are to be played in that imperfectly lighted room is a puzzle— a dark seance is more in keeping with the general gloom cast by lights, supposed to be electric, but which only succeed in appearing dismal, with about as much brilliance as a penny candle.

September 23rd

Two Preston ladies who had been staying in Whalley for a few days were knocked down by a trap near Whalley station on Monday. Walking from the station to the Almshouses, they stepped off the footpath, and a trap coming suddenly round the corner knocked both ladies down in the road. The driver, it is said, continued on his way without stopping to enquire whether assistance was needed. Yet some people tell us the age of chivalry is not yet dead. One lady was seriously injured about the head and chest, and quite unconscious, having to be removed to her temporary home by members of the Ambulance Brigade. Arrived there, the doctor in attendance pronounced her suffering from concussion of the brain and shock. The other lady was little the worse for her mishap. Now doesn't the behaviour of that driver appear contemptible? Had it been a motorist with his car all the countryside would have risen in arms against the brutality of such conduct.

September 30th

The fireworks fete at Oak Hill Park entertained a big crowd of Accrington people. It is the third occasion on which the Park has been alight with Pain's' prismatic lamps within two years. As the proceeds were large it is not unlikely that at some future time the same company will want to provide similar amusement for the multitude. An enterprising Corporation might organise such displays and pocket the profits. It doesn't seem quite the thing for outsiders to make a hundred pounds profit, while the town draws £25; but then if outsiders have the enterprise which some Corporations lack it cannot be avoided. However, the display was a fine sight, and coloured rockets and aerial comets, apart from the set pieces of flaming lights, were well worth coming far to see.

October 7th

A parade of very different stamp was that of members of Park Congregational P.S.A. on Saturday midnight in Accrington. The processionists, or rather their leaders entered several licensed houses with invitation cards for a meeting to be held at the Hippodrome later. Anything in the way of novelty appeals to many people, but apart from being an advertisement I don't see what good such novelties as these are. To induce drunken men to attend such a meeting seems ludicrous. The two gentlemen of the cloth, who had the task of assisting a man who had drunk not wisely but too well to the Hippodrome had not an enviable task. What earthly use is the best logic or sermon in the universe to such a man at such a time? He may be a wretched example of the power of alcohol, but his brain, sodden with drink is scarcely a fitting receptacle for words of wisdom. Then, too, the young people who turn out to see such a parade would be far better in bed, for there are sights even in Accrington at that time of night which are not calculated to edify anyone, let alone the youthful element of the population.

October 21st

Lamentable were the riotous scenes at the Manchester Free Trade hall on Friday and the subsequent arrest of Miss Pankhurst and Miss Kenny. Some say it is a pity

Sir Edward Grey did not answer the questions put by these devoted exponents of Women's Suffrage, and thus have avoided the regrettable disturbance. But, of course, there are two sides to the question. Both ladies, having refused the payment of fine proffered by several prominent people, preferred to work out their sentences at Stangeways gaol. In the intense excitement of arrest, Miss Pankhurst did not gain in dignity: to spit in the face of a constable or assault a member of the force is not the sort of behaviour one would expect from a lady of her intellectual ability and social standing. In fact, the whole proceedings, though Keir Hardie protests their valiant conduct throughout the "dastardly outrage" will do immense good to the cause, are to be deplored even by those who have woman's cause at heart.

October 28th

I must congratulate Union street Wesleyans on the splendid result of their bazaar. To raise over £1,828 at a bazaar, without the aid of raffling, is a wonderful performance.

* * *

Numerous have been the words of sympathy extended to Miss Nellie Hindle, who met with such an alarming accident in Manchester-road on Sunday morning. To leave home in the best of health and youthful spirits, bound for church, where her sweet voice has aided the choir in the singing of many an anthem only to be crushed by a runaway horse en route, seems very hard. I trust her return to convalescence will be speedy.

November 4th

Doubtless, the decision to hand Willow House over to the town for a site for a public library, with the consequent abandonment of the present library, is responsible, to a certain extent, for the decreased membership of the Mechanics' Institution. A decrease of 59 in twelve months is rather a large falling off. Let us hope the decline will not be continued. I regret to note that ladies are answerable for 17 resignations. It is not surprising though that ladies consider themselves rather badly treated. Directors' "ideas of efficiency" and those of lady members evidently do not concur. It is comforting to know that the present income, despite the decline in the membership, will be sufficient to maintain the Institution.

November 11th

I have by me a very interesting letter from the secretary of the Accrington Naturalists' and Antiquarian Society. The cordial tone in which it is written leaves no doubt as to the desire on the part of the society to obtain more lady members. At present there are only two, who—possibly on account of their crushing minority— do not care to join the members on their rambles, thus depriving themselves of much pleasure. Probably some of my readers would find a pleasure in attending the meetings and Mr. Bamber, the secretary, expresses the hope that a few ladies will come forward and give suitable lectures or papers, which would obtain more than usual prominence at the meetings.

* * *

At the annual meeting of members of the Mechanics' Institution, the subject of "ladies' privileges" was brought forward and I am pleased to inform my lady readers that the directors will be pleased to entertain any suggestions which the ladies themselves care to make. Now that is a step -a very tiny step it is true, but still a step- in the right direction.

November 18th

Once more fair weather favoured Mayoral Sunday. In spite of philosophy we are all affected by sunshine and rain, bright or dull clothing, and in these respects the appearance of the processions was a bright display. Military uniforms here, a glistening piece of metal there, and the bright freshness of gentlemen's hats, together with the musical element supplied by our bands, made a cheerful sight and sound.

No wonder crowds of people assembled to see the Mayor walk to church. It was such a brisk sort of morning, too, one felt a joy in being out and about inhaling the fresh

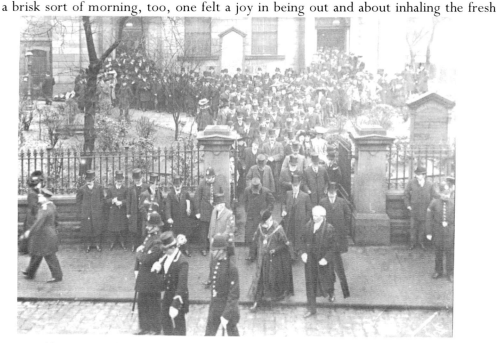

Alderman Rawson leaves the Weslyan Methodist Chapel on Union Street on Mayoral Sunday 1905.

morning air and loitering in the wintry sunshine. The Mayor in his civic robes and chain looked very smart and in the best of health, while his wig and gown made the Town Clerk an imposing and dignified figure.

November 25th

The case of theft brought against the Rishton girl at Blackburn this week is a lamentable one. It is but another instance pointing to the necessity for parents to personally guard their children's welfare. What hope can a child have of success in life when, at the early age of twelve years, she is convicted and heavily fined in a public court for larceny? Years cannot erase such a stigma, and the girl who began by playing truant from school will no doubt in after life bitterly regret the deplorable lapse from honesty. One cannot help thinking that a little more parental supervision might have obviated such a theft, for the unformed ideas and reasoning faculties of a young girl cannot be blamed in such a matter.

* * *

I wonder if any member of the Town Council had occasion to cross Blackburn- road anywhere near the Market Ground on Tuesday night? A connoisseur in mud would have been in his element, for the road was like a map with pools of dirty water. It was impossible to cross without getting one's foot covered with slimy-looking liquid. Might I suggest that, if the Corporation find it impossible to keep the road clean, they might charter ferry boats on wet nights to enable folks to cross without coming into personal contact with the muddy thoroughfare?

* * *

Lady managers have been objected to by members of the District Education Committee, for no apparent reason. In view of recent events, as Mr. Allsopp stated at the meeting, any lady nominated for such a committee had not an enviable position. Personally I consider lady members very useful in such work, and Mr. Beckett said at the meeting that lady members had done work equal to any other member. Then why depose them? "Principle" seems a paltry excuse for so egregious a piece of masculinity. If lady managers are as useful as the male members of the school committees, they ought by all means to be appointed. This very District Education Committee has ere this, I believe, acknowledged the good work done by lady members. Then why seek to exclude, ladies from Great Harwood school management committees?

December 2nd

The two prominent features of Wednesday's Choral concert were the excellence of the chorus singing and the remarkable apathy of the audience. More than an hour had elapsed before any degree of enthusiasm was shown and several good musical items were allowed to pass without eliciting the applause they most certainly deserved. It is just possible—though I doubt the probability—that the stand taken by certain religious dignitaries, who hold that the performance of such sacred works as the "Messiah" and "Elijah" should be followed in absolute silence may have had some weight with Accrington patrons. It must have been positively disheartening for the artistes to sit down after a splendid effort without apparently having stirred the audience. In this respect the occupants of the front seats were sadly remiss. If people only realised what satisfaction and pleasure are given to artistes by ungrudging, unstinted applause, they would surely discard their too evident ennui, and make some small effort to show their appreciation in true English fashion.

December 9th

"Merrie England" has surpassed all expectations. Crowded houses at the Prince's theatre every night testify to the popularity of this year's production. I won't go so far as to say it is better than any yet produced, for the memory of "Mikado", "Iolanthe", "Rose of Persia" and other operas so successfully put on in former years is very vivid. But of its kind it has been admirable. On Monday night, and even since, there have been several little details, insignificant in themselves, but important as a whole, which might have been improved. For instance, members of the chorus at times gazed with languid indifference into the auditorium when they ought to have been showing keen interest in the doings of their fellow actors. It is evident those who are to blame in this respect do not realise that every little gesture on their part helps to the perfection of the whole. One of the young ladies-it were invidious to mention names-has won the hearts of the audiences every night this week by her whole-hearted appreciation of her part. She is really a very minor character in the play, but has made herself agreeably conspicuous by her good acting. That impassivity of expression adopted by one or two, accorded ill with the exciting phases of the opera, and is moreover rather distracting.

Miss Sally Crossley as "Jill All Alone" in "Merrie Enaland".

Then, again, the audience has been treated in the witch's great scene in the forest to a phenomenon in the shape of a fleeting fire. The fire beneath the witch's cauldron actually had the audacity to "walk off" when intruders approached. It was too funny! There seems to have been a scarcity of flowers, too. I have never seen a May festival with so few posies. When Queen Elizabeth approached on one occasion half the men forgot to doff their hats, a sign of homage any Queen has the right to expect from her subjects. These are trifles however, but wise people realise that trifles make perfection.

December 16th

The shower bouquets presented by Mr. J.W. Bridge to the principal ladies last Saturday night were simply lovely! Several were composed of yellow tea roses and pink carnations, while the rest were of chrysanthemums and red tulips. It must be really nice to be a principal at such times. Then, too, I believe that every chorus girl received a box of chocolates from the same generous source. It is to be hoped the "Father" of the Society will not sever his connection for many years to come.

December 23rd

My first duty and pleasure this week is to wish all my readers a Merry Christmas! There isn't much prospect of an old-fashioned Christmas up to the time of writing, as the rain in its steady drip, drip, dripping against the window panes is anything but Christmassy, and very depressing in its ceaseless, monotonous downpour, And the streets—ugh! Luckily there is the excitement of exploring the stores of local tradesmen to counterbalance the monotony. Were ever Christmas goods so absolutely alluring displayed before? Children have been nearly wild with excitement after spending hours viewing tantalising toys and dolls in the shop windows, and wondering in a hopeful sort of way whether Santa Claus will bring them such things. It seems a pity when toys have been brought to such perfection, and can be obtained at such trifling cost, that any little child should be denied that pleasure of having for its very own some tiny souvenir of Christmas.

December 30th

Another year gone. How quickly time flies. It seems but a short time since we entered upon 1905, and now it is my duty and pleasure to welcome another year, and to wish my readers prosperity and happiness during the coming twelvemonth. The weather this Christmas has not been altogether seasonable, but it might have been worse. While there has been no heavy fall of rain, the atmosphere has been too heavy and too damp to be pleasant, and the streets wet and dirty. Those who cry for "snow, snow, beautiful snow!" may yet have their wishes gratified, as there is plenty of time before the end of winter.

1906

January 6th

Apart from festivities, 1906 has opened in an exciting manner, and the first month of the New Year promises to be lively enough. The excitement of the General Election lies ahead, and everybody predicts that to a certain extent this will be a woman's election. Women seem determined to talk politics even though their knowledge of the subject is limited. Before Mr. Balfour's resignation one could have gone amongst one's women friends without hearing politics discussed at all, but now one's afternoons are enlivened by sudden political knowledge which seems to have come to women. Arguments bearing on the present situation have quite taken the place of scandal at afternoon teas. Who shall say it is not a step in the right direction?

* * *

I wish to express my sympathy with Mr. and Mrs. Will Entwisle, who have this week lost their little son Geoffrey. He was such a bright and taking little fellow. His chubby face, nearly always dimpled with smiles, before his illness, had endeared him to many outside his own family circle.

* * *

Quite the most romantic wedding we have had in Accrington for some time was that of Miss Alice Broadley and Mr. Tom Noble, who were married at the New Church on Saturday morning. With the exception of about half a dozen friends the fact that the ceremony was to take place at all was unknown, and the bridal couple were on their way to Blackpool where the honeymoon was spent, before news was noised abroad. The Rev. J. Rendell, who performed the ceremony, played the bridal march as the bride and bridegroom left the church. A love match which sets all convention aside naturally has the good wishes of everybody.

January 13th

Although this is essentially a non-political column, one may comment upon Mr. Winston Churchill's striking personality without fear of rousing party feeling, or in fact exhibiting any. I was glad to see so many ladies at the meeting in the Town Hall on Saturday, it is a sign that members of my sex are eager at the present moment to absorb every bit of political knowledge they can possibly glean. A fine set-up young fellow of about five feet ten inches, with a chest and pair of shoulders which do credit to his physical training in the Army, a smooth face devoid of any pretensions to a moustache, broad forehead, nice eyes, and a generous mouth, Mr Winston Churchill impressed one as being intelligently alert—an impression which was verified when he commenced to speak. His humour touches were as amusing as his serious moments were interesting, which is saying much, but in the minds of many the zenith of his oratory was reached in the peroration, where he certainly soared with infinite skill.

Many ladies were present on the platform, several clothed in garments which bespoke their liberal tendencies with no uncertainty. But if woman desires to be a welcome figure at such gatherings she ought by all means to discard her large and obtrusive head-gear.

* * *

When an efficient way of entirely clearing our streets of mud has been found, and adopted by the Accrington Corporation, I feel sure people will be better tempered and better mannered than at present. To feel sticky slabs of mud being hurled at one's petticoats and one's dainty shoes coming in contact with the horrid, greasy pavement is simply ruinous to clothes, temper, and one's whole bearing. The best dressed man or woman cannot possibly feel serene and at peace with the world with the knowledge that he or she is splashed with mud. The deluges of mud poured on us in bad weather make us long for an ideal mudless Accrington. How delightful that would be!

* * *

Just before two o'clock on Saturday crowds of people were hurrying in one direction. No need to ask where these people were going. They had all one fixed purpose—to see the Accrington Amateur Dramatic Society in "My Friend the Prince." The fact that so many braved the wretched weather, risking the freshness of their gowns on carriage steps, tram-cars, or walking through the numerous puddles, was a great compliment to the dramatic Society. For a more miserably damp day could not be imagined.

January 20th

A pleasant function was the 36th annual Conservative Ball. It was quite a pleasure to recline on one of those comfortable lounges in a corner and watch the gay scene. A beautiful effect was attained by the softened light, caused by a number of evergreen plants gracefully twined around the electroliers, the floor, as usual, was polished to perfection for dancing, and the chairs and comfortable settees arranged on all sides looked most inviting. Not the least sociable retreat was the supper room, carpeted with red felt, and altogether desirably furnished with good things; while a green felting carpeted the staircase and an awning sheltered the entrance to the club. With such cosy accompaniments on all hands, no wonder the dancers proclaimed themselves satisfied and the dance a huge success. The M.C.'s Captain Slinger, Captain Sharples, Surgeon-Lieut. Fitzgerald, Mr. G. W. Pickup and Mr. S Briggs-Bury are to be complimented on their considerate discharge of by no means easy duties.

* * *

The attendance at the Chamber concert didn't appear to be at all lessened by the inclement weather, though one might almost be forgiven on such a night, if the calling of a cosy fire on one's own hearth waxed too eloquent to be resisted. However, a large number of people did resist their own fireside attractions, and voted the concert an evening well spent. Mr. Carl Fuchs and his violoncello are always desirable assets at a chamber evening, but never, I think, did the beauties of his playing appeal so irresistibly as on Friday. At the conclusion of Popper's "Tarantella" the applause was so pronounced that only an additional piece would satisfy, and the musician responded with a soothing and beautiful composition.

* * *

Our Mayoress (Mrs Alderman Rawson) must have retired to rest on Saturday with the satisfaction which only comes with the knowledge of a day's work well done. To have brought a little additional sunshine for a few hours into the lives of 800 poor children by a kindly act of generosity is indeed a splendid day's work. The rousing cheers given to the Mayor and Mayoress by the children proved that their part of the entertainment was much appreciated. The children attacked the buns and coffee with a relish that was good to see, and later exhibited a childish delight in the musical entertainment which must have gratified the artistes. During the evening one of the little guests presented the Mayoress with a very pretty shower bouquet. Mrs. Rawson wished all the children a happy new year and hoped they would grow up to be good, honourable and useful men and women.

January 27th

The Mayor's procession to St. James's Church on Sunday, although the processionists numbered a hundred, was not quite so attractive as usual. The absence of the Volunteers and the Ambulance Corps detracted somewhat from the effect. Luckily the weather was favourable, and people turned out in large numbers to view the procession.

February 3rd

Last Saturday's dog show, organised by the North-East Lancashire Pomeranian Club held in the Central Conservative Club lecture-room attracted prize-winners from all parts of the country. At times the room was too small to comfortably hold the large number of exhibitors and interested spectators. Several of the competitors were very keen, in the black, open, any weight class, so much so, that it was decided to divide the premier honour between Mrs Houlker's "Haughty Carl" and Mrs Ainscough's "Seedhill Perfection." Mrs. Houlker is to be congratulated on her success. Her "Beautiful King of the Sables" won two firsts and two seconds, in addition to "Haughty Carl's" fine achievement, while her fluffy little beauty, "Champion Haughty Winnie," carried off one third prize, and a litter of tiny favourites also won a first.

* * *

While first-class balls seem to have lost their attraction, the dances at the political clubs continue, and every Saturday night hundreds of young folk enjoy the "light fantastic." I can't say the fact pleases me. Organised dances, with responsible persons in attendance and supervision, cannot be very harmful, but these gatherings - I dare not call them twopenny hops - are not an unmitigated blessing.

February 10th

Those unlucky folks who ate potted meat with such painful results must have had a terrible fright. At first it was hoped that only a few had come within the grip, but now it is known that the patients have been numbered by the score, and one of them—poor Bobby Howarth, the popular Church newsagent and cricket enthusiast—has proved fatal. Most of the Accrington cases, I am glad to learn, are doing well, but unfortunately the potted meat which has done all the damage was not confined to one or even two stores and at Huncoat as well as Church there are patients who will require great care.

* * *

The circulation of scurrilous and anonymous postcards has become a positive nuisance in Great Harwood. Having arrived at the conclusion that the senders are residents of the place the public officials will probably succeed in bringing the offender, or offenders, to justice. To be ducked in a pond, as one indignant lady suggested the discovered author should be, seems an altogether inadequate punishment for the abusive literary genius who has written these objectionable missives to district councillors, doctors, and even ladies of the place. A lunatic asylum would seem the most suitable rendezvous.

February 17th

It is a long time since I laughed so much as I did on Wednesday at the jokes and funny antics of the Kentucky Minstrels. Everything went so smoothly—and a first performance, too—that one wonders at what stage of perfection they will eventually arrive. Not the least amusing feature was the endeavour on the part of the audience

The Kentucky Minstrels

to recognise familiar faces beneath the polished black exteriors; by no means an easy task, as the "blacking" was effectual in disguising them for a time. It was laughable to hear the guesses made and the discomfiture of those who guessed incorrectly when a familiar voice put an end to conjecture. The audience was decidedly appreciative. True, a long time elapsed before the point of a joke was fully realised, then a murmur of sound arose from the back of the hall, growing in volume, resembling a mighty wave, until it broke in a flood of appreciative laughter, at the feet of the humorous perpetrator. It was most amusing; one began to count the seconds after a joke before the deluge.

A finer male choir I have not heard for many a long day. Well balanced, they sang with precision and the volume was remarkable. "Comrades in Arms" was splendidly given. With more practice I really think the Kentucky troupe might qualify for choir competition.

February 24th

"Quite the best they have yet given," was the general verdict at the conclusion of last Wednesday's Cunliffe concert. There was a capital attendance, and the majority of the audience were well satisfied with the musical fare provided. Several fresh lady instrumentalists were visible in the orchestra. It seems strange in a town like Accrington, where there is so much talent, that more lady musicians do not qualify for similar positions. Besides the pleasure of being a unit on concert nights, rehearsals provide such excellent opportunities for good, solid practice, that they are bound to be highly beneficial as well as pleasurable

Miss Edith Exley-Smith was scarcely happy in her choice of songs. "Land of Hope and Glory" is about the most colourless song, I have ever listened to. It seems incredible that Elgar, who has written so much delightful music, should be responsible for its composition. It altogether lacks the vivid touches one associates with the work of the brilliant modern musical composer.

* * *

Awhile since golf was regarded as the game of the middle-aged. The man to whom cricket, football and tennis no longer appealed found it a good resource; but now the youth is as keen on it as his elders— more so if possible, and ladies are following the youths' example. I am told there has recently been an influx of lady subscribers on the Accrington links, who intend carrying all before them as soon as they have thoroughly mastered the game.

* * *

I am glad the District Education Committee has at last appointed a lady manager and over-ruled the much-talked-of "principle" of the three Harwood members. Mrs. Dr. Cran was courageous in allowing her name to appear for nomination after the lamentable discussions that have taken place on the subject, but there was absolutely no doubt as to the feeling of the majority of the committee when the votes for and against the election of a lady manager were counted. It seems strange that such a majority could not achieve so desirable an end without so much waste of valuable time in discussion. There is no doubt that the services of a lady will be invaluable in such a position.

March 3rd

There are signs that at last Accrington is awaking from its winter sleep. Many of the drapers' windows are labelled, "Last week of sale," while others have already discarded the striking posters, replacing them with new spring goods, a transformation which has delighted feminine shop-gazers this week. When milliners and drapers disport their new goods one's thoughts turn in joyful anticipation to the bright summer days to come, and the necessary change of raiment.

* * *

I suppose I shall be forgiven if I say that the most appropriate adjective to be applied to the weather of the past few days is "vile." Surely March cannot indulge in as many vagaries as January or February of this year, despite the fact that it is styled, "March, many weathers". These sudden changes from frost to sleet, easterly winds to balmy breezes, sunshine to leaden skies are not good for us. It is to be hoped March will belie all prophecies and be on its best behaviour now that it has been ushered in with so many tears, resulting in such deplorably muddy thoroughfares. The most suitable costume for early spring wear in Accrington is generally of the macintosh order.

March 10th

Looking at the contented faces of Accrington's oldest inhabitants as they sat at the tea tables in the Ambulance Drill Hall, and later when they were treated to a varied musical programme in the Town Hall, on Saturday, none could doubt the huge success of the first Municipal Aged Folks' Treat. Much work, thought, time, and energy must have devolved on the Mayor's committee in the organisation of such a scheme, but no doubt Alderman Rawson and his colleagues would find compensation in seeing "enjoyment" writ large on so many faces as a result of their labours. When so many healthy-looking old folks can be gathered together in this district, capable of enjoying festivities with almost as much spirit as young people, and far more cheeriness than I have seen displayed at many more youthful gatherings, one begins to doubt the logic of the grumbler who rails at the wretched climate of this northern town, and attendant prophecies of short lives. Accrington can't be such a very unhealthy place to live in after all, with so much living testimony to the contrary. The court room was utilised as a smoke room for the old men when they had "tea'd," and the old faces beaming over their long pipes made a suitable subject for the brush of a Dendy Sadler.

Some of the participants pictured at the 1906 "Old Folks' Treat"

* * *

Wednesday's concert in aid of the Ambulance Drill Hall, proved so successful, and so many pretty compliments were paid to the local talented ones, that members of the Clef Club have in contemplation in future years to give two musical evenings instead of one. It certainly was a capital concert. There was only one drawback, and that was the absence of ladies on the platform—so I thought. However, if ladies are not admitted to membership of the club, it seems useless to mention the subject. Yet I see no reason why ladies shouldn't be members.

One of the features of the concert was the suite of five songs composed by a local gentleman, Mr. H. Rigby, of Oswaldtwistle. Indeed, Mr. Rigby contributed largely to the evening's entertainment, for in addition he was first violin in the string quartet, played three movements, with pianoforte accompaniment, of a sonata, and was also a member of a musical trio. Not a small task for an evening.

* * *

Mr. W. Blackburn, another local pianist, besides an Andante and Scherzo from Piano Trio in A, of his own arrangement, was discovered to be the composer of a delightful melody set to a couple of verses of Shelley's, entitled "Love's philosophy." Mr. Bridge Peters was in excellent voice and sang the "Prologue to Pagliacci" with dramatic effect and fine expression. Mr. Joseph Hanson sang "Lend me your aid" (Gounod) very well, but I have heard him in much better voice. A brilliant pianoforte solo was the "Ballade in A Flat, Op. 47" (Chopin), by Mr. Percy Bainbridge. Many people heard Mr. Bainbridge in this capacity for the first time, and numerous complimentary remarks were made about his playing and undoubted ability as a pianist. With such a galaxy of talent at their command, it is rather surprising the Clef Club do not provide entertainments more frequently.

* * *

In Oswaldtwistle much enthusiasm has been displayed over the formation of a tennis club. With Dr. Craig as president, the new club promises to be a success. The site has been chosen in what is known as the "West End," somewhere near the present cricket field. Already the membership for ladies is practically closed, so many have been the applications from the fair sex, who have shown great energy in the matter from the very beginning. To augment its finances the club recently organised a "social," with excellent results. Moss-lane Tennis Club will have to look to its laurels, for I hear members of the rival club are already discussing the advisability of playing matches against Accrington.

March 17th

Bravo! The staircase at the Mechanics' is fixed. In appearance it is certainly an improvement on the old one, and almost—not quite—compensates for the chaotic appearance of the institution these last few weeks. I have not yet heard which room is being placed at the disposal of lady members when the alterations shall be completed. Doubtless the directors are giving the matter their careful consideration. One realises now that the Ladies' room is undergoing a process of demolition, that the "white elephant" was a useful animal after all.

* * *

With so many examples at hand it seems strange that women in our town can lapse into untidiness after marriage, as they so frequently do. Apart from anything else, it seems unkind to a husband for his wife to become untidy, ugly, and assume that "don't care" manner. Doubtless before marriage she was his ideal of all that was fresh, and charming, and by her own carelessness helps to deface this opinion. Men would hesitate to engage themselves to a girl if they thought she would develop with a year or two of matrimony into a sloppy style, with blouses minus their due number of buttons, stockings with holes in, hair anything but nicely coiffured, and untidiness conspicuous in many other little details of her toilette. Many a girl noted for neatness of appearance and proud of her tidy tresses, has been seen to tread this distressful path after marriage. If questioned she will find a score of reasons for her untidiness, but in her heart of hearts she knows, as does every woman, that if she really wished to be tidy nothing can prevent it. It is the duty of every woman be she maid or wife, to make the most of her appearance. "Self-love is not so grave a sin as self-neglecting"; if ladies would only realise the truth of that old saw how much, nicer some of them would contrive to be in appearance.

* * *

One is glad to hear that F. Steiner and Co. have generously promised to extend sympathetic consideration to the widow and child of the man who met with such a lamentable accident last week. The fact that the victim had taken no part in the horse-play indulged in by the apprentices but increases the sadness of the whole affair. My sympathies are with his widow, who as a result of play carried to excess is thus suddenly deprived of husband and breadwinner. Doubtless the apprentices themselves regret the deplorable end to their pranks and will remember it with lifelong sorrow.

* * *

Keen golfers are looking forward to a round of the links in the evening. Play is now possible until well after six o'clock, and every day gives a few minutes longer of welcome light. It is amusing to watch the eagerness of newly-fledged lady aspirants, who fondly believe that more practice will bring to them that mysterious and evanescent thing known as form. Next autumn may find them as far off as ever from the scratch mark, but the merry springtime is full of bright hopes and golfing is a pastime which if it does not always bring proficiency in the game gives desirable bloom of health, brightness to the eye, and a graceful elasticity of movement charming to see.

* * *

Mrs. Mills, in her thoughtful and interesting address at the Co-operative Guild made reference to the lack of tact instanced by such unfortunate occurrences as the one in Downing-street last Friday. Lamentable indeed do the friends of women regard these over-zealous and misdirected efforts of some of the "suffragettes." No advancement to the cause can be accelerated by such persistent worrying of the Prime Minister.

March 24th

Miscellaneous Choral concerts are never quite so interesting as oratorio nights. Wednesday's concert was not one of the best. Fortunately the moderately large audience was a good-tempered one, and allowed itself to applaud items which in more critical moods would not have met with such favourable response. The chorus singing was far from being perfect. Several harsh feminine voices completely marred the effect of some of the pianissimo passages, while the attack throughout was not decided enough. A little more attention to the conductor's baton would ensure more successful results. Then, too, members of the chorus were occasionally regrettably off pitch.

There can be no question that the place of honour on Wednesday undoubtedly belonged to Mr. Arthur Catterall He played superbly! He generated that electric current of sympathy out to the listener, as only a clever violinist with a great love for his art, and mastery of his instrument, can. With regret I heard the last notes of the encore die away and the musician disappear below stairs—I could have listened all night to such delightful music.

Madame Siviter, it was said, was suffering from a cold. That being so, it were scarcely just to judge her altogether by her singing on Wednesday. Her voice was harsh at times, and it appeared quite impossible for her to reach some notes properly, though her head notes are by far the sweetest.

Clarity of enunciation was the only feature of interest in Mr. Henry Brearley's singing. His songs were rendered with almost exactly the same tone-colour, giving the listener the impression that he was incapable of giving vent to much feeling or expression.

* * *

Sunday was a charming herald of spring.

The balmy atmosphere was delicious after the miserably wet days we have had to endure since 1906 dawned. Thoughts of cycling arise with the brief spells of dry weather. Many of us eagerly seize the opportunities of taking a spin presented by the longer afternoons.

March 31st

"A Critic of Critics" has forwarded to the Editor a letter dealing in the main with points mentioned in my reference to the last Choral Concert. He writes:—"*My chief objection to your criticism is the one affecting the chorus. The statement that 'the audience was a good-tempered one and allowed itself to applaud items which in more critical moods would not have met with such favourable response,' makes me think one of two things. The first is that the writer of the words went to the concert in none too happy a mood, and as a natural consequence 'slated' the chorus, and also the audience. The second is that the audience being in a happier frame of mind had no more sense than heartily applaud numbers which were badly rendered. I for one believe the applause given was thoroughly merited. The value of a newspaper to a society is inestimable (take the Opera Society for instance), and while you bewail the shortness of tenors, you evidently forget the fact that undeserved criticism is all against inducing more to join. The Choral Society is doing a noble work under rather adverse conditions, and it must be very discouraging to Mr. Walker and the committee after being thanked, as they undoubtedly were thanked, by the applause of the audience, to have it got forth to the public through your paper that the concert as a whole was poor.*"

I give the preceding paragraph with pleasure. Innumerable references to the Choral Society in previous issues show that I am solicitous for its success. In fact, I have gone further, maintaining that it was one of those excellent institutions which should not be permitted to languish for lack of funds. To suggest, then, that I wish the Society anything but good were surely beside the mark.

* * *

Is it an augury of the sort of thing we may ultimately come to, that this week a party of three ladies and a gentleman engaged a first-class smoker in the American special leaving Euston for Liverpool? My Lady Nicotine is making rapid and unhappy conquests of the sex supposed to be immune, and since the example has spread and is still spreading, the out-look becomes graver. For doctors tell us that the cocaine habit is also increasing among women, and is even more dangerous than the cigarette, which, harmless though it may seem, does not always end in smoke. At the risk of being termed old-fashioned, I personally, do not think the habit, even though it were quite harmless, tends to feminine charm. Apart from any prejudice, the habit in many cases discolours the teeth and carries in its train a perfume that is not dainty by any means.

April 7th

Variety met the eye at every turn on Sunday in Accrington. The weather was gracious, and dozens of girls were to be seen proudly wearing their new summer gowns. Accrington does not always follow the styles laid down in current fashion books, but occasionally the latest fancy in the fashion world is seized upon with avidity. Such seems to be the case this year.

* * *

Some girls wore their winter hats, while others apparently had donned last summer's millinery, which, if one must be strictly truthful, looked rather out-of-date, and not a little "crushed" when contrasted with the more up-to-date specimens. Again, many coats were thrown back, disclosing dainty frills and laces; thus, in the length of a hundred yards, one encountered spring, summer, autumn, and winter fashions—commendable variety in these monotonous times.

* * *

" Blessed be Saturdays and Sundays!" is the feeling connected with all who profit by a cessation from work on these two days; and, when we are treated to such glorious sunshine as prevailed last week-end, this brief respite is doubly blessed. Although the trees are apparently so loth to put forth their green shoots, walks abroad are very enjoyable just now. Clouds of dust raised by motors, cycles, and every kind of wheel, barring the perambulator, whose occupants appear to revel in the sunlight just as much as their elders, and are much in evidence—are the only drawbacks to the pedestrian. In spite of the added annoyances and dangers of motor cars, there appears to be an increase of cyclists on the road. It were well if, when awheel, the riders were to realise that the best way to ensure security is to follow the rules of the road. By this means is danger lessened, and many accidents would be averted were the rules more rigidly adhered to.

April 21st

Accringtonians have this week greatly augmented the Theatre Royal audiences at Blackburn; amongst them habitués of the concert room seldom seen inside a theatre. They are attracted by an Accrington young lady, Miss Ruth Nightingale, an actress of promise, with age on her side. Successful as an elocutionist, Miss Nightingale had a burning ambition to go on the stage, and at length her parents yielded. She was fortunate in being attached to a good Shakespearian company, and the fact that she is now second only to Miss Millie Ford, a charming and capable actress, is striking testimony to her talent, which was early recognise by the management of the combination. Her Accrington friends would gladly have seen her in a leading part, and there was some disappointment when it was found impossible for a second performance of "Romeo and Juliet" in order that is she might take leading lady.

Her characters during the week have been:—Fleance, in "Macbeth"; one of King Edward IV's sons in "Richard III"; Jessica in "Merchant of Venice"; Bianca in "Othello"; and Celia, in "As you like it." Her best effort was undoubtedly as Celia, on Wednesday, when her friends formed the great majority in circle and stalls. There are times when she gives evidence of self-consciousness—due, maybe, to the presence of so many personal friends— and one or two minor defects detract somewhat from a finished performance. She is also perhaps a little too eager occasionally, but that is only natural in one so young at the beginning of a stage career, and doubtless time and experience will erase these trifles.

April 28th

Another instance of the misdirected zeal of ladies who profess to have woman's cause at heart was the lamentable scene which disturbed the decorum of the Ladies' Gallery on Wednesday during the debate of the Woman's Suffrage motion in the House of Commons. As one of the members suggested when the disturbance resulting in the eviction of ladies had subsided, the members would not care to have such a scene repeated on the floor of the House. An exhibition of this kind is not likely to meet with the approval of many of the "demonstrators'" sensible countrywomen either. The strangest feature of the whole occurrence seems to be the alacrity with which the interrupters gave their names to the inspector of police. One can understand an excited "suffragette" uttering an involuntary exclamation, but to forget her dignity to such a degree as the five ladies did on Wednesday is inexcusable. The fluttering of the cotton banner through the bars of the grille was the farcical touch which no doubt brought down the "House." No wonder such a sequel to unwarrantable interruption was the cause of so much amusement among the members. The desire of these ladies to have their names associated with such proceedings in the public press passes comprehension. Martyrs, indeed! Such "martyrdom" is a reflection on the intelligence of the average woman. Doubtless the deplorable incident has but confirmed members in their determination to restrain feminine politicians behind the protective barrier of the grille. It needs no mighty intelligence to foresee the detrimental effect done to the cause by such undignified behaviour. Pity the ladies themselves cannot realise the irremediable damage they are working by their unbridled emotions, and the undesirable public criticism their actions evoke bringing the very name of woman into disrepute.

May 12th

Poverty! poverty! poverty! Was ever a corporation in such dire straits before? Accrington cannot afford a penny rate to keep its people clean! Terrible! What next? It is regrettable that the discussion re new baths at the Council meeting on Monday should have resolved itself more or less into barbed personalities. One has only to visit the St. James-street establishment to realise the dire necessity for new baths. If the stifling aroma which meets the visitor as she descends into the badly ventilated building is not convincing enough, let her disrobe in one of those out-of-date cabins and enter the plunge bath. "It is safe, clean and sanitary as any bath in the country, of its age," says one councillor. It matters not what old tumble-down shanty any other antiquated town is the proud possessor of, the question is whether ours, in sanitation, cleanliness, or safety is suitable for a population such as ours. Emphatically it is not. I speak that which I do know. But to return to the plunge bath. How fares our visitor whom we have left awhile in that wood cabin? Being of a strong, constitution she has possibly survived the distracting perfume and is ready for the bath. The clarity of the water is not such as to enamour her, but if she is brave enough to dive we will hope for her sake, that no jagged tile at the bottom of the bath comes in contact with her cranium.

I am glad Mr. Higham supported Mr. Richard's motion, and had the courage of his convictions. Among other things he said, "It was a disgrace to a town like Accrington that there should not be reasonable facilities for baths. The present, or the late, structure was erected in 1878, when the population was about 30,000. Since, the residents had increased by 50 per cent. Even the plunge bath was too small. It was unsafe at times, when more people wanted to use it than there was room for. Apart from that, if they had a larger and more adequate bath it would be far more largely used than the present one." He also said that he did not agree with Dr. Nuttall that it was more necessary to spend money on education than on baths, and in the interests of the public he would feel compelled to spend money on new baths. Mr. Cameron urged "to throw the bath into the gutter before the paint has got dried on it would not be prudent." His imprudence was in trying to patch up the baths in the first place, and not in realising their mistake in so doing now. Only six, unfortunately, voted for Mr. Richard's motion. I would suggest that the other nineteen ought to be compelled to visit the present baths daily in order to gain practical information against the time when the scheme which it has been arranged the eight slipper baths should be part of, is ready for completion. If the nineteen councillors are then alive, I don't think there would be any apathy, when the subject of baths was re-discussed in Council, nor yet any to suggest that the present baths are anything but a disgrace to a Corporation who profess to have the health of the population at heart, and a blot on a town whose watchword is, or should be, Progress.

May 19th

Oswaldtwistle ladies must have been quite pleased with the Chairman's remarks at the opening of the Liberal Club sale of work on Saturday afternoon. Mr. Hargreaves pointed out that on an occasion of that sort—with the object of raising funds—the ladies were always foremost, and suggested! That perhaps ladies were not quite fairly treated in return, as there was very little provision for ladies in the clubs. It does not seem quite the thing for ladies to work hard to finance an institution and then see all the advantages offered to men. If all men were as broad minded as this particular chairman appears to be on the subject of woman's freedom, there would be greater scope offered to ladies in connection with institutions than at present exist.

* * *

What a pity such broadminded views are not held by the directors of our Mechanics' Institute! Since the alterations the facilities for lady members have been reduced to a minimum, and one sees little prospect of their being much different for some time. They haven't even a private room there now, to say nothing of billiards or any other game. I am voicing the sentiments of a majority, if not all the lady members of the Mechanics', when I say that the present arrangements are most inconvenient.

May 26th

It would be interesting to hear the individual experiences of those motorists who in the bright and promising sunshine of Friday morning set out so jubilantly on their run to Edinburgh. The azure skies of the early morning when the cars assembled in Whalley, looking spick and span, but not one whit less bright than the hopeful faces of their occupants, gave no sign of the unwelcome change that was to come. The cars made a brave show, with their polished coach-work embellished with still brighter metal trappings glistening in the sunlight, speaking triumphantly of chauffeurs' earnest toil. Soon the brightness of the heavens gave place to flying wracks of clouds, and rain came down in torrents, then a strong wind blew mightily, and my informant tells me she saw enough Scotch mist to last her a lifetime. Saturday dawned with no abatement of the fury, and the elements refused to patch up a truce all the way home. All the cars did not reach the Scotch capital, though one cannot but admire the philosophic calmness of those who, failing to achieve their desires, yet reserved sufficient enthusiasm to sample and appreciate the joys of a simple hostelry where warmth and comfort soon lulled all ambitious feelings to rest. Telephones were in great demand in the endeavour of motorists to trace the whereabouts of their fellow sufferers in various places along the trial route, and to inform those at home that all was well.

Their advent in Whalley on the return journey was a rare eight. One realised the beauty of curly hair under such conditions at all events. How dejected some of them looked to be sure. Yet despite the constant wetting some of the motorists retained their cheeriness but one and all agreed that they had endured experiences which they had no desire to repeat. Next time they undertake a reliability run may the weather be more propitious.

June 2nd

Whitsuntide, as a rule the crowning season of the year, is at hand. This annual holiday promises to be colder than the past Easter, when for a brief spell we were treated to a foretaste of glorious summer. It is most discouraging! Several optimists, however, have predicted a departure of those rain-bearing depressions, the most unwelcome guests of May, as a consequence of the heat wave which has advanced northwards from France this week, and which caused the barometers to rise steadily all over the country.

* * *

I am sure the weather we have had is also very trying to the temper. On Sunday afternoon, captivated by a burst of tempting sunshine, many girls sallied forth in their new finery, intent on displaying their charming taste, when lo! ere an hour had passed down the rain came again. Every girl knows how provoking such unexpected showers can be at times, and one couldn't help feeling sorry for the wreckage wrought to chiffons, frills and furbelows on Sunday. Several triumphs in millinery were completely ruined, while frocks showed plainly in how short a time rain spells destruction for delicate fabrics. It was too provoking, as one young lady exclaimed, who, wet to the skin, sought to repair the damage done to what had so recently been a delicious toute ensemble.

* * *

Congratulations to Miss Mabel Bloomer, who has succeeded in winning the coveted post of head mistress of Hyndburn Park new Council school. The committee would have no easy task in choosing one out of so many clever applicants. A sensible and capable young lady, Miss Bloomer is eminently suitable for the position, and no doubt will justify the high opinion formed of her qualification when she enters on her new sphere of labour. The two other young ladies, Miss Evelyn Law and Miss Alice Grimshaw, are also to be complimented on being amongst the last three who survived the cutting down process. May they have better luck next time.

Mistresses and assistant mistresses apparently will have to walk warily towards matrimony, if they value their posts, in future. The decision that henceforth marriage shall be equivalent to three months' notice will he rather a shock to many couples who with joint earnings had hoped to bridge over the first few years of matrimony. Teaching is not such a flourishing profession that such a decision can he treated lightly by those who depend on it for sustenance. Possibly the overcrowded state of things at present is responsible for the change, and education committees have adapted this means to give the "young ones" a chance. Still, it seems rather hard on the married ones that are to be for all that.

* * *

Apparently the goodly company, numbering about a hundred, assembled at Mytton Bridge early on Wednesday morning did not consider otter hunting cruel sport. Many ladies who were included in the assembly followed the hunt with much enthusiasm. For two days, owing to the swollen condition of the river the hunt had been postponed, and even on Wednesday the river was by no means low. Starting from Hodder Foot the hounds and their followers proceeded up the river for some distance before a drag was scented. Just before reaching lower Hodder bridges a faint drag was touched and the "music" began. After passing Lower Hodder the hounds were hot on the scent, and hunted well almost up to Hodder school. Quite half a dozen times they hunted backward and forward between these two places until the otter was sighted by several members of the field. Then excitement grew intense and a good hunt ensued. The difficulties were great and the otter had the advantage of deep water. After nearly two hours' stirring sport the otter eluded his pursuers and vanished up the river. Personally, I consider he had earned his freedom, for besides the cleverness in doubling repeatedly, thus outwitting his would-be captors, the otter must have been a strong swimmer, for more than once he got into close quarters with the hounds, but soon, out-distanced them.

June 9th

June was ever a favourite month for nuptials, but this week the little God Cupid has been exceptionally busy in our midst. Wedding bells seem to have been in the air all week, and if sunshine is any criterion of happiness to be, the brides of this week have assurance in plenty.

A charming wedding was that of Dr. Graham, of Briercliffe, Burnley, to Miss Margaret Tough, daughter of Dr. Tough, of Parkside, Accrington, on Wednesday. A large congregation of relatives and guests were present in St. Peter's Church to watch the ceremony. The bride, who was given away by her father, was wearing a lovely toilette of cream silk voile prettily trimmed with lace, her veil being draped over a wreath of orange blossoms, and her bouquet composed of orchids and white roses. She looked very nice indeed.

* * *

Another pretty though quiet wedding on the same day was that of Miss Ada Jackson, of local amateur opera fame, and Mr. George B. Smith, also at St. Peter's Church. Miss Jackson's bridal gown was of tussore, palest biscuit shade, with vandyked frills giving a graceful appearance to the skirt; a vest of net, lace revers, and a folded silk belt completing the costume. The white chip hat, with its drooping feathers and tulle trimmings, worn with this costume suited the bonny face of the bride to perfection. Her only bridesmaid was Miss Sally Crossley, who looked pretty in a neat costume of cream serge with pleated skirt and short Eton coat, trimmed with tiny velvet buttons, disclosing a vest of white silk and lace; her French, sailor hat was of pink chip with carnations, and ribbon trimmings.

* * *

Congratulations to Mr. and Mrs. (Miss Edith Bannister, of Cannon-street, Accrington), James Watson, who were married on Wednesday at the Church of the Sacred Heart, Accrington. The bridal toilette was of fine cream cloth, of costume persuasion, with exquisite silk coatee, opening over a vest of white net, in which the bride looked exceedingly well; she also wore a becoming hat. Her attendants, four in number, were all very young, and looked remarkably sweet. The three little maids, Misses Dorothy and Clare Buckle, and Miss Rachel Taylor, were dressed daintily in pure white exquisitely embroidered; with large hats, and carried rose-decked wands. A white sailor suit was worn by Master John Bannister Buckle, who also carried a wand decorated with trails of roses.

* * *

Members of the North-East Lancashire Automobile Club have been invited to a meet and garden party on June 13th, at Chadswell, the country residence of Mr. and Mrs. Tom Higham. By the way, Mrs. Tom Higham is becoming quite a clever golf player. Partnered by Mr. A. B. Scholefield, she contrived to qualify for final in a mixed foursome competition for prizes presented by the captain of the Lytham and St. Annes links on Wednesday. In the final Miss Cran and Mr. W. R. Ballantyne defeated Mrs. Higham and Mr. Scholefield.

June 16th

A large and fashionable company of guests and interested spectators filled Wesley Chapel on Tuesday afternoon, when Mr. Chas. Douglas, of Manchester, was married to Miss Annie Bunting, of Quarry Hill, Accrington. Fortunately the sun shone brightly until long after the ceremony, thus enabling the beautiful toilettes of the ladies to reserve their pristine splendour coming and departing from church.

Of rich white satin, the bridal gown was simply fashioned, with skirt devoid of superfluous trimmings, just sweeping the ground behind, and bodice adorned with fine, lovely lace in berthe form; the poufed elbow sleeves also edged with frills of similar lace. The sheeny whiteness of the satin suited the expressive, beautiful face of the bride perfectly, and the filmy net veil above the rather large wreath of blossom, when thrown back, made a delicate and appropriate setting. Her bouquet was composed of white roses and lilies of the valley.

* * *

The weather for Mr. and Mrs. Higham's garden party at Chadswell on Wednesday was not of the brightest, but luckily, though dull, rain was not included in the afternoon's programme. In the Hodder district the roads were terribly dusty, and feminine occupants of the cars rather resented the effect on coiffures and toilettes, for it is impossible, however many wraps one puts on, to quite exclude dust, particles. The roads were much pleasanter nearer Accrington, where rain the day before had acted like some huge watering cart.

* * *

Fortunate indeed are those young people connected with Oak-street Congregational Church, who to-day start for their Continental trip, under the able guidance of Miss Higham. Very few ladies, however kindly disposed towards their fellow beings, would care to undertake such a task, but Miss Higham never appears to shirk any effort which will give pleasure to others. Unselfishness is a praiseworthy trait in anyone's character, and when coupled with Miss Higham's unassuming disposition is still more to be appreciated. She is one of those who "do good by stealth, and blush to find it fame." Most of the beauty spots in and near the Italian Lakes and the Swiss Alps are included in the fortnight's programme, outlined at length in Tuesday's and to-day's issues by Mr. Jno. Higham, M.P., and one may be forgiven if one breaks a commandment in coveting some of the joys in store for the party during the next fortnight, as they view the manifold delights of Nature in such beauteous spots. I trust their generous leader will also find some amends for her generosity in watching the pleasure of others, as she so richly deserves.

June 23rd

Quite a pretty spectacle was the marriage of Miss Ellen Hargreaves and Mr. Joshua Hayley at Cannon-street Chapel, which was the rendezvous of a goodly number of the fair sex, and presented a picture well worth seeing on Wednesday. The bride comes of a well-known family, her father, Mr. Laycock Hargreaves, being a familiar figure in the town. She looked very beautiful as she walked up the aisle on the arm of her father, who gave her away. Her dress was of ivory spotted Brussels net over ivory satin and chiffon; and her veil, of Honiton point lace, with orange blossom, presented to her by her cousin, was a very pretty and dainty acquisition. Her maids, her two sisters, Misses Bessie and Annie Hargreaves, were dressed in pale blue silk, taffeta with chiffon insertion, and Tuscan hats with white straw and ostrich plumes and pink roses and hyacinth. The couple, who are spending their honeymoon in Llandudno, have my heartiest wishes for their future welfare.

* * *

Bathers at Burnley's public baths for the municipal year just closed numbered 120,669, and the receipts: were £1,434. Such a total does not indicate that the Burnley Corporation have any cause to regret the erection of decent bathing. establishments. There is every reason to hope for the financial success of our new scheme for the erection of public baths recently drawn up by Mr. Newton, the Borough Engineer. It is comforting to know that sometime in the near future we may hope to indulge in swimming in our own town without present discomforts.

June 30th

That hardy annual, the cricket match in aid of the Children's Society, was again a success on Wednesday. Fortunately the sun smiled on the project, and all went merrily. Arrayed in flannels, the gentlemen wielded the bat with praiseworthy energy; one of their number who, it was said, had not played for eighteen months, scored heavily, receiving quite an ovation as he came off the field. The policemen played a sturdy game also, making a capital score, but the time limit had been reached ere they were through, so the match was proclaimed a draw. The Chief and Mr. Carter undertook the duties of umpires, the latter having filled a blank caused by Mr. Charlie Critchley's inability to discharge his usual office. With no less prowess did the ladies "wield" the provisions. In the early afternoon a bevy of fair maids carried round strawberries and other fruits, a record sale resulting in this department. In the cutting-up rooms, and behind the tea urns several familiar faces were to be seen, the owners engaged in piling trays full of good things for the hungry spectators. Mrs. Canter was the leader. Although one or two were heard to grumble the majority of those who were waited on by the young ladies appreciated their zeal to the full. Even the grumblers, had they been permitted a glance "behind the scenes," where energy and patience were required to make arrangements—for the cricket-club house, not being designed for such affairs, is not replete with every luxury .and convenience— would have had nothing but admiration for the girls, who smilingly overcame small difficulties, and sallied forth triumphant with laden trays. It is expected the proceeds will amount to £50 or a trifle more.

July 14th

The marriage of Mr. Watson, of Blackburn, and Miss Browning, of Accrington, celebrated at Christ Church, on Tuesday afternoon, was interesting and charmingly arranged. Fickle all morning, the weather changed suddenly just before the time fixed for the nuptials, and glorious sunshine honoured the event. A large number of people, mainly of the feminine persuasion (the sterner sex profess to abhor weddings, and judging by the number of ladies without cavaliers at recent local affairs of this kind, they obviously live up to their ideas on the subject), assembled in the church long before the marriage was solemnised. Sweet peas, lilies, and a variety of green plants adorned the interior; bunches of simple white sweet peas decorating the pretty carved oak pulpit, while an awning did duty as a covering from porch to church gates. Behind the choir were to be seen a number of children, members of Miss Browning's Sunday school class, who appeared to take an eager interest in the proceedings. In addition to having special seats in church, the young people the night previously had been permitted to survey the many beautiful wedding presents, among which was a rose-bowl presented to their teacher by themselves, and were finally made happy with boxes of sweets. Very few brides on the eve of their wedding have time or thought to make others happy.

The bridal party looked perfectly sweet as they came into church, headed by the bride leaning on her father's arm. The bride looked lovely indeed in her beautiful wedding gown of silk chiffon made in the form of a princesse robe, with transparent yoke and collar-band of fine white lace, the skirt having pretty lace insertions across, and down to meet the multitudinous tiny frills adorning the hem and multiplying at the back to form a short train.

July 28th

Pretty and impressive—one of the chief social events of the year—was the wedding, at Cannon-street Baptist Church, Accrington, on Tuesday, of Mr, George Lawson Macalpine, eldest son of Mr. G. W. Macalpine, J.P., Broad Oak, and Miss Margaret Eadie Peters, younger daughter of Mr. John Peters, J.P., Glenlyon, Whalley-road. Both families are widely known and respected. The bride and bridegroom, who have been teachers at Willow-street Sunday School, are much esteemed for their good qualities; the latter holding a responsible position at his father's Altham collieries, and taking considerable interest in public affairs and in the work, of Cannon-street Church and School.

The nuptial ceremony, fixed for 1-30, aroused intense interest. Although admission was by ticket, a precaution necessary in order to prevent a crush, there was a crowded congregation, most of the seats, including the galleries, being occupied soon after twelve o'clock, when the doors were opened.

Everything was auspicious for the happy event, the fickle weather turning to glorious sunshine. It was a bright and joyous scene, a flutter of excitement and expectancy, and a hum of voices pervading the edifice prior to the arrival of the bridal party. A crowd outside awaited the coming of the bride. Mr. W. I. Hunt, the organist, played selections.

The lovely floral decorations were much admired. The delightful effect was considerably heightened when the guests began to arrive. The ladies were beautifully attired most of them carrying splendid bouquets of varied tints. Mr. and Mrs. G. W. Macalpine, their youngest son Geoffrey, and Miss Macalpine, of Paisley, entered the front seat opposite the communion, whilst Mr. and Mrs. John Peters occupied the front seat on the other side.

A murmur spread through the assembled people as the bridegroom, attended by his brother, who undertook the duties of best man appeared on the scene, and many marvelled at their sang froid. Throughout the ceremony the bridegroom showed not a trace of nervousness. This is worthy of note, as often the bridegroom is only one degree more self-possessed than the bride. About half-past one the bride, attended by the bridesmaids, entered the church and was the cynosure of all eyes as she walked up the aisle to the communion, amid general expressions of admiration. The bride, tall and graceful, given away by her father, was charmingly attired in ivory duchesse satin skirt with long train, trimmed with Brussels lace, finished off with rosettes, and had a draped bodice with Brussels lace bertha. The yoke was composed of ruck tucks in net, and hand insertion. She wore a veil of Brussels net and orange blossom, carrying a lovely shower bouquet of roses and lilies of the valley. The reception was at Broad Oak, Mr. G. W. Macalpine's residence, about 130 guests being present. The newly wedded couple had a hearty send-off for the honeymoon in Switzerland and other parts of the Continent, their stay extending over five weeks.

The workpeople at the Accrington and Great Harwood collieries and the workmen at the firm's brickworks, about 1,500 in number, will be given a trip to Blackpool to-day.

* * *

Having only just returned from a delightful holiday in Wales, where each member of an easy-going party chose his or her own method of enjoying each successive day, I feel privileged to talk of these things. It is wonderful what rapid strides have been made in the designs of bathing costumes in recent years, for fashion exercises her sway in these things, scarcely less than in the ballroom, and ladies are to be seen disporting themselves in bathing attire perfectly designed to meet the susceptibilities of Madame Grundy, yet lacking the ugliness of old-time bathing costumes. The only things which apparently are impervious to the advancement of the times are the wooden structures known as bathing-machines. They are certainly the most comfortless places ever invented, and one feels pretty much like a caged animal while disrobing in them, to say nothing of the startling gruff voice which penetrates through the cracks with the command to "stick fast ma'am," followed by a lumbering and rolling journey to the sea's edge, drawn by an old cart horse. If one is well-balanced the chances are the journey is made without other mishap than a few bruises, but if, on the other hand, the bars of the doors are imperfectly screwed on, as sometimes happens, there is a glorious prospect of being pitched headlong into the sea before one has prepared for ablution. 'Tis very exciting, but one would willingly dispense with this form of excitement in favour of more modern and less dangerous wooden huts. They always remind me of Accrington and its tramcars. How go-ahead people can tolerate either is one of life's mysteries.

August 4th

As the "Observer" goes to press a day earlier than usual owing to the August Holidays, it is impossible to ascertain with any degree of accuracy how many weddings are booked for the first two days of the Fair. But the number is declared to be as large as ever. It is, after all, not surprising that so many couples should choose August Fair for their nuptial ceremony. You see they are able to go on their bridal tours without loss of wages, or rather without additional loss. I hope that all the couples united in matrimony in Accrington within the next few days may have complete happiness.

* * *

"Scribbler" in Tuesday's "Observer" very properly called attention to the state of our only river—the Hyndburn. It was my bad luck to have to cross Bull Bridge several times during the early part of the week. The stench from the river was abominable. And the water was as black as ink. I wonder when our councillors will tackle this very serious business. We hear of new schools and new mills and new library, but no effort is made to cleanse our abominable river. The new schools are being forced upon us, it is said. What a pity some central authority does not also compel us to make the river bed something like decent.

August 11th

Looking spick and span after the installation of electric light and a thorough cleansing from floor to ceiling, the Prince's Theatre, Accrington, reopened on Monday with "Somebody's Sweetheart," a piece which has given great satisfaction to the folk who, for various reasons, have been compelled to stay at home this holiday time. Accrington seemed deserted in the early part of the week, but the theatre audiences showed that some had remained at home. It has been a slack week in Accrington. Shops closed, the town has been unusually quiet. Shopkeepers of to-day are fortunate as compared with tradesmen of, say, a dozen years ago. I suppose tradesmen must have holidays like the rest of folk, and they richly deserve the brief respite Accrington Fair brings. The misfortune is that people have not accustomed themselves to preparing days in advance; they must be educated to the new order of things. I confess that my sympathies are on the side of the shopkeepers. They are kept to the grindstone all the year round, and we must submit to the inconveniences of a deserted town. As time goes on we shall get accustomed to the new order of things. I frankly admit that it is rather awkward when the housewife is unable to buy bacon and butter, but that is because we have not been properly trained.

I began my notes with reference to the Theatre. The introduction of the electric light throughout the building ought to be cordially welcomed by all local thespians. Gas lights on and above the stage are dangerous, and it must be consoling to frequenters of our only Theatre to know that gas has been entirely superseded by electricity. The change has been costly, but I believe it will be mutually beneficial to the management and to theatre-goers. Our Theatre, so far as lighting is concerned is up to date, and that is something. The electricity is to be generated from a gas plant in a building separated from the Theatre, thus ensuring absolute safety.

* * *

Chatting with an official at the railway station this week, I learned that this August had broken all records. The bookings at Accrington station on Friday night and on Saturday were simply astonishing. "What is the distinctive feature of the bookings?" I asked, and the reply was "Long distance. We never booked so many for the West of England as we have done this year." "And how does Blackpool fare?" "Well, Blackpool continues an easy first, but the difference is not so marked as in times gone by. We had splendid trains for the West and South of England." "And Douglas?" I asked. "Oh, the Isle of Man has beaten all previous years. You see, while a few years ago Liverpool and Fleetwood took all the passengers there are now other routes— Barrow and Heysham. But Fleetwood holds its own, and will continue to do so, because the trains run to the quay and there is absolutely no trouble with the luggage."

September 1st

The Rev. J. S. Balmer, of Blackpool, is to be admired for having the courage of his convictions. His omission of the word "obey" from the declaration of a bride at a recent wedding seems to have aroused general comment. If, as he says, a Nonconformist minister is not legally required to ask a bride to say "I will obey," why in the world was the custom first started? This rev. gentleman declared that he omitted the word "obey" because he did not wish to place the wife, the weaker vessel, at a marked disadvantage. If this omission is only a precedent followed by others, there ought to be a preponderance of Nonconformist brides in the future. Although one doesn't like to think that husbands take a mean advantage of this clause in the marriage ceremony, there is nothing like being on the safe side. Personally I do not see why, if there is going to be a change, the bridegroom should not take upon himself to "obey" his better half. Had this been the case formerly no doubt the custom of saying, "I will obey" would have been banished from the wedding service long ago.

* * *

Mothers may be forgiven if they experienced a sense of relief on Monday when the school- doors opened to receive the noisy lads and lasses who for weeks past have made confusion in their homes. Such lengthy holidays undermine the discipline which is such a necessary part of school life, and no doubt teachers will have experienced some little difficulty in keeping their charges in order this week. When I was a girl at school, the week following the summer vacation always seemed the most tedious of the whole year. Nevertheless I have no sympathy with those people who prate about not having any holidays. One often hears an elderly man or woman saying, "We never had such holidays when we were children, and did very well without such nonsensical ideas of going away from home to spend a few weeks every year. One feels sorry for such a one. Never to have realised the joys of thorough relaxation from the daily routine which a week or two at the seaside ensures seems very lamentable. At any rate if they had so indulged possibly they would not have descended into a narrow groove which admits of no broad-minded sensible ideas on the subject of holidays now.

* * *

I understand the committee who have the matter in hand have under consideration the scheme for electric tramway service in Accrington. Those concerned have visited many towns and inspected various cars, so we are hoping in the near future to have a really ornamental as well as useful means of locomotion. We deserve something handsome and comfortable to replace the makeshifts so long and patiently endured.

September 8th

A few days of charming summer weather sufficed to make people hysterical about the "intolerable heat." Last week-end certainly was unbearably hot; but if it rains a day we hear foolish complaints about our uncertain climate. Thus it would seem that our degenerate generation is never satisfied. Unfortunately we have no clothing suitable for the tropical heat endured while the heat wave spent itself, and many makeshifts had per-force to be resorted to. "Scribbler" said he envied the ladies their white gowns, but I assure him they were very little use in warding off the terrific glare of the sun on Saturday and Sunday. Many ladies who wore those pretty open-work blouses which looked so refreshingly cool discovered that Old King Sol had shown his scorn of such devices by duplicating in red and white the embroidery design on their fair skins. As the red sun-burn marks turn to brown before they disappear altogether it would really seem as though these cool-looking fabrics had their disadvantages. I feel very sorry for the smart young girls who discarded stockings and shoes in favour of sandals to walk along dusty roads to Whalley, especially as in all likelihood they were not used to this style of foot-gear, and it takes a certain time to become inured to that kind of thing. It makes one feel positively hot to think of their baked feet. A crusade against what is called "The curse of the collar," and a suggestion of a decollete costume for men is the latest fad, and no doubt a result of the recent heat. The suggestion is not an agreeable one, for the result of such transformation would be anything but pretty, though linen collars must be unbearable on hot days.

Surely we anticipate our seasons rather unwisely. One reads of men who were playing football on Saturday and had to be carried from the field unconscious, smitten with sunstroke. Football must have been intolerable in the broiling heat. No wonder many players collapsed. It would be too hot watching the game I should say. I saw a number of people swimming in the cool waters of the Hodder, and voted that far-away the finest amusement.

* * *

Hearing of the exploits of lady bargain- hunters at that marvellous institution, the shilling sale in Church-street on Tuesday, one cannot marvel at the report of a lady being crushed to death, which comes from Missouri. Fighting to get to the counters, the place was nearly wrecked by a crowd of women, and while one was killed several were severely injured and had their clothes torn to shreds. Undoubtedly some things are managed better in England than America. Although there was much crowding and jostling in Church-street, thanks to the good management which necessitated the closing of doors at intervals throughout the day, and the sense of decency which is not entirely lost to feminine bargain-hunters even in Accrington, the chase on Tuesday resulted in nothing more serious than loss of temper. The word "bargain" to the majority of women appears to be more efficacious than the proverbial red rag to a bull.

September 15th

Having absorbed several smaller institutions, the North-East Lancashire Automobile club is now an important organisation, able to place 200 cars of various makes and designs on the road at a day's notice. And their treatment of the crippled and poor children of the district on more than one occasion shows that motorists have a generous as well as a "selfish" side. Far from me to offer such a suggestion but I know that some people hold the view that motorists think of nobody but themselves. This feeling, I fancy, will gradually die away. Acts of kindness recently made public demonstrate that at any rate motorists are endowed with human nature just as much as some of those people who are everlastingly calling them.

* * *

How terribly sad was the motor accident which put an end to a bright young life on Sunday night. Sorrowful indeed must have been the hearts of Mr. and Mrs. Pierce, of Oakwood-road, when their little son Allan, aged six summers, who had left them but a little while before to join a playmate across the way, was carried home lifeless. His unconscious rush in front of a passing motor resulted in such mutilation of his poor little body that life must have fled immediately. Although there was no suggestion of recklessness or neglect, one can imagine that the very sight and sound of a car in future will cause the grief-stricken parents to shudder. One can only hope that Time, the great healer, will use his soothing power to assuage their great grief.

September 29th

The prolonged spell of fine weather we have enjoyed has almost obscured the realisation that winter is close at hand. Usually at this time of the year cotton frocks and summer millinery have been discarded, but who cares to think of gloomy days and warm clothing while the sun shines so lavishly, enabling summer games and a hundred and one pleasures only possible in pleasant weather to be continued? All too soon the trees will bedeck themselves in their beautiful coppery tints, and the fall of the sere and yellow leaf will be followed by the unlovely bareness of winter.

* * *

Already pleasant social evenings are being planned to fill the coming long nights. Next Wednesday, I see, a concert promoted by Mrs. J. Carter in aid of the Cannon-street bazaar funds to be held in Willow-street School. A neat little programme intimates that eight well-known local artistes will be in evidence, and judging by the well-chosen songs and other musical items the concert ought to be excellent. It is practically the first of this season's concerts, and I understand in connection with bazaars and other institutions there are to be a large number this winter, so socially Accrington will not be dull.

October 6th

Mrs. James Carter is to be complimented on the very enjoyable concert she promoted in aid of the bazaar fund in Willow-street School on Wednesday evening. From start to finish the musical programme was successful, and I understand the financial proceeds also are good. One good feature of the concert was the strict adherence to printed items—there is nothing more provoking than to have a programme which becomes useless owing to the vagaries of artistes. It was rather a mistake to omit the interval, even though time was short, for a few minutes breathing space allows the audience to relax somewhat, and Wednesday's assemblage would have been all the better for a little relaxation—they were apathetic to the point of frigidity. Of course, hats and coats are not conducive to comfort in a hot room, but Accrington audiences seem loth to part with out-door apparel at many of our concerts, thus annoying those who sit behind their hats, and bringing discomfort on themselves by wearing clothing utterly unsuited to heated concert rooms. In some towns ladies would never dream of appearing thus, and it only requires one or two influential ladies to lead the way, and this custom would be abolished in Accrington. It is a well-known fact that many—I don't say all—ladies are prone to follow the lead of those whom they consider social superiors. One often hears the question "What is So-and-so wearing at this affair?" "So-and-so," who is supposed to be correct, probably follows her own inclination in the matter, unconscious that others only await her decision to go and do likewise, like a flock of sheep.

* * *

Those motorists, including an Accrington gentleman, who were fined at Lytham on Thursday for having exceeded the 20 miles an hour speed limit would not regard motoring as an unmixed blessing, or police traps as very desirable institutions. Defendants complained of the police not having stopped them at the time and no wonder for the fines all told amounted to £35. Poor motorists! When balloons supersede motors as some day they may, will there be a speed limit on them also I wonder? If not, there should be no question as to the future of ballooning as a pleasurable pastime for without tyres and police traps it should certainly flourish.

* * *

Fortunately the motor accident which befell Mr. Briggs-Bury and his guests last Saturday resulted in nothing more serious than a few scars and bruises. Combined with the inevitable shock to nerves, cuts and bruises are bad enough in all conscience, but the results might have been much worse.

October 20th

An interesting programme has been compiled for the first of the season's Cunliffe concerts on November 7th. Among other artistes the services of Miss Marguerite de Forest Anderson the American lady flautist, of the Queen's Hall concerts, have been procured. A lady flautist is certainly a novelty at an Accrington concert, and if she but be as clever as her name is lengthy, she ought to be worth hearing. These concerts are always popular, and the orchestra, I hear, is in excellent form just now.

* * *

Having seen the crowds of people who arrived in Blackpool on Friday and Saturday to view the motor races, and knowing most of the hotels along the promenade were full of visitors—motorists and their friends-staying for a few days solely on account of the trials, it is difficult to fathom the objections made by some of the ratepayers of Blackpool against these affairs. Saturday's crowd must have brought thousands of pounds into Blackpool, which at the end of a season, would not otherwise have happened. Motorists as a rule are not sparing of expenditure, and if one only reckons that £1 per head—in many cases considerably below the mark— was spent, what a huge gain this represents for the town. In addition there were thousands of people along the promenade, lining the barricades, who did not possess cars, nor perhaps ever hoped to, but who took a keen interest in the races, an had evidently come for the purpose of seeing such a battalion of cars. Each of these would require food, even if they were day "trippers," another gigantic source of profit to shop-keepers—so why grumble? The result of the motor trials to many of the shop keepers, to say nothing of hotel proprietors, garage companies and so on, must have been a little gold mine. The races are certainly more exciting to competitors than spectators, as the cars fly past so quickly. Mr. Havelock Lonsdale, of Accrington, was the fortunate gentleman who carried off the first prize—a lovely silver cup—in the standing mile handicap for touring cars confined to members of Lancashire clubs, with his 30 hp. Daimler.

October 27th

The Backhaus concert on Wednesday was a decided success. For once in a way an Accrington audience was unstinting in its applause, and the artistes no less generous in their responses to encores. And the audience was so great that some parts of the Town Hall were uncomfortably crowded.

In a column mainly devoted to ladies— though I am glad to know these weekly jottings afford some pleasure (possibly amusement) to men—it would seem the right thing to give Madame Ella Russell the place of honour, but there is no denying the fact that Backhaus, with his great recitation, honestly earned by his superb pianoforte playing, was the lion of the evening.

* * *

Madame Clara Butt and her husband, Mr. Kennerley Rumford, are to visit Accrington in December—on the 12th to be correct—to give a farewell concert in the Town Hall previous to taking a tour round the world, which it is expected will cover two years. Their concert party includes Miss Esta D'Argo and Mr. Phillip Simmons. The programme is an interesting one, and no doubt will provide another very enjoyable evening for music lovers.

* * *

The suggested ladies' subscription dance, which, by the way, has not advanced very far beyond a suggestion yet, is likely to have many supporters. I do think there ought to be a special clause in our pin money allowance this winter. Everybody I know seems to be contemplating a concert, dance, or some other kind of entertainment to eke out bazaar funds, or with some other legitimate excuse. Of course, all those sociable evenings will add to the brightness and pleasure of young folks this winter, and all but a few very narrow-minded people realise that the amusement of young people must be catered for. If their elders find so much gaiety contagious- well it won't do them any harm to be inoculated with a little of youth's lymph for dullness.

November 3rd

How dark and depressingly dreary the almost ceaseless rain has made this week! It is not much comfort to know that people directly connected with the water supply for our reservoirs have been happy in the thought of abundance for some time to come, as a result of the heavy downpour. Nothing is more distressing to the temper, either, than continual drizzle. One can appreciate a good steady downpour even when, as during last week-end, it is varied by a good solid descent of hailstones, but a ceaseless drizzle, with its accompanying murkiness, is never acceptable.

It is a pleasure to draw the curtains, shutting out such dreariness, and turn to an inviting armchair near a cosy fire, with one's favourite book, handy; but to continually be toasting one's feet begins to pall after a time, and besides makes people rather selfish.

It is well that hostesses realise this, and minimise the danger of becoming selfish by entertaining to the best of their ability just now. Some people have got into rather absurd ways, though, during recent years. Many ladies insist on entertaining lavishly or not at all, whereas a cup of coffee, sandwiches and cake, plus a bright musical evening, are as much as most young folks desire. I am glad to see one or two ladies in Accrington have initiated the fashion of having their "at homes" in the evenings. It is such an informal and jolly way of entertaining, and enables gentlemen as well as ladies to participate. If music takes the place of perfidious gossip, so much, the better. Anyhow, it is a pleasant step in the right direction, and possibly others will follow the lead and contribute their quota to the general enjoyment.

* * *

Inspector Garvey

On Tuesday Inspector Garvey, a familiar figure in the Accrington borough police force, completed twenty-five years' service. He has, it is stated, no intention of retiring on a pension—as, of course, his years of service entitle him to do—just yet. When I was younger the rather severe face of the inspector inspired me with something akin to awe, but since then I have learned that behind that stern exterior there is a kindly heart, which many a time has helped to lessen the suffering of some poor human being. Honest and straightforward men—and women too—need not fear this sturdy minion of the law, and it is to be hoped that for many years yet he will continue to help along the course of law and order in the town.

November 10th

To help worthy local institutions is always a delight, and I have special pleasure in drawing attention to the excellent programme announced for next Wednesday by the Accrington Clef Club, in the Ambulance Drill Hall. The club holds its gatherings in a portion of the Drill Hall, and a good "house" will enable the members, not only to do something in return for the kindness shown them, but to hand over a substantial sum for the benefit of the local Ambulance Brigade. Ladies are not included, but that is no reason why we should not give the Clef lot a helping hand.

* * *

The Cunliffe concerts gain in popularity every season. Despite the very unfavourable elements out of doors, a large number of people assembled in the Town Hall on Wednesday and were apparently well satisfied with the music provided. I was glad to see many ladies had removed their hats before entering the concert room, as the Cunliffe concert patrons are usually among the worst offenders. There remained many, of course, who were not so thoughtful, due maybe in some cases to the scarcity of cloak room accommodation, but in the majority to love of display. One can forgive an invalid, or an old lady who from motives of health has to retain her headgear, but those who appear to regard a concert as an effective show-room for their millinery are beyond forgiveness. To see and be seen appears to be their only aim in concert-going. I am not exaggerating. One young lady who, during the greater part of the musical programme let her eyes wander up and down the room, occasionally craning her neck to assist her vision, I happened to meet subsequently. Her knowledge of "Who's who?" at the concert, and what every lady wore, was surprising. Not content with their apparel in some cases, she must needs supply portions of their private history as a setting. "But how went the music?" ventured another lady visitor. "Oh! the music was very nice," replied the inveterate gossip, immediately launching into a description of the lady flautist's gown, her youthful style of dressing, her hair, mouth, possible age.

* * *

Church is indebted to the trio of ladies who have been instrumental in forming a District Nursing Association for the township by soliciting subscriptions to the amount of £100. In addition, the energies of Miss Cole, the secretary, Mrs. B. Bury, and Mrs. Furness have resulted in the promise of annual donations from local gentlemen and firms in the district. Almost immediately a qualified nurse will be ready to help the poor people of Church in cases of distress.

November 17th

Accrington folk had a musical treat offered to them on Wednesday evening, but I am sorry to hear that only a comparatively small number attended the Clef Club concert in the Ambulance Drill Hall. Maybe the execrable weather had something to do with this, and possibly also Carl Rosa operas at Blackburn. It surely cannot be that the interest in good music is on the wane locally; but surely the efforts of the Clef Club are deserving of better reward. Social events so far this winter have followed one another in such quick succession that possibly some of the concert goers are feeling the demands on time and purse. It is worthy of note that—barring the brave array of members in immaculate evening dress—ladies predominated in the audience. Surely this was magnanimous, for it is well-known that ladies are excluded from membership. May I add that some of my own sex of unquestionable ability would be an acquisition to the club? It wouldn't be a bad idea for ladies to form a Clef Club of their own, and join forces with the gentlemen on concert evenings.

* * *

Sunday was an ideal day for Mayoral procession. No wonder people turned out in thousands to see the newly-elected Mayor, with his attendant townsmen, walk to church. And the procession was well worth seeing, too. A fine figure looked Mr. Higham in his robes, with the handsome chain glinting in the sunlight, preceded by the mace bearer, as spick and span as it is possible for a mace bearer to be. The Town Clerk, in wig and gown, always an imposing figure at these functions, looked rather warm, although there was a nip of frost in the air. One of Accrington's grand old men, Mr. William Entwisle, J.P., was also in the procession, and could give points in his bearing to many a more youthful citizen. The

Alderman Thomas Hiaham

volunteers in their uniform added a touch of colour to the scene, but I cannot say the "music" of the bag-pipes was inspiring—at any rate to English folk. The service in the church I thought was not of the high order one associates with Oak-street. The choir did not sustain the reputation previously earned. The Mayoress and the Mayor's mother were present, and evinced keen interest in the proceedings. I wonder why Mayoresses never go to church officially. If they did the drab aspect of frock coats would be varied by the charming colourings of ladies' gowns and hats. What a pity they don't, though there wouldn't be room for outsiders in any church in Accrington if ladies were asked to join the procession.

November 24th

There is good news for the friends of the Accrington Choral Society. The president, Mr. W. Haworth, J.P., has generously come forward with a gift not only sufficient to pay the Society's financial obligations but to enable the season to commence with a substantial balance in hand, having handed over to the treasurer the sum of £200.

Now, how can the public of Accrington, and especially patrons of the society, show appreciation of Mr. Haworth's kindness? In many ways. They can, and I hope will, support the Society with such enthusiasm that the treasurer will never again be on the wrong side. After Mr. Haworth's handsome gift there ought not to be an empty seat in the Town Hall on Wednesday.

December 1st

Despite the execrable weather a large number of ladies, dressed in pretty gowns and charming millinery, attended the Mayoress's "at home" on Thursday. With all due respect to the Mayor, who looked remarkably well as he assisted the Mayoress in receiving her guests, he was but a secondary consideration at this function. All eyes rested on the splendid figure and handsome face of the Mayoress as she, with natural and becoming grace, welcomed the visitors. The gathering was not quite so cosmopolitan as on a former interesting occasion, and as it wasn't market day, string bags, oranges, etc., did not appear, though I saw one baby in arms awed into silence like several of its elders, who, seated in grim state, watched the proceedings interestedly. Miss Hannah Higham, a daughter of the Mayoress, flitted about the room and apparently enjoyed the function immensely. Mrs. Higham (the Mayor's mother), in black silk coat, and bonnet, chatted amiably with the guests, now and again handing round cakes and sandwiches from the little tables near. Mrs. Albert Higham very smartly gowned in a black and white costume, with short bolero edged with ermine, above a white blouse, and a large picture hat, looked well and Miss Higham, in neat tailor-made wine-coloured costume adorned with silk braid, wore an extremely handsome sable fur.

The chief-topic of conversation was of course the forthcoming Mayoral receptions, to which many people are looking forward with pleasurable anticipations.

December 15th

By comparison with some of the old hands, who, I understand, have been on the staff a score of years—from the very first number of the "Observer" in fact—I am indeed a junior in the profession. But that does not preclude me from joining with the rest to offering congratulations on this the fortieth anniversary of the paper. I suppose the old 'uns would scarcely include me in their own happy circle—for I believe the "Observer" lot are a very happy family— but they, as well as the Editor and all the rest, have my best wishes. May they continue in this happy situate, and may the "Observer and Times " continue to flourish.

* * *

The fact that some time must elapse before the charming personality and beautiful voice of Madame Clara Butt will be again in evidence at an Accrington Concert, owing to her impending foreign tour, was an additional stimulus to the prevalent desire to hear her at the concert on Wednesday. Those who heard the singing of the famous contralto's opulent voice for the first time were almost to be envied their experience, for the sensation of first hearing such a gifted songstress is one of the memorable things of life.

* * *

The Mayoral receptions this week have more than fulfilled the pleasurable anticipations. Thursday's guests talk of the nice chats they had with friends, and the capital entertainments supplied for their enjoyment, but the dancers who on Friday "chased the glowing hours with flying feet," especially the young people, have still more glowing tales to tell of happy hours due to the generosity of the Mayor and Mayoress. On January 4th there will be a children's dance, and in the evening a ball for young people, and I hear there are still more festivities to come in February.

December 22nd

My first duty and pleasure to-day is to wish all my readers a very happy Christmas. Everybody is looking cheery, and the shops are quite gay in Accrington. There are still a few unpleasant creatures who maintain that Father Christmas is a humbug, but having done honour to him for so many years many of us would be loth to bid him farewell forever. No doubt the pampered and petted children will be made happy, but it is sad to think how many poorer ones there are even in Accrington to whom these simple joys are denied.

* * *

Where toys have been displayed this week there also have gathered groups of boys and girls amusing to watch. With eyes as big as saucers they have coveted those charming dolls or that pretty doll's house, with verandah and windows all complete, or this butcher's shop with joints of beef and legs of mutton; displayed on hooks, to say nothing of the soldiers and horses and carts in which the hearts of boys for ever delight. Oh! they have had such a splendid time gazing on all these wonders and supposing, only "s'posing," some of these pretty things might find their way into "our" stockings on Christmas morning.

December 29th

Not without regrets shall we bid adieu to 1906. The year has in several ways been an auspicious one, and most of us will be able to look back upon it with kindly feeling and pleasant memory. May 1907 be another such. That every one of my readers may have a bright and prosperous New Year is my sincerest wish.

1907

January 5th

It is to be hoped, now that the Christmas festivities are ended, that our local bands will cease from troubling, and "Auld Lang Syne" and "Fine old English Gentleman" be allowed to rest in peace—for at least another year. If I had my way, that "fine gentleman" would never more be resuscitated. Although fond of music, I find the bands one of the great trials, of Christmas time, and when one resides in the midst of generous neighbours the reiteration of "Fine old English Gentleman" becomes well nigh maddening. Robbed of its old-time significance by the impartiality with which it is now administered, this music is more than tedious.

Of the way in which these limited repertoires have been delivered I will say little. One can understand how tired the instrumentalists themselves grow of playing these items time after time, and there is always a gruesome interest in following the straying instrumentalist, and wagering whether he will get to the correct pitch before the conclusion of the piece. When there are two or three of this type in one band, the result to the musical borders on tragedy.

* * *

Yesterday's Mayoral entertainments to the little ones in the afternoon, and to the "young people" in the evening, were most successful functions. The arrangements were well planned and admirably carried out. Both gatherings were much enjoyed, and the young people highly appreciated the hospitality of the Mayor and Mayoress. In the afternoon there were not far short of 300 youngsters, many of them prettily dressed. And weren't they happy! It was good to see them enjoy themselves, and must have given supreme pleasure to the Mayor and Mayoress and other members of their family. The evening dance, attended by about 400 persons, mostly young, was charming.

* * *

I am glad to hear that suffering patients in the Victoria Cottage Hospital have not been neglected this Christmas-time. Miss Carpenter, the matron, informs me that since those pretty decorations of holly, mistletoe, Chinese lanterns and festoons of greens bearing cheery mottoes, were erected, the patients have had a comparatively happy time. Doubtless those young people who have sacrificed a few hours on different evenings to entertain with songs and other music a few of their less happily-placed fellow creatures need no outside commendation to realise the happiness they provided.

One young fellow whose leg had been badly damaged said the singing helped him to forget the pain of the bones that were knitting together, and he thought the people were very kind to come. This is typical of the gratitude of others, more or less bluntly expressed.

Perhaps the most interesting specimens in the female ward are the two wee babies, who occupy the pretty little swing cots in the centre adorned with fresh muslin draperies tied up with pale blue bows. These babies are rather startling examples of what can, and frequently does, happen to little mites through wilful neglect or ignorance of mothers. Both are burdened at the outset of life with delicate constitutions and defects caused by neglect which years of care cannot obliterate, one of the two, aged several months, only weighing now what he ought to have weighed at birth. Fortunately under the gentle care of the kindly matron and her assistants the two babies are progressing, favourably, but what chance can two little chaps have with such a poor start in life, and all, perchance because their mothers had not the knowledge necessary to rear healthy little lives? It is a great pity every girl is not taught during her school days a few of the necessary truths of life and equipped with a knowledge of the responsibilities of motherhood, which in later life would be of much more service to her than either Euclid or algebra.

January 12th

Were Mayor and Mayoress ever so kind- hearted and generous? On Saturday the poor children had their treat, and right well did they enjoy the good things provided for their delectation. It did one's heart good, as one old lady remarked, to see so much enjoyment written on their beaming faces. When photographs of the Mayor and Mayoress appeared on the screen cheers from hundreds of grateful children rose like a huge tidal wave and dissolved in a flood of sound, which in its spontaneous sincerity could not fail to express their gratitude for the favours lavished upon them.

On Thursday the Mayor and Mayoress gazed on quite a different scene in the Town Hall. Again they were host and hostess, but handsome ladies, attended in a few cases by gentlemen, had taken the place of the poor children, and although the guests this time did not cheer, they were doubtless none the less grateful for the kindnesses of the Mayor and Mayoress.

On Thursday evening the police force were entertained to supper by the Mayor. Really, for thoughtfulness in entertaining there never was such an ideal couple; they seem to have included everybody in the town they could possibly think of, to share their Mayoral hospitality. Three cheers for the Mayor and Mayoress!

Hip! hip! hip! hurrah!! It doesn't look much in cold print, but is quite as hearty, if not as noisy, as the children's cheers.

* * *

The Mayoral young people's dance was magnificent, but there were one or two blemishes for which, of course, neither Mayor nor Mayoress could possibly be held responsible. At one time quite half a score young fellows were on the platform without lady partners, partaking of the refreshments, while many young ladies were down in the room without cavaliers.

Even if these youthful gentlemen were non-dancers it was surely their clear duty to ask members of the fair sex to accompany them on to the refreshment platform and attend to their wants. As the girls looked exceedingly pretty this grave omission could only be attributed to the colossal selfishness of the young men, who perhaps as they advance in years would be heartily ashamed of such conduct.

Another point:—As Friday night's dance was essentially for young people, it was scarcely fair that married ladies should monopolize the attentions of young men when by doing so they were robbing young girls of their rightful partners. Perhaps the ladies themselves did not give the matter a moment's thought or they would have observed the disappointed looks of several young people whose charms certainly entitled them to more attention from members of the opposite sex of their own age. I merely mention this matter because I know many of the girls— some of them at a dance of this elaborate kind for the first time—felt very sore about it.

January 19th

Wednesday's Conservative Ball eclipsed all previous efforts in recent years. The committee are to be complimented on the huge success they achieved. All the arrangements were admirable. Numbering close upon two hundred, the guests had a delightful time, gentlemen for once in a way being most attentive. Great interest centred around Sir George and Lady Bullough, the latter winning all hearts by her charming ways. Simplicity was the keynote of her pretty pale blue satin gown, relieved on the corsage with exquisite lace, the skirt being fully pleated from the hips; she also wore a string of diamonds around her throat, and a tiara of emeralds, and she was one of the most striking ladies in the room. Ever and anon her long gown became entangled round her feet in the dance, but she freed, herself with easy grace from its folds smiling bewitchingly the while at her partners. She was most energetic, and one seldom saw her seated while a dance was in progress. Similar energy has been evident in all her movements in the town since her arrival on Wednesday afternoon. On Thursday morning, accompanied by her two sisters and brother, she visited Hyndburn Park School, professing herself charmed with all the school arrangements, which was a much handsomer type of elementary school than she expected to find in this country. In the afternoon, after a motor spin in the country, she went through Bullough's works showing a keen interest in all the departments of this huge hive of industry, while on Friday morning she was at the Police Station witnessing the distribution of her weekly bounty to the poor of Accrington.

* * *

It was good! to see some of the older ones enjoying themselves to their hearts' content at the Old Folks' Treat on Saturday. Quite the most touching incident, I thought, was the Mayoress' presentation of little gifts to the young girl entertainers from the Theatre. She also bestowed upon each little face a motherly kiss, which no doubt was quite as much appreciated as the gifts by the girls, who looked surprised to be so honoured.

January 26th

I am glad to hear that the opera is "going strong." By opera I mean, of course, the production the first week in February by our Amateurs. Perhaps it would be more correct to use the plural and say productions, for this year our Amateurs are giving two operas, "Trial by Jury "and "The Sorcerer."

* * *

"*Why did women want to get into Imperial Parliament?*" quoth Councillor Townsend. "*Did the women want a quarrel at their own firesides when there was an election?*" Why shouldn't women be content to bowl all the time when by desiring to bat they ruffle the tempers of their poor, dear husbands, whose political opinions should not be met with domestic opposition or criticism, especially at national match times, lest a quarrel ensue? Don't you see, man can lay down his own laws on his own hearthstone now, but if woman were permitted a Parliamentary vote she might have the audacity to bring her intelligence to bear on political opinions, and his giddy, supremacy might totter and fall by the way. What a fall that would be—it might break the peace of marital bliss for a time—and if the fall be rapid it might even smash one of those pretty hearth-stone tiles. How dreadful! Surely ye "suffragettes" have not counted the cost of your entry into Parliament! Says Councillor Townsend, "*There is a broad distinction between men and women. One is masculine, the other feminine; one is rational and the other emotional.*" Purely declamatory again! "*Women seem to forget that the greatest forces have proclaimed them inferior to men. The Church excluded women from the pulpit on the basis that they were inferior.*" If true, even the Church is not infallible in its beliefs, though Councillor Townsend thinks it is quite justified in taking up that position. "*Therefore women, instead of trying to get into men's domain, should keep in their own.*" The question naturally follows, which is man's and which woman's domain? A man's saying that a special sphere is alone woman's domain doesn't make it so, nor yet does his idea that she is inferior ensure her inferiority? Personally I agree with Mrs. Mills, who does not admit that women are intellectually inferior to men, given equal opportunities. "*The first thing a woman thinks about is how she is going to get wed. It is her study and thought from morning till night,*" says Coun. Townsend. This is a gross libel on the sex, and as one of its members I resent such a sweeping statement, even in a general sense. As Mrs. Mills pointed out, in some cases, owing to the low wages given to women by the laws of man, some women are obliged to turn to matrimony as their only means of carrying on existence, but I am not prepared to accept Mr. Townsend's statement that even these poor creatures consider nothing but matrimony. What a dull time they would have, to be sure!

* * *

Next Monday and during the week, the people of Accrington will have a chance of showing appreciation of one of our best institutions by buying the pretty flowers exhibited in the Town Hall made by cripple girls and boys from the Industrial Training Homes. The exhibition is under the patronage of the Mayor and Mayoress, and I hope will be as successful as a cause devoted to the betterment of suffering and crippled humanity deserves. To say nothing of helping the poor cripples, the flowers they make are well worth purchasing, for they are exceedingly pretty—only second to those one sees in Nature's flower garden.

February 2nd

Parliament is making things pleasure and secure for the servant class as a whole, and mistresses are still crying out that they cannot procure the help they require. In East Lancashire especially, where mills and other works abound to attract feminine employees, the domestic servant question is becoming a pressing one. There appears to be a growing distaste for domestic service in that particular class whence servants of the past have emanated. No doubt the solution of the servant difficulty will eventually be found in the day servant who has her evenings free. Such an arrangement would interfere largely with our present system of social entertaining, which, to a great extent is carried on in the evenings, and naturally mistresses do not take to the idea kindly. In households where hospitality is conducted on a simple scale this arrangement need not necessarily be a great hardship if the maid, after setting everything in readiness for the evening meal goes home after tea. Anyhow, that is what will probably happen unless many better class girls now acting as companions and lady helps will boldly step into the breach and qualify themselves to take all save the very roughest duties. Unfortunately the difficulty with "better class" girls is invariably their supposed dignity which prompts them to refuse to do things which a daughter of the house would do willingly.

* * *

What a terrible shock the boiler explosion last Friday at Huncoat, and its fatal results, must have been to the two families concerned. The sympathies of everyone have been roused by the sorrow and sudden bereavement thrust upon Mr. Birtwistle, who in so short a time has lost both wife and daughter. The Hartleys, mother and two daughters, were more fortunate in escaping with their lives, and though badly injured there is hope of their recovery. Thousands of people have visited the house this week to view the damage, and hundreds more accompanied the burial cortege to the cemetery. Although one cannot commend such morbid curiosity, it is to be hoped the wreckage was a valuable object lesson to those inclined to be careless in these matters.

February 9th

It is evident that the two operas performed by our local amateurs this week have not appealed to popular taste as other Gilbert and Sullivan productions have done in previous years. Though, perhaps, not so interesting as later works, the manner in which the amateurs have performed "Trial by Jury" and "The Sorcerer" this week certainly merited more patronage. Were similar creditable productions given by amateurs in Burnley, Bury or Wigan the theatres would be crowded every night with delighted spectators eager to show their appreciation. But in Accrington this year some people have considered the purchasing of tickets an awful bore because they didn't particularly care for the operas. Having paid 5s., or 2s. 6d., as the case may be, and put in an appearance at the theatre they apparently felt they had done their duty nobly. Of the encouragement necessary to convince the actors that, besides helping local charities they had provided enjoyable entertainment at the cost of much time and energy, they never thought. One night this week the "house" was particularly frigid. Surely our amateurs deserve more applause than they have received. Applause is helpful.

For the performances this week I have only words of praise. I do not say they have been perfect in every particular, but taking them on the whole our amateurs have done exceedingly well and I certainly have not yet seen an amateur society to surpass them.

February 16th

Mr. and Mrs. Sinclair must have been gratified by the pretty silver tea service presented to them by the members of the police force to mark their "silver wedding." It is always nice to know that one's efforts are appreciated, and the presentation of such a handsome token, along with the good wishes and praise of Mr. Garvey—who was for the time being a mouthpiece for the whole force—could not fail to convince the "Chief" of the appreciation in which he is held.

* * *

Thanks to the efforts of those energetic secretaries, Mr. Harry Heap and Mr. R. Crossley, that pleasant Gents' Subscription Dance was revived at the Conservative Club last night. It has, I believe, flourished on seven different occasions at the Liberal Club and Town Hall, and last night's affair was no less brilliant than its predecessors, and certainly quite as enjoyable. The gentlemen are always extremely attentive on these occasions, as, of course, they ought to be, for the pleasure and success of the dance rests entirely in their hands—so far it has not rested in vain. To the abundance of gaieties we have experienced in our town this winter, it was a pleasant addition. In the name of the ladies I say, "Thanks, gentlemen!"

March 2nd

Local interest in the Cunliffe concerts shows no signs of waning. Again on Wednesday evening an interested crowd assembled in the Town Hall, attracted by the musical fare provided for the second of this season's concerts. The programme was both long and varied; perhaps a little too varied to please any one person entirely. But no doubt such variety provokes wider interest in our little community if it does not always educate whatever critical faculties listeners may possess.

Some interest attached to the appearance of Miss Lucy Nuttall, a young contralto who was complimented by the judges at the Blackpool Festival. It was not her first appearance in the town, however, as she previously sang at one of the Mayoral receptions. "My wish for you," her first song, was very prettily delivered.

On the whole the concert was enjoyable, although many ladies still persist in wearing hats. There is absolutely no reason for such eccentricity, as promoters of the concert provide cloak-room accommodation free of charge.

March 9th

A number of trees were planted on a plot of land in Blackburn-road, Haslingden, on Saturday to celebrate the first "Arbour Day" in connection with the "Beautiful Haslingden Council" This Council, promoted with the commendable aim of beautifying the town by planting trees, flowers, etc., was inaugurated in 1906, and as its members number sixty-eight, there is no doubt residents appreciate the scheme. The originator of this pretty idea, Mr. Joseph A. Wilkinson, has undertaken the duties of secretary, while Mr. A. Smethurst, J.P., is the president. Although Haslingden will never be a Southport, or a Buxton, it is worthy of note that already the organisation has done much good work.

* * *

Accrington might with advantage follow the lead of these enthusiastic Haslingden people, who are doing their utmost to encourage householders to cultivate their front gardens and adopt window boxes. If our townspeople would attend to their small plots, the appearance of the town would certainly be greatly enhanced. If every house sported its window box, and every garden its flowers what a charming place this would be.

* * *

There are many attractive features prepared for the decoration of the Town Hall assembly-room during the latter part of next week, when Cannon-street Baptist bazaar is to be held, and some of the stall-holders are wearing fancy costumes. There is nothing in the way of raffling to attract the gentlemen, which in my opinion is rather a mistake. As one man remarked in my hearing the other day, "You've no idea how beastly awkward a chap feels when there is no raffling at a bazaar. It isn't as if we regarded raffling merely as a gamble; no spirit of greed or gain prompts us to put in sixpence, or a shilling, for an article which very probably we don't want. If we get it we are satisfied, if somebody else gets it we are still content. There are heaps of namby-pamby women's things at bazaars that fellows, especially bachelors like myself, don't care about, and one cannot be stowing away refreshments all the time, or wear half a dozen buttonholes at once." Poor man! The only advice I can offer you bachelors is take your mother or your sisters with you. If you don't care for that plan take somebody else's sister. Providing your companion is of the feminine persuasion, she will be happy to help you to spend your surplus cash. You may lose her in the crush, but, if this happens, there are the "side-shows," which I am told are to be specially interesting, as a last resource.

March 16th

Assuredly bazaars are not going out of fashion, in Accrington at any rate. The proceeds from Cannon-street Baptist bazaar on Wednesday, the opening day, amounted to £1,050. I am inclined to agree with the Mayor, that bazaars are the very finest institutions for raising money. Like the poor, they are always with us, and it is surprising how much money is available to support any and every kind of bazaar in our town. Rather a gloom was cast over the opening ceremony by the illness of the Rev. Charles Williams, who, however, in the midst of his suffering had not forgotten to send a note wishing every success to the affair and regretting his inability to be present.

* * *

It has been stated more than once in recent years that the ladies of the present generation have neglected the art of the needle. This is not the case in our town as instance the work turned out in huge heaps for this bazaar. One lady's "show" to-day is equal I am sure, to a dozen or more of bazaar workers in grandma's day. Of course, nowadays the ladies have private show-days in their own homes, and as there is a good deal of competition amongst the fair sex, Mrs. Jones strives hard to show as many goods as Mrs. Smith. I don't suggest that this leads to jealous envy, for we all know that such an emotion never—well hardly ever, enters, or has any connection with bazaars. This spirit of competition certainly helps to swell bazaar funds considerably, but the dear ladies sadly overwork themselves on that account. Men do not understand the bazaar fever, and during this "working for bazaar" period, have shrugged their shoulders in disdain as they sauntered off to play billiards, observing that they'd be jolly glad when the bazaar was over, and the feminine members of their households returned to their normal quiet, and the place not all strewn with bazaar goods.

March 23rd

Saturday was Children's Day at Cannon- street bazaar, and Miss Phyllis Bury and Master Geoffrey Macalpine officiated as opener and chairman respectively. They performed their duties in a charming manner, and with rather more sang froid than is often displayed under similar conditions by people many years their senior. When two such young people perform these ceremonies with easy grace now, what may we not expect of them in later years? Judging by Master Macalpine's short speech, delivered in an intelligent way, we are certainly justified in expecting great things from him in the future. Let us hope that in more ways than one he will someday be competent to wear the mantle, which in the natural order of things descends from father to son. Miss Bury's speech was short, but very prettily given; she also gracefully acknowledged a bouquet, presented along with a short speech, by Miss Lucy Lightfoot. All the young speakers were not so self possessed as these three. The ordeal of addressing the crowd was too much for a sensitive little girl, who, however, overcame her pardonable weakness in a "plucky" manner which won the admiration of everybody. Finally Miss Ashworth moved a vote of thanks to Miss Bury and Master Macalpine, which Master Hunt seconded. The total proceeds of the bazaar amounted to £2,540 19s. A very creditable result.

* * *

Politics, generally speaking, find no place in this column. Nor is it on political grounds that I am about to refer to the lady candidates for whom the electors will be asked to vote next Monday. Rather do the poor and needy women and children up at Pike Law prompt me on this subject. There are many people quite ready to argue that there is no need for women on Boards of Guardians. Among sensible people this theory was exploded long ago, but there remain still a few of the Rip Van Winkle type, who, in the face of all the good work done by women in the past, insist on maintaining this old- fashioned view. Home is certainly a woman's sphere, but there is no reason why that sphere of usefulness should not be extended. And, after all, the workhouse is the only home some people can lay claim to. Why should the inmates, especially the women and children, be denied the brightness and sympathy of women guardians?

* * *

There is a portion of Poor-Law work which seems to me to be the special province of woman. Think of the poor old women needing relief in their last days. With all due respect to the gentlemen, however kind-hearted they may be, they cannot supply the consolation and sympathy needed to bring a ray of sunshine into these lives. Then, too, there are the ill-treated and deserted women who have been betrayed, and as a last resource have taken refuge in the only home open to them. Is it likely that these stricken ones would confide their troubles to any but a woman? How much the influence of a good and sympathetic woman must mean in such cases as these, cannot be overestimated. To the sick women in the infirmary, women as ministering angels are essential; and last, but by no means least in their manifold needs come the children. Those poor little boys and girls deprived at the outset of life of a mother's love and care—how necessary it is for them that women should have a hand in their upbringing. What can a man know or understand of the motherly instincts, common to every woman worthy the name, which enable her to guard and guide the little ones aright? It is not sufficient for the children or the women that they are comfortably housed and do not want bread; it is a woman's counsel, intuition, care, attention, and loving sympathy that they need most.

* * *

That Miss Higham in her capacity as lady Guardian has supplied some of these mental as well as bodily needs, is well known. One has only to note the moistened eye, quivering lip, and voice softened with emotion of many an aged dame up at Pike Law, when the qualities of Miss Higham form the topic of conversation to realise how invaluable her help has been to them. Nor is Miss Higham's good work confined to the workhouse alone. In Accrington many poor homes where aged, sick and helpless invalids exist have been made happier by the timely assistance and wise counsel of Miss Higham. For many years she was one of the staunchest supporters and worker's of the Accrington District Nursing Association, and even now finds time to assist in the good work done in connection with the Victoria Hospital. Not many weeks ago her enthusiastic aid helped to make the Flower Exhibition in the Town Hall for the benefit of the poor crippled girls a great success. For twelve years she has cheerfully worked for the good of the men, women and children of Pike Law with most happy results. Need I say more? A record of twelve years' invaluable help speaks for itself, and I hope every member of my sex—or of the opposite sex for that matter—who can influence a vote in South Ward on Monday, will exercise that influence to ensure Miss Higham's return to Pike Law, where she has proved her great usefulness by fruitful labours these many years.

March 30th

The death of the Rev. Charles Williams comes as a great shock. Had it occurred a week or two ago, his passing away would not have been so much of a surprise, but latterly, since his removal to a Manchester Nursing Home, where an operation was successfully performed, better hopes were entertained of his recovery, and he himself declared that he hoped to pull through all right. Now he is dead, the nation has lost a noble and hard-working man—strenuous in all good work. The Baptist denomination is deprived of one of its foremost advocates; from Accrington has been taken one of the most influential public men of the district, and his son and daughters mourn a beloved father. Early next month the wedding of one of his grand-daughters was arranged to take place, so that the death of the "Grand old man" of local Nonconformity just now is doubly sad, casting as it will a gloom over the nuptials. The family have my deepest sympathy in their grief and sorrow.

April 6th

Another handsome donation of £250, from Sir George Bullough, has been added to the extension fund of the Victoria Hospital. With the £500 each contributed by Mr. James Cunliffe and Mr. G. W. Macalpine, the subscriptions now in hand make an imposing total. Three examples of generosity such as these are worthy of emulation, and it is to be hoped many more contributions will follow, as there is still a large sum of money required to defray the cost of the extension.

* * *

An old lady assured me the other day that not for seventy years has there been such a gloriously fine Easter as this one. Easter, 1907, will certainly be long remembered as a record holiday-time of unbroken fine weather. Cloudless skies and prolonged dazzling sunshine have seemed almost uncanny with many of the trees still looking so wintrily black. But there is no doubt the atmosphere borrowed from a sunny June has worked wonders with all vegetation. The hedgerows are putting forward shoots of green now, and the buds are beginning to swell on many trees. Lambs gambol across the fields in playful fashion, and the songs of the birds are gaining in crescendo every day.

* * *

Impressive indeed was the funeral service last Saturday. Cannon-street Church was filled with mourners, who listened with many outward tokens of grief to the brief and pathetic address delivered by Dr. McLaren. A still larger crowd assembled to escort the remains of the Rev. Charles Williams to the Cemetery. It was said that when the hearse containing the coffin, with its three wreaths significant of the simplicity which distinguished the "Grand Old Man" in life, reached the Cemetery gates, the tail end of the procession was just passing the Town Hall. Many an eye was wet with tears, and it must have been some comfort to the bereaved family to know that their departed relative was held so high in public estimation.

April 13th

Owing to the recent death of the Rev. Charles Williams, the wedding on Thursday between his grand-daughter, Miss Alice May Entwisle, and Mr. John Threlfall Kenyon, son of Mr. J. T. Kenyon, of "The Mount," was a very quiet affair. Big preparations were being made, including a reception and dance, in which a large number of people were to be the happy participators, until the fatal accident happened to the Rev. Charles Williams. It was only natural that thoughts of the great man's funeral should obtrude themselves upon the minds of his nearest and dearest during the wedding ceremony, occurring as it did so recently. Had death not intervened to upset all previous arrangements, this wedding would have been an exceptionally pretty one.

After the wedding reception at "Lynwood House," the happy pair departed for London, en route to Bournemouth, where the honeymoon is being spent. On Tuesday the workpeople at Oak Vale Mill presented their employer's daughter (the bride) with a pair of handsome bronzes.

April 20th

Although Mr. William Haworth's donation of £1,000 to the extension fund of the Victoria Hospital is such a generous one, it has surprised very few people. Mr. Haworth is a generous giver to any and every object which commands his sympathy or arouses his interest. Would we had more of his type in our midst. Some people, no doubt, find such magnificent examples difficult to imitate, but they should remember that small sums from smaller sources are just as acceptable.

* * *

The top-spinning season has already begun. Usually the children do not buy their whips and tops till May, but the exceptionally fine weather this year enabled them to antedate their pleasures by several weeks. Of all games tops are perhaps the safest to be indulged in nowadays, for street dangers are so numerous with so many motors about, that a game which keeps children to the pavement is to be commended. Only the rare ill-humour of passers-by is to be feared with a top.

May 4th

Magnificent! Although the appeal for funds for the extension and endowment of the Victoria Hospital—an admirable institution which serves Accrington and the towns around—has not been issued—promises already made known amount to £12,000. This, of course, includes the £6,000 voted by the Bradley trustees—£4,000 for endowment, and £2,000 for the Bradley ward. Since I referred to the needs of the Hospital a fortnight ago munificent donations have been announced. Messrs. Howard and Bullough, Ltd. (including the individual gifts of the directors and Sir George Bullough, the head of the firm) are contributing £2,000; and this week comes the gratifying intelligence that Messrs. S. and J. Briggs-Bury, members of a well-known Accrington family, are sending £2,000 to the endowment fund. The gift of Messrs. Briggs-Bury, in memory of their parents, will be especially acceptable, because it is to a fund not so readily appreciated by the general public as a building fund. People give to buildings and extensions who do not realise the great value of endowments. If an endowment fund of say £20,000 could be raised, it would relieve the Board of Management of our Hospital of considerable anxiety, as the revenue would be forthcoming even in times of local or commercial adversity.

In another part of, today's paper the Editor asks for subscriptions for a Children's Cot at the Hospital. The suggestion is a good one and will, I am sure, commend itself to readers of this column.

* * *

Much to the disgust of opera lovers, and amateur societies the country over, the brightest and most popular of Gilbert and Sullivan operas has been banned. The reason for the prohibition was the "buffoonery" of certain parts in the "Mikado." The Lord Chamberlain also pointed out to the secretary of the Middlesbrough Amateur Operatic Society, who appealed against the mandate, on account of their forthcoming production, for which all arrangements had been made, that Middlesbrough Amateurs were wanting to play "The Mikado" on the very day that Prince Fushimi arrives in England. The Lord Chamberlain's decision, of course, upsets all the arrangements of the Accrington Operatic Society, who had chosen the "Mikado" for their next production.

* * *

Miss Mary Ramsbottom, daughter of Mr. Hannibal Ramsbottom, on Tuesday left Accrington for America, where she is shortly to be married, I understand, to Mr. Harry Chapman, son of the late Mr. Chapman, of Broad Oak Works, Accrington. Bon voyage, and a happy life in the States.

May 18th

A week's holiday! Is it a good or a bad augury? Depends entirely on circumstances, I suppose. A week's stoppage of the greater part of the looms in the district will help to even matters as between spinners and manufacturers. But what of the workpeople? They are scarcely prepared for a week's holiday. For the August holiday they are getting ready weeks and weeks ahead, putting money into holiday clubs and saving in other ways. It is a little unfortunate the decision to close the factories has been arrived at so near the holiday. To the railway people the closing of the mills will mean much—a big increase in holiday and a considerable diminution of goods traffic. Blackpool will reap the benefit , because people are not prepared for longer distances.

May 25th

A large number of interested spectators assembled in Cannon-street Chapel on Wednesday to witness the nuptials of Miss Jane Annie Maud (Daisy) Oldham and Mr. Bridge Baron Peters. Members of the church choir, and favourites with the congregation, the interest evoked was not surprising. The bride looked exceedingly pretty in a gown of ivory silk voile, mounted on silk moirette foundation; the swathed corsage had a yoke of embroidered chiffon, while the sleeves of voile had deep epaulettes mounted with ribbons, and studded with pearls; festoons of the voile finished with ribbon adorned the skirt, which had a panel of embroidered chiffon to match the yoke, outlined with pearl embroidery. She wore a pretty hemstitched net veil, embroidered at the corners in white silk, through which her black hair, simply arranged in coils at the nape of the neck, gleamed with pretty effect. The bridal bouquet was composed of white flowers, and the bride wore a handsome gold chain bracelet, the bridegroom's gift.
After the ceremony the happy pair left for London, en route to Ventnor in the Isle of Wight, where the honeymoon is being spent. The bride's travelling costume was of brown faced cloth, relieved with white trimmings, and hat to match.

June 8th

Everybody has been grumbling more or less about the wretched weather we have endured this last six weeks. High hopes were entertained of the sunny disposition of June, but alas! our hopes have been completely "washed" away during the first week, by the almost incessant downpour. Personally, I have no adjectives left with which to voice my disappointment— there has been such a run on my store of uncomplimentary epithets lately.

* * *

A good deal of interest was manifested in the wedding of Miss Hilda Logan, daughter of the Rev. Moffat Logan, of Canon-street Church, to Mr. Charles Johnson, on Wednesday. Since her arrival in Accrington a few years ago, Miss Logan in her own sweet way has done much to endear herself to the hearts of members of her father's congregation. Last week the girls in her Sunday school class presented her with a handsome framed photograph of themselves —a token of their love and esteem—and a Bible was the offering of members and friends of the Sunday School. Although the guests at the wedding were confined to relations, and just a few old friends, many people braved the weeping elements to be present in church.

June 15th

Mr. William Entwisle's birthday on Wednesday was celebrated by the customary drive. Sawley was the destination, and about forty members of the family enjoyed the picnic, Mr. Entwisle, looking hale and hearty, despite, his six and eighty winters, was one of the happiest in the crowd.

June 29th

By no means sad were the blind people of Accrington and district who were driven to Chadswell on Wednesday, and entertained by the Mayor and Mayoress of Accrington at their pretty country house. Charmingly situated, the front door of the house commands a fine view of the valley right up to Clitheroe Castle; while to the left lies Hodder with its many beauties; and soaring to the right, Longridge Fells. It was strange at first to hear the exclamations of delight from the lips of the sightless ones as they "saw" the varied beauties of the landscape, and ecstatically drank in the charming surroundings. But this uncanny feeling was soon dispelled when one recalled the fact that at least one blind man present visits the football and cricket fields regularly to "watch" the games. None more interested or enthusiastic than "Tom" while a match is in progress. So keenly excited does he become at times that he has been known to kick the person seated near him on the stand as the player scored the goal. The scores, too, he knows accurately, and discourses fluently on the various phases of the matches he "sees." Old John Ingham amusingly brought the Mayor to task for allowing the standards for the electric tramways to be erected just where blind men least liked blocks on the pavements during his Mayoralty. This was the only complaint he could bring against the Mayor during his term of office. In replying, Mr. Higham expressed regret that the standards were a stumbling-block to the blind, but hoped that to these additional landmarks they would soon become accustomed.   One very touching incident occurred during the proceedings. A surprise had been prepared for the Mayoress by her blind admirers in the shape of a smart basket, the first article made at the new Institute in Avenue Parade, laden with pretty flowers, given, I believe, by Miss Moffitt, of Holly Mount. Roses, geraniums, sweet peas, and various other beautiful flowers graced the basket, which a little blind girl had the honour of presenting. For a few moments the Mayoress was quite overcome by this unlooked-for gift, and was unable to speak. Later she, in a graceful little speech, thanked the donors, and said how pleased she had been to receive their basket of flowers, and to entertain the blind.

Happy, and perhaps a trifle tired, the picnicers boarded the vehicles before dusk fell, unconsciously forming an example of contentment which many of their more fortunate fellow mortals would do well to imitate.

July 6th

Mrs. John Higham's feelings on discovering that her boy had fallen from a railway carriage during a journey from Liverpool to London, must have been harrowing. Newspaper accounts differ considerably as to the facts, but that the boy was standing with his back to the door when it flew open, hurling him to the ground, seems quite clear. At the time of writing he was reported to be progressing as favourably as could be expected, though he must have had a terrible shock, and the injury to his head is said to have been serious. How he escaped death seems almost miraculous. The sympathy of readers of this column, especially that of mothers, will, I am sure, go out to Mr. and Mrs. Higham and all the members of their family.

* * *

Can anyone suggest a word which adequately describes the weather of late? Too dreadful for words, surely. On Thursday, just about three o'clock, when the Mayor and Mayoress were ready to receive their guests in the Town Hall, the rain came down in torrents, accompanied by reverberations of thunder and flashes of lightning. One can scarcely blame people if they refused to brave the elements on such a day. Even a man feels qualms about venturing far afield in such wretched "stuff" while ladies with frocks to navigate are liable to all sorts of mishaps. However, those who had the courage to venture forth—and they were many—were well rewarded on reaching the Town Hall. The carpeted stairs, lined with lovely plants, looked more than nice, and cosy after leaving the grimly wet aspects of things and people out o' doors, while the assembly-room, with its pretty decorations, appealed, irresistibly.

July 13th

Rain has much to answer for this year. It has spoiled many out-door festivities locally and further afield, and on Wednesday it scored another "success" by marring the annual cricket match for the Children's Society. It was a great misfortune. The police had worked very hard, not only in disposing of tickets, but in all the arrangements. It was their wish to make Wednesday's gathering a record, and in all probability would have succeeded had the weather been favourable. But, unluckily, a beautiful morning was succeeded by threatening clouds, and about three o'clock, when the fair sex were wending their way to the Accrington cricket ground, or were about to leave home for the match, a heavy shower fell—one of those persistent, clothes-soaking showers with which May and June made us only too familiar. The result was disastrous. Many who had bought tickets never reached the ground at all, and the receipts at the "gate" did not exceed a sovereign. Thanks to the generosity of Accrington tradesmen, the supply of provisions for the afternoon tea was abundant. Of strawberries there were many, many baskets—but who could enjoy strawberries and sugar in a downpour of rain? The pavilion became so crowded that the ladies in charge of the afternoon tea, and the young maidens who had volunteered to act as waitresses, were unable to proceed with their work. Serving edibles to visitors seated on the stand is child's play to dispensing tea in rooms crowded with people driven indoors by the rain. Everybody felt sorry for the ladies at the tables and for their white-robed attendants. Theirs was a task nobody envied.

Fortunately the sale of tickets in advance had realised about £40, so that the rain interfered with the pleasure of the patrons to a greater degree than with the match receipts. Think of it. Forty pounds in shilling and sixpenny tickets in about ten days! The police did not begin their labours as early as usual because they had just been engaged in collecting for the Fresh Air Fund, having raised about £75. Naturally they wanted to give the townspeople a little breathing space. And this prompts me to ask—is there a town of similar size in all England where so much is done for the helpless as in Accrington? Verily no. The blind, the sick, the poor children and the aged people, the cripples and the "unwanted" children are in turn provided for. I sometimes wonder where all the money comes from and how it is gathered together.

* * *

It is not my province to deal with the cricket match. That is fortunate, for I don't understand cricket. But I was able to pick up a few points by listening to the boys. The Gentlemen batted first, and had scored about 60 when there was only one wicket to fall. Some of the batsmen had fallen easy preys, I gathered. One "medico" from whom great things had been expected was bowled the first ball, and I overheard one "Brook" trying to induce the reporters to print "Fitz's" "duck" in red, or failing that, in caps. Of course the language was without meaning to me. I also heard something about "good old Hab," who, I learned, was captain for the Gentlemen. That, I suppose, is his pet name on the cricket field—I don't know. Well, he and his son Richard were the last men in, and the score stood at 69. "Declared," I heard somebody say, and on inquiry I gathered that the captain for the Gents had called his men off, leaving the Police to get an equal number in something under 60 minutes. "A 'cute bit of business," I heard someone say, and another whispered, later on, "Captain Harwood—(umpire, I think they called him)—wanted him to play another over, but he said, "Nay, I might be "out","." From which I gathered—well, I give it up as I am not versed in cricket phraseology.

* * *

After a brief interval players seemed enthusiastic about resuming the game, although to me it appeared foolhardy, as the ground had become "soaked," and rain was still falling heavily. "Give 'em a chance," I heard one of the Gents say. And they— the Police, I suppose—had their chance. And didn't the lads on the pavilion shout. "Ducks"—not ducks swimming on the cricket ground, but cricket "ducks"—were plentiful, I gathered. First one and then another went to the crease, only to retire almost immediately. A great cheer announced the advent of P.C. Baron, an old hand at the cricket matches, as well as a splendid salesman—of tickets. (You see, I am picking up the threads). Well, I saw the man with the ball throw down his cap, take a long run behind the wickets, deliver his ball, and then—the stumps at the other end were dislodged, and Baron—the hope of his side—came back to the pavilion, just as "Fitz" had done. Thus the man most, feared on either side had shared the same fate. What a happy ending. Something was said about "six for five"—a bit paradoxical, I thought. Soon after, the gentlemen with the great white coats—umpires, I understand (two genial fellows in the persons of Captain Harwood and "the Chief")—left the ground, and "once more" there was "a draw." I think if I attend a few more matches I shall be eligible for a post as cricket expert on the "Observer."

* * *

Much excitement was caused in Rishton on Wednesday by the pretty wedding of Miss Amy Clayton, daughter to Mr. Robert Clayton, J.P., and Dr. W. H. Horner. It was quite the biggest affair that has been seen in that neighbourhood for some time. The wedding was in the parish church, where soon after the mid-day meal crowds of gaily dressed women flocked to witness the tying of the nuptials. The bride was gowned in a dress of white muslin de soie, embroidered in a design of wheat ears and lovers' knots, carried out in silver tissue and chiffon, with a wide border of duchesse satin. After the ceremony a reception was held at "The Turrets." On the lawn in front of the house a large marquee was erected where Mr. and Mrs. Clayton received the guests. The honeymoon is being spent at the Ardennes.

July 20th

Who, seeing the happy faces of the poor cripple children on Wednesday, from beginning to end of that glorious ride to St. Annes, could doubt the successful result of the Mayor's happy idea? The motor cars made a fine show as they assembled before the Town Hall, with their excited occupants. One by one the numbered cars started on their journey, with a short interval between each, to avoid too much dust en route. One or two drivers, with more enthusiasm than wisdom, passed the cars in front and caused a little discomfort, but on the whole the wheelmen considered the comfort of their little guests rather than their own desires, thus obviating unpleasantness. Eyes sparkled and cheeks glowed, as the glories of a motor trip unfolded themselves to the delighted "one-day" motorists. What a time they had, to be sure! A halt was called at Leagate, where mine host served refreshments to the children and attendants. Then on again to St. Annes, where the Mayoress received her guests. There followed several hours' enjoyment on the sands, succeeded by tea,

A car prepares to pick up its passengers for the 1907 Children's outing to St Annes

including delicious strawberries and cream, and innumerable sweets, and other dainties. All the arrangements were good, and the Mayoress managed everything splendidly. Sweets galore were given to the children, each car possessing at least one big chocolate box. A supply of chocolates, the gift of Master Gratton Lee, was much appreciated by the youngsters. It is a day that will long be remembered by the little cripples of Accrington, and the cheers of gladness will echo for weeks in the proud little hearts of the Mayor and Mayoress's guests.

August 3rd

Mrs. E. A. Riley (Haslingden) has my hearty congratulations. Not only has she, been awarded a non-stop certificate for the Scottish Motor Trials, but being first in her class has received the gold medal. She drove a 20-horse Belsize, and her points totalled 966.375, the second car being a Coventry Humber (964.2). In the hill climbs Mrs. Riley was an easy first, gaining 99.975 points, the second on the list being credited With 83.2.

* * *

One of the features of local summer holidays for many years has been the large number of weddings. This year there appears to be a falling-off in the interesting unions. It is not that any fewer couples than formerly want to get married. The indications are that a larger number than ever have carried love to the point of readiness to marry, but the obstacle is that houses can't be got wherein to set up housekeeping. The dearth of houses is almost universal over East Lancashire. In

Accrington and the district, Blackburn, Burnley and many other places cottages can't, as the saying is, be got for love or money, and a large proportion of those anxious to enter the wedded state are said to have made up their minds to wait till speculative builders take heart of grace to provide the needful.

It's a thousand pities that entrance upon hymeneal bliss has to be deferred for such a reason Why not marry and go into lodgings for a time? Well, East Lancashire young' couples as a rule don't like the idea of lodgings. For the most part they have saved money, with a view to have households of their own, and can look forward to being in comfortable circumstances. The motion of renting a portion of a house from another is repugnant to them. They naturally want privacy, a hearth and home of their very own. What is the reason builders don't go in for the erection of cottages on a much larger scale, when they would be sure of having them all occupied as soon as ready? Fear of the rates is said to be the greatest stumbling-block, and there is a misgiving that the prosperous times of the last couple of years won't last. If by a stroke of a magic wand hundreds and hundreds of new cottages could be in readiness in places like the Accrington district, Blackburn and Burnley to-morrow morning they would all be snapped up before Saturday night. But would they continue to be tenanted in future years ?

August 10th

The holidays for 1907 are over—for many of us. We cannot say we do not want them again as the Mayor said of the old trams. Holidays are always welcome, and very often they are all too short. There is one great drawback, though, and that is that work now seems a great hardship. Ah, well, we shall soon get in harness again, toiling away and looking forward to the short relaxation Christmastide brings. Christmas! Seems a long way off, doesn't it? And yet there is no holiday between.

* * *

The weather during the holidays has been "mixed," on the whole a little better than the average. We generally associate August Fair with very bad weather. While there have been some heavy showers, there has also been plenty of sunshine, and at the seaside the conditions were distinctly favourable. Blackpool was very busy in the early part of the week, though I don't think so many Accrington folk went to Blackpool as usual. Liverpool, with its fine pageant and the Channel Fleet has attracted an enormous number of visitors. Quite a number of Accrington people went to see the Fleet in the Mersey on Wednesday and Thursday. Taking warning from the experience of those who were "stranded" on one or other of the ironclads for several hours the previous day, they seemed to be content with a view of the exterior of the battleships, either from the landing stage or from one of the steamers sailing round the Fleet. It was a great sight—fourteen battleships in a line three or four miles long, and, by way of contrast, a couple of wooden vessels which at one time did duty for this country in time of war. The war ships are now somewhere near

Blackpool and Fleetwood, and doubtless many folk will endeavour to see them to-day.

* * *

There is a consensus of opinion that the new electric trams are a vast improvement on the old steam-drawn cars. Personally I have not taken my initial ride, but I am told that they run smoothly and are very popular, with Oswaldtwistle folk especially. That is not to be wondered at. From the tram termini at Church, or from Church railway station, up to New-lane, is a long stretch—a most monotonous walk. The new trams will be a great boon to Oswaldtwistle, and the enthusiasm shown on the opening day and since is proof that Oswaldtwistle appreciates Accrington's efforts in this direction. It was a happy idea of somebody's to suggest that the first cars should be driven by ladies. Probably more ladies use the cars than gentlemen, and it was a nice compliment to them to select three of their number to regulate at the wheel on this auspicious occasion.

That they did their work well everyone agreed. The Mayoress, who led the way, is a good "driver"—at any rate the Mayor said so, and he ought to know. Then came Mrs. Rawson, the ex-Mayoress, followed by Mrs. Arthur Bury. Many friends would have been glad to see Mrs. Aitken at the wheel also, but that was impossible.

* * *

The Pot Fair certainly does not grow any less. It is, I think, bigger and more attractive this year than ever. And the crowds that gather round the stalls—bargain-hunting as "Scribbler " would put it—are countless. To walk round the Pot Fair, keeping one's eyes and ears open, is real fun. I get far more enjoyment out of it than I should in a noisy seaside scramble. The little sallies of the salesman, the retort of some "Lancashire witch," the assurances of the seller and the doubtings of the buyer, with the attendant facial expressions, are to me great fun. The Accrington Pot Fair is a place for the study of human nature.

* * *

No fewer than eleven couples were joined in wedlock at Immanuel Church, Oswaldtwistle, on Saturday, and as will be seen from a report in to-day's paper, there was the unusual incident of a double wedding, brother and sister going through the pleasant ordeal. Weddings have been unusually numerous in Accrington district during the past fortnight. Where the couples are going to live I don't know. Houses, I am told, cannot be had for "love or money" unless you are prepared to buy, and newly-married couples are not always in that favoured position. Quite a number of weddings are still "held up," I believe, owing to inability to get houses.

August 24th

It is satisfactory to learn that the traffic on the newly-created electrical system between Accrington and Oswaldtwistle continues highly satisfactory. The receipts, I notice, keep up wonderfully well. That this section of the tramways will pay, and pay

1907 saw the long awaited introduction of electric trams in Accrington

well, there is not a shadow of doubt. But I am not concerned about the financial part of the arrangement.

There are one or two drawbacks in the new single-deck cars, the remedy for which is

Alderman and Mrs Thomas Higham at the controls of Accrington's first electric tram

largely in the hands of the passengers themselves. Each end of the car is supposed to be for smokers, the centre compartment being reserved for non-smokers. Thus a lady entering a car from behind has to pass the smokers—and sometimes spitters—before reaching her seat; on the other hand smokers have to pass the ladies to get to their den in the front part of the car. If smokers would only exercise care there ought to be no occasion to complain, but unfortunately they don't. They smoke and spit, and spit and smoke. It is their privilege to smoke—in the reserved compartments—but they have no right to spit, and I hope the authorities will be very severe with men guilty of this most offensive practice.

Another point. The cars are nice and clean. But it is very difficult to keep them clean. Some mothers are so careless. They let their children stand on the seats, unmindful of the passengers who may follow. Often enough the children are eating cakes or sweets and the seats become very dirty. I appeal then to women in charge of children as well as to smokers. Let us all try to keep the cars clean; let there be no smoking and no filthy language.

* * *

Local theatre-goers have had exceptional fare this week, At the Prince's, Accrington, the boards have been occupied by one of the best Shakespearian companies it has been my privilege to see in Accrington. The week has been a very successful one at Accrington, and will, I hope, encourage the management to bring more high-class companies.

August 31st

"Much happiness" to Dr. and Mrs. James Spence Geddie, whose wedding at Royds-street Baptist Church on Thursday created a good deal of interest. The bride was Miss Isabel Alice Bardsley, eldest daughter of Mr. Joshua Bardsley, of Milnshaw House, Accrington, and very pretty did she look in a dress of white soft satin trimmed with lace. After the honeymoon in Scotland, Lowther Place, Whalley-road, will, be their residence.

* * *

Congratulations to Miss Mary Ashworth, of Accrington, upon her appointment to the position of headmistress of the new Council Infants' School at Epsom. Miss Ashworth's selection is the more noteworthy in that it has been made without even so much as an interview, nor has there been any special influence at work in her behalf. It is entirely because of her educational qualifications and the excellence of her testimonials that the choice has fallen upon her. Like many another successful teacher, Miss Ashworth's school career commenced at Willow-street and afterwards she was trained at Stockwell. From being assistant at Burnley Wood Infants' School Burnley, she was appointed to the head mistress of Habergham, and for the last three years has held a similar position at Coal Clough Council Schools, Burnley.

* * *

I wonder what the women of Oswaldtwistle think about the proposal to buy The Rhyddings and throw the grounds open as a public park? I fancy they will be enthusiastically in favour of such a scheme, whatever the menfolk may say about rates and financial considerations generally. How nice it is to be able to go into a pretty and well-kept park and enjoy an hour's leisure over a book perhaps, or with one's sewing or embroidery. And how much a mother appreciates being able to take her children to such a place and let them romp for an hour or two while she sits by finding pleasure in their gambols and the pleasant surroundings. I hope the ladies of Oswaldtwistle will bring to bear an appreciable amount of "moral suasion" on their husbands and brothers on this question of a park.

* * *

We are getting on. The emancipation of woman—if she needs emancipating—is surely at hand. Are you aware that women are now qualified for election as Mayors? Who will be the first candidate? How would it be on some future occasion to elect Mrs. Higham as Mayor and Mr. Higham as—I was going to say "Mayoress," just by way of turn and turn about? There are ladies, I feel sure, who could not only grace the Mayoral chair, but carry out the duties of the office with tact and ability. I'm afraid, though, it will be a long time before we get a candidate for such an office from among our sex.

September 7th

Of special interest to the very wide circle of friends will be the marriage on Wednesday next at Immanuel Church, Oswaldtwistle, of Miss Frances Mary Townley and Mr. John William Holgate. The bride is the daughter of the late Dr. Townley, of Oswaldtwistle, and sister of the Medical Officer of Health for that township, and the bridegroom is the son of Mr. Stephen Holgate, of Rock Mount, Altham. The wedding, which is fixed for 2 o'clock, will, I hear, be a very pretty one, with a service fully choral, and there will be a large number of guests.

* * *

I am glad to hear that Oswaldtwistle, like most other towns hereabouts, has now got a District Nurse of its own, and it is pleasing, too, to find that Dr. Townley, who undertook the formation of the Nursing

The wedding of Dr. Townley's daughter, Frances Mary, at Oswaldtwistle Immanuel Church

Association, has had no difficulty in enlisting the help of fellow-townspeople so far as financial matters go. Over and over again I have come across cases where the help of District Nurses has come as a boon and a blessing to the sick and the halt, and Oswaldtwistle, I feel sure, will soon appreciate very thoroughly the work of its nursing sister.

* * *

On a very considerable scale are the improvements and re-decorations that are just now being carried out at Cannon-street Baptist Church, Accrington, and I am assured that when the re-opening of the Church takes place a week or two hence members of the congregation will be very agreeably surprised by the transformation that will have been wrought. Not only in the matter of decoration, but of lighting also, there will be a great improvement. Electricity is, of course, being introduced as the illuminant and no pains are being spared to make the lighting thoroughly effective.

* * *

I do hope the two enthusiastic bargain- hunters whom "Scribbler" told about on Tuesday got something really worth the having for their long and wearisome vigil. Imagine standing out in the cold, deserted street from three o'clock in the morning until after eight waiting for a shop to open, so that they might have the first pick of the "great bargain sale!" Not for all the bargains in the world would I turn out at 3 a.m.; to do any such thing needs, I should think, courage and resolution of a higher order than I can claim to possess. But what about the risks of colds and influenza and pneumonia, and goodness only knows what besides? "Bargains" secured in such a way may possibly turn out to be very dear in the end.

September 14th

What a glorious spell of weather we have had this week! In the midst of so much sunshine it is difficult to realise that the time of the sere and yellow leaf is at hand.

* * *

To stand outside a shop in a pouring rain, from before five o'clock in the morning till the doors opened at nine, in order to purchase a costume at a shilling sale is scarcely a commendable feat of endurance, as I pointed out last week. Especially when, as in a recent instance, a more "pushful" if less patient "shopper" secured the coveted prize in the sudden rush when the doors were opened. Could absurdity go further? To stand for hours in the rain risking health, more valuable than a hundred costumes, and then to be baulked of the much-longed-for clothing.

September 21st

My deepest sympathy goes out to the Rev. D. Jerman, pastor of New-lane Baptist Church, Oswaldtwistle, and his wife in the heavy bereavement they have sustained. Death always brings grief in its train, but when as in the present case it cuts off quickly and unexpectedly a charming seven years old daughter, the wound is all the sorer. Mr. Jerman's daughter was stricken down, and on the very same day that the doctor pronounced the illness to be due to diphtheria she succumbed. The distressing event cast quite a gloom over the anniversary services at New-lane Baptist Church, on Sunday, as the little girl was beloved by all.

September 28th

The Children's Cot Fund is slowly but surely mounting up. One-half the sum required to endow a Cot has been subscribed. There are still 5,000 shillings to raise. How has the money to be got together? There are many ways of rendering help. Concerts and entertainments ought to be organised during the winter months, and little sales of work promoted by the children would bring in substantial sums. One or two such sales, I hear, are in hand. I wish them every success. So far, the schools in the district have done very little. I commend the scheme to the teachers of the district. Collections at Sunday Schools, and at day schools too, would be excellent. And the operatives might give a helping hand by mill collections.

October 12th

My first duty to-day is to offer congratulations to the young ladies of Whalley-road who took part in a most successful children's bazaar in the grounds of Dyke Nook (Mrs. Jonathan Barnes) on Saturday afternoon. The girls had worked very hard to achieve success, but not one of them ever anticipated realising £20 2s. The girls initiated and carried on the sale unaided by more experienced hands, and when Mrs. James Cunliffe attended for the purpose of formally opening the bazaar she and other ladies who had gathered together were simply astounded at the wonderful collection of articles, many of them made by the children themselves.

The names of the Whalley-road workers sent to me are—Emily Barlow, Gladys Barnes, Alice Broughton, Fanny Broughton, Nellie Calverley, Marjorie Cunliffe,

The young Whalley Road fund raisers

Kathleen Kenyon, Lizzie Bateson, Marjorie Webster, Kathleen Wilson and Lucy Lightfoot. The photographic group will interest not only those who took part in this very successful venture but many others besides.

* * *

Christmas is coming. True it is still more than two months distant, but how rapidly will November and part of December speed if we are but treated to fine weather. Plum pudding season is certainly drawing nigh. Everything will be dearer this winter, and so this delicacy will cost more. The price of flour is up, so are currants and raisins, and spices, and eggs will be dearer too. It behoves the careful housewife to make her puddings in plenty this year, though for who knows, with the prospects of a railway strike, whether there will be a famine in joints and turkeys and geese and all the other Christmas fare. It is just possible, even if one were able to buy food in such a contingency, that there would be no coal available to cook it. Rosy prospect, indeed!

* * *

Miss K. A. Whittaker and Mr. Bridge Peters's concert drew quite a large audience to the Town Hall on Wednesday evening. It was good to see so many well-known Accringtonians occupying the reserved seats. Local talent should not be overlooked, even though the winter ahead of us promises concerts galore. Patrons, too, in the majority, arrived in good time, and so the uncarpeted floor did not become so annoying with the sound of passing feet, as it might otherwise have done. The two local artistes had a cordial reception.

I was pleased to see so many ladies take advantage of the cloak-room facilities to leave their hats below stairs. A small minority only, in the reserved seats, wore hats. This is a step in the right direction, and it is to be hoped the ladies will be so considerate at every concert of this kind during the winter. It is only the fear of appearing conspicuous in many cases that makes the fair sex stick so lovingly to hats at concerts in Accrington. One often hears the remark, "I should like to go without hat to this affair, but if all the other ladies wore hats, how silly I should feel." You wouldn't think many of the Accrington ladies were so afflicted with self-consciousness, but they are—poor dears!

October 19th

Rapid progress has been, and is still being, made with the laying of tram-lines in Accrington. Whalley-road, to the terminus at Clayton-le-Moors, is now in good running order, and the lines in Burnley-road are nearing completion. Soon the cars will be running merrily along there also. By the time that and Manchester-road are finished, there should be quite a number of people in Accrington, apart from workers, able to lay tram-lines. Lively interest has been evinced in the proceedings by the G. P. all along. The welding together of the lines has created more than ordinary interest. It is seldom that the welding takes place without a crowd of spectators closely following the process. And for the uninitiated let me say that the process is well worth watching. Children are delighted when the blue flame leaps up through the covering, and their elders watch the descent of the iron shavings which when burning dislodge the metal disc, and thus proceed to weld the lines beneath. No wonder the welding process is followed with such keen interest.

October 26th

If rehearsals are anything to go by, our Amateurs will make a splendid show in the "Mikado" in December. Principals are getting well into their work, I hear, and the chorus is strong, especially the males. Mr. Weathersby, who coached the "Rose of Persia," is again to take control. In accordance with the resolution of the last annual meeting, patrons of one guinea will be entitled to six tickets instead of four for a sovereign. This, I think, is a step in the right direction. Five shillings per seat was considered very high by some people, and the price is now reduced to 3s. 6d.

* * *

"One of the best ballad concerts we've had in Accrington for years," declared a musical enthusiast, as we descended the Town Hall stairs on Wednesday evening at the close of the "Ada Crossley Concert." To that opinion I cordially subscribe, and, so far as one could judge from the short conversations in the vestibule and in the cloak room, and even outside the hall, it represented the views of a great many others besides. To some it was a disappointment that Mr. Percy Grainger, who has come to the front as a pianist with such remarkable rapidity, could not appear, but his place was filled by an equally brilliant pianist in Herr Benno Schonberger.

"Where's Percy Grainger?" yelled a raucous voice in the middle of the hall when Mr. Hamilton Earle came to the front of the platform to announce a change in the programme. Later on, in answer to the cheering which followed Ada Crossley's double encore, Mr. Earle again appeared and said Madame Crossley desired him to answer the question put by a gentleman in the hall. No one could complain, he said, of the absence of Mr. Percy Grainger when they had as a substitute a pianist of such world-wide repute as Herr Schonberger. (Hear, hear, and applause from all parts of the hall). As might be gleaned from the newspapers, Mr. Grainger had been commanded by the King of Denmark and Queen Alexandra to play at the Greig memorial concert at Copenhagen, and was at that moment on his way from that Capital. If, added Mr. Earle, the gentleman was very anxious to hear Mr. Grainger, he would have the opportunity at Blackburn the evening following. Interruptions are very rare at Accrington concerts, and the snub administered by Mr. Earle was heartily relished. True to promise, Mr. Grainger put in an appearance at Blackburn on Thursday.

November 2nd

The wedding of Mr. Maxwell Kenyon, son of Mr. R. W. Kenyon, to Miss Ruby Rendell, daughter of the Rev. J. R. Rendell, aroused quite a flutter of excitement in feminine Accrington on Tuesday afternoon. The ceremony was performed at the New Church, where for so long the bride's father has been the pastor, and with which the bridegroom's family has been identified for generations back. Apart from the esteem in which her father is held, the bride has done much good work in connection with the New Church, and won the affection of its members.

November 9th

The playing of the band was proclaimed the best feature of Wednesday's Cunliffe concert. When one considers the indifferent achievements of the principal artistes on that particular night, this is not such a eulogistic statement as at first glance appears. The orchestra did nothing worthy of note during the first two selections. Improvement came with "Three Bavarian Dances" by Elgar. That instrumentalists should have different opinions about how music should be played cannot be avoided. But different ideas about the method and exact moment of attack are deplorable, especially if too rigid time is maintained by all parties afterwards. The one-mindedness—if I may coin a phrase—of the violinists in Halle's band is their greatest charm. It would pay Cunliffe's men to visit these concerts in Manchester occasionally. The overture to "Hunyady Laszlo" (Erkel) was one of the best contributions of the band. Barring the faultiness of one or two wood-wind instruments at critical moments, and the uneasy start of the cornet in the opening theme it was remarkably well done. The flute variation in the second melody was tastefully and painstakingly played by Mr. Darbyshire. The Barcarolle "Les Contes d'Hoffmann" (Offenbach) was a dainty composition, prettily played. "Faust" was faulty in parts, but the finale lacked nothing in brilliance.

November 16th

Sunday was a lovely day for a Mayoral procession to church. Old King Sol favoured the Mayoral parade by shedding lustre on the glittering impedimenta of office, from his regal throne, and the Honourable Jack Frost honoured the parade also. Between these two worthy gentlemen there was evidently agreement as to the worth of our Mayor. Without them the parade would not have been nearly so picturesque. The Mayor's chain and robes never look so well as when King Sol chooses; the polish on the mace, carried by the spick and span mace- bearer, shines with added brilliance, and the Town Clerk looks happier in his wig and gown on a fine day. Tall hats of councillors, magistrates, and other prominent townsmen retain their shiny aspect by virtue of the sun's good offices, and the Artillery and Rifle Volunteers, Ambulance Corps and police are smarter also, to say nothing of the Fire Brigade, whose helmets on such days remind one of an advertisement for somebody's polish. Even the pipers look warmer in their kilts, and the spectators in their serried ranks are infinitely nicer minus dripping umbrellas.

As a lady, I cannot help thinking that if one of my own sex were "mayor," the procession to church would gain in picturesqueness—and dimensions. I don't see why, now that ladies are eligible for the Council, our present Mayoress should not be "mayor" when Alderman Higham is tired of his office. With her husband as aide de camp, I'm sure Mrs. T. E. Higham would make an excellent lady "mayor." And wouldn't she have a picturesque following on Mayors' Sunday? Silks, satins, laces, picture hats and frills and furbelows would appear in their thousands, for if Alderman

Alderman Higham delivers his speech on Mayor's Sunday, 1907

Higham is a favourite amongst the men of Accrington, his lady is equally popular with the ladies
Even now I don't see why ladies do not join in the parade. Why shouldn't the Mayor in the first place walk by the side of his Mayoress, and the Town Clerk bring his wife?

* * *

The handsome new Public Library in St. James-street is nearly completed, and will soon be ready for use. Wasn't some sort of provision for the ladies promised in the "Mechanics" when this library was opened? True, as a director points out, there are very few lady members left now—the taking away of their room decreased the ladies' membership. It wouldn't be a bad plan to invite several suffragettes to Accrington, and put them on the track of the directors. Persistence is their strong point, and persistence and continual jogging of memories seem necessary when only men are on the directorate.

November 23rd

The report of another little effort for the Children's Cot Fund comes to hand. Five little ones in the neighbourhood of Clement-street got together quite a nice collection of useful articles as well as a few dolls, dolls' clothing, and playthings, and these were offered for sale at a miniature bazaar in the yard of 8, Clement-street, on Saturday, the sale being formally opened by Nurse Stevenson, who expressed the wish that the bazaar, held for such a worthy object, would be attended with success. The sale realised 43 shillings, and this has been added to the Cot Fund. The names of the promoters are Rose, Violet, Servetus and Fuchsia Leaver, and Alice Ann Nuttall. Miss Stevenson was presented with a bouquet.

November 30th

Even allowing for the unfortunate time chosen for the second visit of Backhaus, the great pianist, to the Accrington Town Hall, it was most disappointing to see so thin an audience as that which little more than quarter filled the assembly-room on Wednesday evening.

Five minutes before Wednesday's concert commenced everything about the Town Hall seemed absolutely cold and frigid. It was quite depressing to survey the rows of empty chairs and forms, and to reflect that it was for this one of the musical geniuses of the day had come to Accrington. But once the concert had commenced all these things were forgotten in the whole-hearted enjoyment of a generous banquet of delightful melody.

December 7th

In the words of Barnum, "The Mikado" is the "biggest and best show" the Accrington Amateurs have given. Need anything more be said? Well, yes, perhaps a few sentences will be expected. The Mayor, who saw the show on Wednesday, declared that he had never seen, and did not hope to see, a better performance of "The Mikado." I entirely agree. Certainly such all-round excellence has never been seen in this district before.

Thursday night was a record. Fourteen hundred people passed the doors, and money was again refused. Again the pity of it. I believe that more than 1,400 have been crowded into the Theatre before, but never at an opera. It is splendid—would have been better had the Theatre been larger. My compliments to Coach Weathersby, Conductor Hanson, Chairman Bury, and all the rest. How sorry they will be when the curtain falls to-night and all is over.

December 14th

Lady Bullough has sent 100 shillings for the Children's Cot Fund in the name of her baby, Hermione Bullough.

December 21st

Mr. Walker, the conductor, in particular, and Accrington Choralites in general, may congratulate themselves once again, for Wednesday's concert was a marked success. There is always a stronger choir for "The Messiah" than on any other occasion, and

This group benefitted from Lady Bullough's generosity when 600 children enjoyed a Christmas party in the Ambulance Drill hall in 1907

from beginning to end the chorus singing was infinitely superior to many previous efforts. The opening chorus, strange to say, was the least effective of the evening. It was a pity the attack was not better; it was in striking contrast to "For unto us a child is born" and "Lift up your heads," which were the best of the choruses.

* * *

One bachelor fewer. I am glad. There are too many bachelors in Accrington, and some of them very eligible men, too. Mr. W. J. Newton, our Borough Engineer, is no longer among them. Some of us had "given him up," as the saying goes, but we were wrong. It gives us hope for other prominent townsmen. I heartily congratulate the bride (Miss Edith Randall) and bridegroom, though why they should run off to Leeds, keeping the wedding a profound secret, I don't exactly know. Mr. Newton was at the Choral concert on Wednesday evening, so that he must have been pretty early astir on Thursday morning. The news of the wedding came as a great surprise at the Town Hall. Only one official had been informed of the coming event, and he was told the night before, in order that Mr. Newton's absence might be explained. The Surveyor has been so busy with the construction of the tramways that I don't know how he found time to think of getting married. I don't suppose the honeymoon will be long, but I hope it will be a happy one.

1908

January 4th

Ladies may be pardoned if they did not conform to the wishes of the committee and remove their hats while watching the progress of the play by the Accrington Amateurs on New Year's Day. On Wednesday it was bitterly cold. Out of doors the cold blast blew, and whenever a door was opened the cold air was wafted in on the poor victims huddled together inside. Visions of Christmas log fires floated through my mind all afternoon, and I longed for a blanket or a foot warmer, or at least a cup of hot tea.

January 18th

The Old Folks' Treat, so generously provided by the moneyed classes of our town on Saturday, was a very enjoyable affair. The Mayor and Mayoress seemed to be supremely happy in the entertaining part, as did the elder Mrs. Higham, whose smiling face the old folk were glad to see. Like many of us, she has a long time yet to live before attaining the age of the oldest quartet in the room, and I hope she may live to be present at many similar gatherings. The Fund for the Aged is not confined to a treat once a year. It is used for sending old people to convalescent homes and to other places where health may be improved and enjoyment may be enhanced.

January 25th

The Council Chamber was the scene of jest and merriment on Saturday afternoon. The presentation of wedding gifts to the Borough Engineer and Mrs. Newton, from the Town Council and the Corporation officials, was most happily planned to precede the opening of the Carnegie Library. A graceful speech delivered by the Mayor accompanied the gift from members of the Town Council. The handsome, fruit and flower stand left nothing to be desired in the way of beauty. Of most exquisite workmanship, the centre flower vase, with its beautiful fretwork design, rests on an ebony stand; around this three smaller vases are placed, and between each of these on a scroll of silver depends the daintiest of little round bon-bon dishes with fretwork edges. A most lovely gift!

To Mr. Aitken, the Town Clerk, was entrusted the presentation of the officials' gifts—a beautiful silver candelabra and candlesticks bearing monogram and suitable inscription. After the remark that it was rather a nervous undertaking for himself to take up, as, having been so long married he had lost touch with all those niceties of expression that were associated with such happy occasions, the Town Clerk fairly let himself go. I had no idea our worthy Town Clerk had such a fund of fatherly advice to bestow in the cause of matrimony. Many of our young ladies, I am given to understand, have, since hearing of these words of wisdom (pity they could not hear them firsthand), forsworn golf and laid their hockey sticks aside, and have decided not to dance over-much this season. Instead, they have turned their attention to the making of pies, and are learning to cook, and to sew and knit, so that some bachelor may regard them as pearls of domesticity. To qualify as excellent cooks and housekeepers is now the aim of every maid in Accrington.

With the remarks of the Borough Engineer about "the cold and icy region of bachelorhood" ringing in their ears, Accrington bachelors must surely sigh for the "genial summer of woman's influence." "Take up your cross and leave the arctic regions of masculine aloofness and gladden by your protection and sympathy some fair creature of the gentler sex," is the advice of Mr. Newton. "Go to her home and first sample your beloved's cooking before making up your mind," says our Town Clerk

* * *

An epoch-making occasion in very truth was the opening of the Carnegie Public Library. Quite apart from the grandeur of the building, which gave so much pleasure in its fresh and utilitarian beauty, the afternoon had many interests. It is only on days of such import that so many representative townsmen are heard expounding their views from one platform. Each speaker in his own way had something of interest to talk about. On one subject they were all agreed—that the mental uplifting of the people and public libraries are synonymous. "Public libraries are the poor man's university," one speaker quoted from Carlyle. I sincerely hope there will be many graduates in our new school of knowledge. Surely public talent for reading had never fairer setting for its development than this new library provides.

Afternoon tea in Willow-street School proved an enjoyable finale to the proceedings. Here the ladies, led by the Mayoress, earned their quota of praise. The small tables in both rooms were charmingly adorned with flowers and trails of smilax, and soon the thirsty speakers and their attendant listeners were regaled with dainty fare. Tongues that had been silent throughout the speeches in the lecture-hall were loosened, and folks chattered and laughed and thoroughly enjoyed the social intercourse thus afforded.

February 15th

The Mayor looked supremely happy on Monday, when from the little platform erected at one end of the Lecture Hall of our Public Library he thanked the gentlemen of the county who have been generous enough to lend beautiful pictures in order that we in Accrington may, for a short time, have the chance of gazing upon some of the best works English artists have produced this last century. It is not a big exhibition, but it is a good one. And the collection would have been much larger had there been room to show the pictures. Many paintings had to be regretfully refused because there was not room to display them. The more the pity. It is not only a very excellent collection, but a representative one also—descriptive of the growth of water- colour art in this country, and embracing many very fine specimens in oils.

* * *

From the lovely works of art to dirty streets may seem a big drop, and the complaints one hears on every hand must be my excuse. Never have our streets, and especially our main roads, been so dirty as during this winter. The tramway construction may, in part, be urged as an excuse with regard to the main thoroughfares, but the tramways were finished long ago, and still our footpaths have been in a disgraceful condition. I often wonder why the Corporation don't make free use of hose pipes for washing the footpaths. Surely the plea of shortage of water can no longer be set up.

February 29th

On one or two occasions I have not been able to offer unstinted praise when referring to the concerts of the Robert Cunliffe orchestra. I am therefore all the more pleased to be in a position to say that Wednesday's performance was an unqualified success. With the playing of the band I was especially pleased. It was a marked improvement upon the last concert. Congratulations to Conductor Hanson and Leader Gaggs.

March 7th

The performance of the comedy, "One Summer Day," at the New Jerusalem Schools, Accrington, on Wednesday evening by a number of local amateurs was an artistic success.

The comedy provided a pleasant evening's entertainment, and will doubtless run quite as smoothly tonight, when it will be repeated.

March 14th

There is probably no one more popular amongst temperance workers in Accrington than Mrs. Jeannie Walker, of London, and her visit to the town this week, at a time when temperance questions are so much before the public, has proved quite an attraction. Mrs. Walker has addressed three meetings, on Tuesday and Wednesday in the Gospel Temperance Mission Hall, under the auspices of the Accrington branch of the National British Women's Temperance Association.

There was a large assembly in the Hall on Tuesday afternoon, when Mrs. Walker addressed a special meeting for women, her subject being, "Mother and child." Mrs. Dr. Nuttall presided. The lecturer described the physical action of alcohol on the system and how it affected children. She made a lengthy reference to the slums of our towns, and these she attributed to the drink evil.

At the close a vote of thanks was passed to Mrs. Walker and Mrs. Nuttall on the motion of Mrs. Pickard.

March 28th

A "Well-wisher" writes from Lytham that she considers my remarks on the Choral concert too severe. It is passing strange how innocently-penned paragraphs, which strive only to be accurate, arouse unwarranted indignation in some quarters. My dear "Well-wisher," your remarks, which, by the way, are purely declamatory, are not convincing. Beauty, we are told, exists chiefly in the eye of the beholder. With like truth your gauging of my remarks discovered a defect which was non-existent. That sounds rather paradoxical, perhaps? As to the other reference in your note. If you are musical and attended this particular concert, you would have appreciated the beauty of my reticence on that point. However, it is evidently your will to misconstrue my good intentions, and you know the adage—so why waste precious time trying to convince you that your opinion is entirely an erroneous one. In parenthesis permit me to inform you that I have only the good of our Choral Society at heart if I sometimes—very humbly—point out their mistakes.

* * *

Has anything been done in the direction of providing a ladies' room at the Mechanics' Institution? If steps are not taken promptly, I fear there will be another decrease in membership. What becomes of all that talk about the splendid facilities the directors were going to offer to ladies, who were urged to submit to temporary inconvenience? And now, one hears, the room so grandiloquently described as the future ladies' room has been let to the town as a school attendance office! Revenue, revenue, revenue!

April 4th

Regret will be felt that Mr. James Kenyon has decided to resign, at the close of the present season, the post of secretary of the Kentucky Minstrels, which he has held for three years since the formation of the troupe of entertainers, who whilst amusing the public have done so much for local charities. Mr. Kenyon has had a full share in the no easy task of organising the minstrels and the success of their performance is an indication of the amount of hard and judicious work he has put into the affair. Although pressure of duties in other directions constrains him to resign the post, which he has filled with great satisfaction to all concerned, I hope that an effort will be made to induce him to reconsider his decision. I understand that local charities will benefit this season to a larger extent even than last through the efforts of the Kentucky Minstrels, who gave an entertainment at Haslingden on Saturday to a crowded house in aid of the Ambulance Association of that town.

April 11th

I am beginning to think ours is a model little town in one way. An appeal to the charitable impulses of its people never miscarries. There are now nine pictures presented to the new Art Gallery by the residents of Accrington; pictures that would do credit to any town. When Mr. Will. Haworth spoke so enthusiastically at the opening of the Carnegie Library, of the picture gallery and the organ which might some day grace the Town Hall, one regarded these idealistic flights into the future as beautiful, but not possible of realisation for years and years to come. Now, within a month of the closing of the exhibition, there are nearly a dozen pictures in hand. The Mayor is to be complimented on having so successfully launched the scheme in Accrington.

* * *

It is quite possible that the tradesmen of Haslingden will one day spend their Whit Friday holiday in New York or Boston, returning by the midnight flying machine; only they'd require more than eleven and a half hours for "doing" the stores across the Atlantic. On the whole, the present arrangement seems more comfortable. It is only by force of contrast one realises comfort. Ryde, in the Isle of Wight, is the tradesmen's destination this time. The double journey will be 680 miles at a fare of 13s. Only sixteen hours will be spent in travelling. The demand for tickets for this "outing" proves beyond a doubt that many men enjoy this way of holiday-making. So much energy condensed into a day of twenty-seven hours makes one feel old. Everyone to his taste, say I.

May 9th

It ought to come as a warning to parents with young children that during the month of April there were in Accrington seven deaths from whooping cough, all in children under the age of two years. Not only is the illness distressing, but, in young children, very, dangerous, and it is almost unthinkable—and yet such is too often the case—that there are parents who will wilfully and knowingly expose their little ones to the danger of the infection, either through sheer carelessness or the desire to "get it over," seeing that in the view of some woefully ignorant mothers their children are bound sooner or later to have every illness to which the infantile flesh is heir. No wonder we hear more and more of the duty that lies with educational authorities to teach girls in school something of the duties and responsibilities that will rest with them in later life.

May 16th

Very successful was the juvenile fancy dress ball held in the Conservative Club, Accrington, on Wednesday night and organised by the Misses Hindley, of Blackburn, for the benefit of the younger pupils at their Accrington and Blackburn dancing classes. About eighty children, in addition to the Accrington Provident Co-op. Morris Dancers, took part in the affair, and there was also a large attendance of spectators. Many of the costumes—especially those worn by the young ladies taking part—were extremely pretty, while the boys seemed to go in more for the humorous or picturesque. It is impossible to mention in detail all the many curious, striking and pretty costumes worn, but one character must at least be referred to, and that is "Britannia," represented by little Phyllis Hartley, who is but two years old.

With regard to the dancing itself, the children and the Misses Hindley are certainly to be complimented upon the number and variety of the dances learnt by the former—the Cecilian, the Harrovian, the Motor Polka, and so on. How many grownup folk could dance them?

May 23rd

There was not a very large attendance at the local branch of the N.S.P.C.C. on Monday. Probably, as the Mayor suggested, the people of Accrington consider the society well and firmly established, and are fully satisfied with the way the work is done. According to the balance sheet there was a deficit of something under £2, but as the treasurer has received subscriptions of about £50 since the close of the financial year, the adverse balance is only on paper. A very satisfactory state of things indeed. The ladies in this, as in other organisations, are prominent helpers. The Mayor acknowledged the estimable help they were to the Society, and hoped that they would continue in their good offices. It is to be hoped the treasurer, Mr. J. Beckett, will reconsider his decision to retire. The Society owes much to his good work since its establishment in Accrington, and his withdrawal would mean a great loss to the local branch. He and the secretary (Mr. Crossley) have served the Society for eighteen years. Mr. Crossley intimated that he also was wishful to retire, but the central office would not hear of both officers withdrawing at the same time, and he had agreed to continue for another year in the hope that Mr. Beckett would also yield to the wishes of the central office and the friends of the Society.

June 20th

June, the month of roses, is quickly passing. With one or two deplorable exceptions the weather has been passably fair so far. One night this week the air was deliciously summerlike, and on the horizon a gorgeous sunset spread itself in flaming opulence, while to the nostrils came the refreshing scent of new-mown hay. One or two of the Accrington farmers have begun to cut the meadow grass already, for owing to the heavy rains in May much of the grass is in good condition. Quite the nicest part of the summer is the grass-cutting season, and if only one could blot out the wretchedly wet days which appear at intervals, one might lull oneself into the belief that there is going to be a little bit of real summer this year.

* * *

Oak Hill Park is a stirring place these summery Sundays. Tram-loads of people bound for the park give some indication of the numbers that make their way there, while scores more walk in from all parts of Accrington. The promenading is gay to see, for the summer gowns are out for good now. All kinds of people congregate there. Young folks singly, and young folks sweethearting; here and there an old man and his lady quietly taking the air; groups of young men talking sport; and the mischievous army of little boys who find the three-sided pagoda at the top of the park infinitely more attractive than the band. Then there are the younger people still, whose chief interest seems to be in watching the ducks and swans, and observing that fine peacock spread his magnificent tail. It is impossible to be dull in the parks on Sundays, for when the people have tripped home to tea, and the walks are almost empty for a brief space of time, the rooks make a noisy concert overhead, and the smaller birds chirp and twitter and warble their evensong.

* * *

"A glorious fire!" was the verdict of the assembled crowd on the Tenement on Friday night. We have had many a blaze in Accrington, but none to equal this in point of brilliance. The most impressive moment was when the roof fell in. An awed silence followed the collapse, and there was a lull in the flames also for a few seconds, then the tongues of flame leapt up brighter, greedier, than before. It was a rare treat for the children who managed to escape the vigilance of the paternal eye for the nonce. Many arrived barefoot as well as hot-foot on the scene. Ladies had in many cases donned wraps and macintoshes above their night apparel. Everyone sympathised with the artistes who lost their properties in the fire, but I am glad to hear that the misfortunes are not so serious as at first reported. With insurances at such cheap rates it seems strange that artistes run such great risks. For an expenditure of a few coppers per week they could insure all their "props" and also, if deemed necessary, cover themselves against loss of engagements by such calamities as that on the Tenement. I hear that a very handsome permanent structure is to be erected on the ashes of the old Hippodrome.

* * *

Summer! Not for a while have we had such a long spell of glorious weather. With a hammock under a bough, a book of verses, and unlimited lemonade, one could be quite happy. It is only when such energetic folks as the Accrington Policemen v. Gentlemen play a match on the cricket field that one becomes uncomfortably conscious of the intense heat. Even the joy of sitting on that newly-painted pavilion and eating luscious strawberries could not quite compensate for the absence of the hammock picture of ease. The cricketers vowed that they hadn't had such a "gruelling" for ages, and there wasn't a spectator who looked deliciously cool. At the commencement the seats were pretty well baked by the sun and felt like hot bricks. Perhaps the hottest people, though, were the waitresses. Spectators never realise what a difficult business the dispensing of teas is at such a function. They invariably clamour wildly for tea, but the sun had been so overpowering on Wednesday that they were more than usually impatient, forgetful of the fact that the cricket pavilion is not the best of places for the preparation of afternoon tea. Many of them entered the pavilion, making confusion worse confounded for the waitresses. If some of those impatient spectators could have a glimpse behind the scenes they'd realise that the neat-handed Phyllises have a good deal to do. The young ladies arrive in fresh-looking muslin gowns, white for the most part, and with dainty little cloths on trays ready for tea and cakes. If the freshness of the frocks and tray-cloths endure one hour the young ladies are lucky. Some clumsy person is sure to upset his tea close enough to splash the dresses, and another kindly-disposed creature gives an unconscious jerk at the elbow just at the critical moment. But this is not all. Cups and saucers usually run out, and those spruce maids join in the "washing-up" to hurry things up a bit. The wonder is they manage to be so charming in handing round the tea. But, bless you, they find quite a lot of pleasure in doing the work. They have the satisfaction of knowing that their efforts are being expended in the children's cause. In my admiration of the bevy of fair waitresses I must not forget the older hands who stay indoors arranging the fruit and pouring out tea. Ably led by Mrs. James Carter, they triumphed over heat and confusion nobly.

* * *

The policemen won, as they deserved to.
And they won handsomely. The gents were completely out-played, and the tail-end of the team fell away so quickly that the tenth man was not ready and had to don the flannels in double quick time. It was a proud day for Sergeant Baron and his men. Baron was all smiles. Of course the gentlemen took their defeat with good grace. They confessed that the better team had won. And if you were to ask a policeman, he would tell you that the men who usually wear blue, but who on Wednesday were spick and span in white, would have been victorious on several previous occasions had their opponents "played the game" instead of "playing for a draw." Captain Ramsbottom will have to get together a stronger lot if he means to win, for the Bobbies are a determined crew.

* * *

Including Wednesday's match the police' have raised not far short of £600 for the Children's Society by these annual gatherings. Isn't it splendid? Wet or fine, they always make financial success assured by selling tickets in advance. They are irresistible in regard to the sale of tickets as they are with the ball.
A conversation I overheard on the stand, at the cricket match on Wednesday afternoon prompted me to make inquiries about the entertainment of the teams which follows the match. It is a rather delicate matter, but plain speaking is infinitely better than misconception, especially when such a noble cause is in question. Everybody agrees that the police deserve encouragement, and reasonable people will not grudge them the social to which they were treated, but people seem to be under the impression that the treat comes out of the funds raised for the Children's Society. I am glad to be able to state that the entertainment of the teams is defrayed by the generosity of a number of gentlemen who take a lively interest in the police efforts for suffering children.

July 11th

July is likely to be a favourite month for marriages among members of the scholastic profession in Accrington this year. The Accrington Education Committee's decision to penalise female teachers who marry after August 1st is sure to hurry hesitating parties to seal the marriage contract at once, or not at all. Opinions vary as to the wisdom of this decision. The great point raised by Alderman Cunliffe was that it was impossible for any woman to adequately manage a home, and also attend school in the capacity of teacher. Either one place or the other would be neglected, and as a member of the Education Committee he did not want it to be the education department.

One young lady I have in mind is about to be married. She is mistress of an infant department in our town, and admittedly one of the most up-to-date and efficient teachers in the town. If she does, not marry before August she is practically expelled from school life. Does it sound on the face of it that such plans are good for education? Teachers should be chosen on their merit as teachers, irrespective of their domestic arrangements.

Such prohibition as the Accrington Education Committee have decreed, from a teachers' standpoint, certainly penalises love and wedlock. It will prolong many engagements indefinitely, break some, and to avoid spinsterhood, ladies of the profession will have to betake themselves to other towns where resolutions on the matter are less stringent. I would suggest to some of them that they join the suffragists and have a hand in the making of laws.

July 18th

The Cripple Children's Motor Outing to St. Annes on Wednesday was, unfortunately, marred by a serious accident near Kirkham, by which a Blackburn tradesman and his son were rather badly injured, and the return journey was spoiled by a continuous downpour of rain. The collision was bad enough, but it might have been worse. The front of the tri-car on which young Bradbury was riding, was shattered to match-wood, and the wheels were contorted almost beyond recognition. The riders had a lucky escape, and the members of the Mayor's party rejoiced that things were not worse.

The incident was disconcerting, and in fact cast a gloom over the picnic. Those in the vanguard already at St. Annes wondered why their fellow motorists were so long on the way, and when, one by one, the belated cars arrived, the "latest news" was eagerly sought. The Mayor and Mayoress, who have recently gone through very trying times, were naturally much upset by the reports of the mishap, and were pleased to learn from later arrivals that the results were not so disastrous as at first feared.

The sympathies of the party went out to the Hacking family as well as to the injured men. Only the day before the esteemed owner of the car had been laid to rest in Altham Churchyard. Mr. W. H. Hacking had promised the use of his car, and the family only acted as Mr. Hacking would have wished in sending the motor, along with another car belonging to his nephew, Mr. Burton Hacking. It was particularly unfortunate that the late Mr. Hacking's car should be the one to come to grief. Dr. Hanna happened to be among the later arrivals, and was able to make the best use of the surgical outfit Mr. J. D. Lonsdale has carried in his car for the last two years or more without being required. May a similar, or still larger, period elapse before the outfit is again needed. Other members of the party, able to render assistance, lost no time in getting to work. Though unlucky, Mr. Bradbury and his son may consider themselves fortunate that medical aid was at hand.

Mr. Douglas Hacking, the only member of the family present, took charge of the injured men after Dr. Hanna had dressed their wounds and bandaged their legs, driving them to their home at Blackburn. The complement of cars which had left Accrington a couple of hours earlier was thus reduced by two, but fortunately accommodation could be provided in the cars bringing up the rear. Delay was unavoidable, of course, but the children in the rear cars were eventually carried on to St. Annes and cordially received by the Mayor and Mayoress. Meanwhile those who had arrived in the cars in the vanguard had a right merry time at St. Annes, knowing nothing of the misfortunes of those who came along later.

July 25th

That was a very interesting ceremony in the Hospital grounds on Saturday afternoon. The widow of the late Mr. James Bradley— now Mrs. Westwell— had been asked to lay the corner-stone of the ward which is to perpetuate his memory, and right well she did her work. To the Bradley trustees, of whom Mrs. Westwell is one, the late Mr. Bradley left a large sum of money to be distributed, at their discretion among the poor of the district, and £6,000 was voted for the Bradley ward—£2,000 for its erection and £4,000 for its endowment. The Bradley ward is only a portion of the extension now in progress. It is a big scheme and the enlarged hospital will require a considerable sum every year for its up-keep. Every effort helps and if the Children's Cot, adequately endowed, can be presented to the committee at the opening of the hospital, those associated with it will have cause for congratulation.

August 1st

It was very unfortunate that rain rendered an out-door sale of work impossible on Saturday afternoon. The grounds of The Hollies at Clayton-le-Moors, the residence of Mr. and Mrs. Arthur Wilson, were looking at their best, and they had been elaborately decorated with bunting. It was intended to have the articles arranged on one long stall, provision being made for afternoon tea and games in another part of the garden, but rain upset all plans. Luckily, however, All Saints' School was at the disposal of the little workers, and thither the goods were taken when all hope of "clearing up" had been abandoned. Arranged on the stalls, the useful articles, and the fruit and the sweets and the button-holes and other flowers made a pretty show. There were any number of assistants, and the unfavourable weather did not deter patrons from doing their part in helping the good cause. The sale was attended by probably 300 persons, and notwithstanding the reduced prices of the articles left towards the close of the afternoon the result was most gratifying, £42 being raised— one-half for the League of Pity and the remainder to the Children's Cot at the Hospital. The Rev. F. Lindon Parkyn made an excellent chairman. His opening remarks were very happy and well received. Mrs. Appleby's speech was short but appropriate. She is always ready to help a good cause, especially when the children are concerned. The Rev. J. R. Rendell and Mr. A. E. Britcliffe respectively proposed and seconded a vote of thanks to Mrs. Appleby, and this was passed with acclamation.

August 8th

A pretty and interesting wedding was celebrated at the Whalley Road Congregational Church on Tuesday, when Mr. J. P. Acroyd, B.Sc., science master at the Accrington Technical School and eldest son of Mr. S. Ackroyd, of Darlington, was married to Miss Mabel Bloomer, head mistress at Hyndburn Park Council School, elder daughter of Mr. Robert Bloomer. The officiating minister was the Rev. J. R. Ackroyd, B. D., of Northampton, brother of the bridegroom. Another brother of the bridegroom, the Rev. G. W. Ackroyd was best man. Mr. N. M. Hyde, B.Sc, was groomsman. The bridesmaids were Miss Jennie Bloomer, sister of the bride, and Miss Belsey, cousin of the bride. The bride wore ivory chiffon taffeta with veil and wreath of orange blossom and carried a shower bouquet of white roses and lilies of the valley. A short reception was held after the ceremony at Whalley Road Congregational School, and later the wedding guests had an enjoyable drive to Whitewell. Mr. and Mrs Ackroyd left after the reception for Rievaulx Abbey, Yorkshire, where the honeymoon is being spent.

There were many handsome presents, among them being a pretty brass drawing-room clock, presented by the teachers and children at Hyndburn Park School.

August 15th

Accrington would have been a dull place indeed this holiday time were it not for the fairs, on the Tenement and Market Ground. The latter place afforded amusement in plenty. It has been great fun listening to the flowery eloquence of the vendors who live their lives to the sound of clattering pots and "Going! Going Gone!" They were often amusing, though at times almost vulgar in their endeavour to make a sale. The gullability of the public is in no wise diminished. The number of pots perfect— and otherwise that have passed from the stalls into the expectant hands of the buyers is alarming. I sincerely hope the buyers have not been alarmed when reaching home to find their crockery devoid of the beauty and perfection claimed for it by the vendors. One cannot blame the sellers, for it is their business to persuade people to buy.

Though I certainly think a tax should be imposed on the people who import such a collection of vases and ornaments into Accrington. In a strong gas light, a vendor's eloquence transforms a thing of ugliness into a bargain, and a bargain hath such an attraction to the female eye.

* * *

It is not only the hard-working poorer classes either who so love a bargain. Scarcely a lady in Accrington could resist the joy of "just looking round, you know," during a pot fair. Being of the sex I yielded to temptation and spent an interesting though not intellectual time marvelling at the resource of the vendors, and the avidity with which the bystander swallowed their eloquence. "Dazzle" or something like that, was the appropriate name printed on one stall.

A strident voice attracted attention,:— "Now, ladies, isn't this a lovely jug? Real Royal Devon ware, and no mistake about it. Beauty, that! Just the sort of jug to fetch a penn'orth o' stout in, or (an after-thought this) a drop o' milk. I've eightpence bid. Yer wouldn't let a lovely jug like that go for next to nothing, now, would yer? Did yer say a shilling, ma'am? Shilling! Shilling! Well, I'll keep it myself, and be hanged to yer. Yer can go for your stout in a salmon tin for all I care." This sounded rather a dangerous temper with, so many pots handy, so I drifted away. A woman who would make a suffragette of the noisier type now claimed attention. "What shall I put up next? Here's a cheese dish. It's on the latest improved principle. If you get this dish your cheese won't smell, or go mouldy, or oily, or dry. It's a wonderful cheese dish." It sounded wonderful, too, and I might have capitulated instanter but the pattern on the dish was so "loud" that I doubt whether any self-respecting cheese would have dwelt therein long. I wandered away to the sound of "You've got a bargain, ma'am, and your cheese won't smell—it won't smell at all." A ruddy face appeared above an adjacent stall. "Come here for a bargain, ladies. The best stall on the fair. Now what do you think of that for a mug? Real hand-painted and as light as air. There isn't another like it on any other stall. I've threepence offered. Shall it go at threepence? Going! Going! gone!—I've another here with a grand view painted on. Now who wants this one at threepence? Absolutely the last one! Right you are." And the second artistic achievement vanished into willing hands. At another stall a boy who ought to have been in bed was selling small cups and saucers at the rate of two for a penny, while an older and stouter specimen of the sex backed up the hoarse childish voice with interjections such as "Go it, Percy," "Sell 'em some more," "Real bargains to-night," and so on.

After all, a pot fair has its advantages. I don't know any institution like a pot fair for the study of human nature. You see all types of humanity at a pot fair. I have attended more pot fairs in Accrington than I care to remember, and yet I have learned much this week. For real fun the pleasure fair on Ellison's Tenement is not to be compared with the pot fair on the Market Ground. It is an "education" of a very peculiar sort.

August 22nd

Those of us who took our holidays at the Fair week will have been congratulating ourselves that we fared much better in the matter of weather than those who may happen to have been away from home this week. True, there was not much rain until Thursday and Friday, but all week, save Sunday and Monday, the days have been decidedly cold and sunless and no longer is cool summer attire desirable or safe. The fact is, of course, that autumn is drawing on apace, and almost before we have realised the fact winter will be with us again. Already the daylight hours are becoming fewer, and with the longer nights comes a revival of the desire for such pleasures as music, the drama, and the hundred and one social amenities the circle in which we live affords us.

September 12th

It will interest a host of lady friends to hear that Miss Bessie Newton, daughter of Mr. John Newton, High Mount, Accrington, is to be married to Mr. Reginald Street, son of Mr. Robert Street, of Edenhurst, Timperley, Cheshire. The marriage, I am informed, is to take place on Thursday, Oct. 1, at 2 p.m., at Holy Trinity Church, South Shore, Blackpool.

* * *

The marriage of Miss Cicely de Hoghton, second daughter of Sir James de Hoghton of Hoghton Tower, and Mr. Pearce Cecil le Gendre Starkie, son of the late Colonel Starkie, Huntroyde Hall, near Padiham, has been arranged to take place on September 29th, probably in London.

September 19th

Accrington has been gaining undesirable notoriety this week. The treatment of Mrs. Robinson, a leading member of the Women's Social and Political Union, who tried to express her views on the franchise for women on Ellison's Tenement on Monday night was anything but fair. Every right-thinking Accringtonian will lament the fact that a woman, and a stranger to boot, received such a disgusting reception from the youth of Accrington. And not the youths alone, for many girls added their shrill screams and cat-calls to the noisy cries of the boys.

As Mrs. Robinson remarked, "It is very evident that the young people of Accrington are in urgent need of educating how to treat a woman." One cannot but admire the pluck and determination of a lady who, after having her speech so rudely cut short by lusty voices singing comic songs and shouting, with at intervals loud reports of fireworks adding to the discordance, stated that she was not at all cowed, but intended speaking on some future occasion in Accrington.

Mud throwing, though bad enough, was not the most reprehensible part of the disturbance, for some cowardly hand threw a bottle at Mrs. Robinson as she was going to the station. Fortunately this dangerous missile missed its mark. Had I been Mrs. Robinson, all muddy as she was, and hoarse with her efforts to obtain fair play and a fair hearing, I'm sure that nothing on earth would induce me to face such an ill-mannered mob a third or even a second time. One of "Scribbler's" favourite maxims, "Discretion is the better part of valour!" would soon loom large on my movements in this locality ever after. In fact to withstand the brutal attack of a set of hooligans in an exposed place like the Tenement, where also, owing to the re-building of the Hippodrome, missiles and mud are too plentiful, was rather wonderful—more wonderful than wise. Such courage and determination make of her a keen advocate for the cause.

It is to be hoped, if Mrs. Robinson ventures in our midst to speak again, that her pluck and endurance will meet its reward; for a woman who can smile and remain unafraid in such trying circumstances should have something to say worth listening to. Moreover, "No man (or woman either) should suffer any disability on account of opinion." Certainly no woman should be called upon to suffer mud- throwing and kindred indignities because she has an opinion on the enfranchisement of women.

September 26th

Last Sunday was the wettest day experienced for months. Even rain-seasoned Accrington passed remarks. The thickness in the atmosphere was unpleasant and depressing all day, while the darkness caused by the fog and heavy downpour at midday caused the grids and gutters to choke in such a fashion that one wondered whether returning churchgoers would have to swim or paddle home. Several beautiful flower-bewreathed hats and their tulle and chiffon sisters in the millinery world, went out for the last time on Sunday. Limp and draggled and sticky they emerged, while several ostrich feathers reared themselves on once white head gear in pathetic uncurled attitudes, eloquent of the rough treatment of the elements. A poor white feather in front of me at evening service had been so drenched that it resembled a fringed skipping rope. It was impossible to avoid seeing it all through the sermon, and somehow the harvest decoration, sermon, and text got all mixed up in this picture of abject misery on a lady's hat.

October 3rd

A deputation waited upon Miss Higham this week to invite her to become the Liberal candidate for Higher Antley Ward. If Miss Higham accepts the invitation, she will be the first lady member of the Accrington Town Council. But whether she accepts or not, she must feel highly gratified that the invitation has been extended. She was the first lady Guardian at Higher Pike Law Workhouse, and her zeal and untiring energy at the workhouse are well-known. I have heard it said that Miss Higham is worth any two men in the Boardroom. And there is no doubt of the high esteem with which her fellow Guardians regard her. She is also a great favourite with the inmates.

* * *

Mr. John Rhodes has certainly the courage of his convictions. All who knew him grant so much. Another point in his favour is that, whatever his subject, he never bores his audience. His frank criticisms of sections of the community, at Accrington Discussion Class on Sunday evening, were quite refreshing. His subject was "Some Lancashire failings," and in parts, as one of his audience said, "he fairly laid it on with a trowel." In such a company Mr. Rhodes was bound to be appreciated, and the cries of "Hear, hear" were oft repeated.

One of the first failings Mr. Rhodes referred to was the lack of desire for education evidenced by parents putting their children to work at the earliest opportunity. He argued that the withdrawal of children from education at an early age was not confined to those who put forth the excuse of straitened circumstances. To earn "good money " seemed to be all the ambition most fathers had for their sons

Mr. Rhodes must have been a model youth. Up to being married at thirty, he said, he dare not be out after ten o'clock at night unless his father knew where he was, or for a good reason. What a change among the youth of Accrington. Parents must be more or less to blame for the flooding of our streets close on midnight with young boys and girls, who appear to have nothing whatever to do with their leisure hours. Surely parental control has deteriorated.

* * *

Mr. Rhodes's criticism reminds me of an incident. A few months ago, I saw a small girl and boy, aged about six and four respectively, sitting on a doorstep in one of our main roads. "Topsy," I said to the little maid, who sadly needed a bath, "isn't it time you and your brother were in bed? How is it you are out so late?" "Mother's gone to the 'Hip,' " was the prompt reply. "But where's your father?" "He's gone with mother." And these two little bairns had to wait out of doors until their parents had finished their amusement at the " Hip."

October 10th

Water water in the tap, and not a drop to drink—unpleasant to drink rather. Every morning this week the water in Accrington has been "fishy" both in smell and flavour. Whether the Gas and Water Board people have been dropping copper sulphate in the reservoirs and the fishes have been having their revenge again, or some junior has been mixing up the gas and water taps one cannot say. One heard, not long ago, that Accrington was a capital health resort, but for scented water the authorities have gone one better than some well-known spas this time. On Wednesday, when I drew my morning bath, the aroma, which I could liken only to diseased fish, was horrible. Ugh! My glass of hot water was even worse, for no amount of boiling excluded the horrid smell or dispelled the fishy flavour. I'm expecting a report that the water is quite harmless, but it's decidedly disagreeable, anyhow.

October 17th

An excellent society, the Society for the Prevention of Cruelty to Children, has long advocated the need for legislation with regard to the terrible mortality caused by the overlaying of children. The society has also deplored "the thoughtlessness of parents who left fires unguarded, with the result that children have been burned to death. Harsh censure in the courts of justice has not been sufficient to impress upon mothers the need for simple and precautionary measures for the safety of their infants. Others besides people interested in the N.S.P.C.C. will be glad to see that the Children's Bill, whose provisions cover the two chief causes of fatal mishaps to infants has passed the third reading. A clause adopted by the Commons on Monday will hold a person criminally guilty who whilst drunk overlays an infant. Another clause will make it criminal for parents who neglect to take, proper precautions, against the danger of their children being burnt. Mr H. Samuel said the Government attached the greatest importance to that clause. In England and Wales there were every year 1,400 cases of children burnt to death through unguarded fires, and these represented only a small proportion of the suffering which arose through the same cause. In many other cases the child was permanently injured. These figures are alarming and when one considers that a thoroughly strong fireguard can be bought for a shilling, the omission of the safeguard seems all the more criminal.

October 24th

An interesting programme has been compiled for the first Chamber Concert of the season on October 30th. Several capable artistes have been secured for the evening, but to many local people the inclusion of Mr. Alwyne Brown's name as accompanist is of special interest. Mr. Forbes, who so successfully accompanied the artistes at one or two Chamber Concerts, is a difficult man to follow. However, if Mr. Alwyne Brown has the sympathetic touch which was so charming a feature of his father's (Mr. Thalberg Brown) playing in the days gone by, a good future awaits him. Mr. Alwyne Brown has been a student of the pianoforte for many years, and though still only a youth, I am given to understand that he has travelled far on the road to success as a pianist.

October 31st

Unhappily, for women and children, the uncertain phase of the unemployed question looms blacker, uglier than before. The signs and portents are that the lockout is to proceed, and a statement made by a leading operatives' official indicates an extension of the lockout until at least the end of the year. There are signs of acute distress in many Lancashire towns, and even Accrington will not go unscathed, though Accrington is not likely to feel the pinch so keenly as many other places.

The long line of men out-of-works who stand waiting before the Town Hall each morning, in the hope of having some employment given to them is a sign that the bad trade and stoppage is touching Accrington. The Mayor has this week opened a distress fund, which, it is hoped will alleviate much of the want in a number of families in the town. Alderman Higham has generously started the fund with a contribution of £20. The Mayor referred on Monday, at the Council meeting to a number of old people who will get their pensions in January and are prohibited by the Act from receiving any poor relief without jeopardising their pensions. In the meantime these old folks are in dire need; and these also this fund is intended to benefit.

* * *

Sentence for being guilty of conduct likely to provoke a breach of the peace by inciting the public to "rush" the House of Commons on October 13th was passed on Mrs. Pankhurst, Mrs. Drummond and Miss Christabel Pankhurst at Bow-street, London. They refused to find sureties for their good behaviour for twelve months, choosing to go to prison in order that they may thus, as they think, advance their cause. In default Mrs. Pankhurst and Mrs. Drummond were sentenced to prison for three months, and Miss Pankhurst for ten weeks. Prison is not the cheeriest of places in which, to spend Christmas Day, nor yet to begin a New Year. One cannot but admire the courage of these three ladies whose determination to bring their cause to a successful issue has been, and apparently still is, indomitable. It was not surprising that tears came to the relief of overwrought nerves in court. Each lady made a speech in her own defence, and in the delivery of their speeches Mrs. and Miss Pankhurst completely broke down and sobbed. The prisoners were transferred to Holloway in the "Black Maria," and the van was followed by a number of members of the Women's Social and Political Union.

* * *

With the methods adopted by these extreme Suffragettes we may not all agree, but all must admit the ability displayed by Miss C. Pankhurst in defending herself and her colleagues. The Suffragettes have ever grown bolder since the imprisonment of their leaders. They stormed the House of Commons on Wednesday evening so successfully as to seriously interfere with the business of the senators. Gaining access to the Ladies' gallery, a round dozen of them created a disturbance, shouting "Votes for women," and when the attendants rushed to remove them it was found that two of them had been literally chained to the "grille" behind which women-folk are compelled to stand to view the Commons. They were locked to the "grille" by padlocks, and portions of the partition had to be pulled down before their "release" could be effected. What will be the end of it all? The sooner some settlement is come to the better.

November 7th

The youthful musicians at last week's Chamber Concert were responsible for a most enjoyable and interesting musical evening. Even in musical circles youth may compare favourably with the long practice and experience only possible to age. What these young musicians lacked in experience they undoubtedly compensated for by freshness of style on Friday.

Much interest centred in the playing of the accompaniments by Mr. Alwyne Brown, the young son of the late Mr. Thalberg Brown, whose name during his life in Accrington was always associated with the best in music. To say that Mr. Alwyne appears to have inherited the sympathetic touch and expression that were the chief charm of his father's playing is indeed high praise. He came through the ordeal on Friday with flying colours. A nervousness in his demeanour that would have been quite pardonable on such an occasion was not discernible to the casual observer. All the accompaniments were well and painstakingly played. Early in life Mr. Alwyne Brown offered evidence of musical gifts and now his advanced playing prophesies a rosy future. I wish him every success in the profession he has chosen.

November 14th

Cunliffe concerts seem to be gaining in popularity. A large audience assembled in the Town Hall on Friday week, and the general opinion appeared to be that the concert was remarkably good. If Mr. Hanson and Mr. Gaggs heard one half the remarks uttered in praise of the orchestra they would be proud men that evening. Perfection we do not expect, but the band seem to be approaching nearer the high-water mark each year.

November 21st

The Clerk of the Weather Office apparently looks with favour on Mayoral processions. Sunday was no exception to the succession of fine days for this most interesting event. In point of numbers the procession equalled, if it did not actually surpass previous years. Prominent men of the Liberal party were present in goodly numbers to do honour to the new Conservative Mayor, Mr. John Clegg Lupton. Many Conservatives who are not always in evidence when Liberals are being thus honoured helped to swell the procession. The wholehearted support by Liberals, one hopes, will furnish a precedent for Conservatives on future occasions. Politics, it is said, have no place when civic honours are in question. While admiring the imposing procession led by the police, followed by the mace-bearer, the Mayor in his chain and robes of office, the Town Clerk in wig and gown, and all the lesser lights, one could not help thinking what a different sight Mayoral processions will be in Accrington when a lady honours and is honoured by mayoralty.

The newly elected Mayor addresses the assembled outside the Town Hall in November 1908

Crowds turn out to see Mayoral processions, but if ladies joined the ranks no church in Accrington would be big enough to hold the congregations, and one can imagine the thousands who would, come to view the street display.

November 28th

The report of the Mechanics' Institution was not satisfactory from a financial point of view. The small balance with which they started the year, a little over £7, had been turned into an adverse balance of over £14. The Chairman in his speech made an appeal to the townspeople for help to support the institution, and expressed the hope that in the future, instead of losing members they would increase them. Another forty or fifty honorary members would relieve them from anxiety. It seems a pity that such a noble institution should languish for lack of funds. In recent years the lady membership has declined considerably. The taking away of the ladies' room was the first blow to the lady members' list, but many relying on the intimation that another room would be provided as soon as the Public Library had been established, and other alterations made in the Institution, remained amongst the subscribers. With what result? The room that was to more than atone for the removal of the old ladies' room, viz., the old public library department, has been let as a school attendance office at a rental of £20 a year. The ladies' room has never materialised, and shows no signs of so doing. This is not the only grievance the ladies have against those in authority. With the room vanished several fashion papers in which ladies were interested. In the newsroom, where ladies now look for these books there is an ever dwindling stock. As a lady remarked the other day, "If it wasn't for the past honourable record, I wouldn't remain a member another year." But surely in these days we shouldn't be depending on "past records" to maintain an institution of this kind. Is there not one gentleman on the list of newly-elected and re elected ones who is sufficiently interested in the ladies to help to supply a suitable room and literature for them? If my memory be correct, the wives of some of the directors in the old days worked hard to establish a ladies' room, and thus supplied a long-felt want in the town.

* * *

I am pleased to learn that the Linen League recently formed in connection with, the Accrington Victoria Hospital promises to be a great success. The object of the League, as my readers know, is to ease the burden of administration of our hospital by making itself responsible for the provision of all linen and garments that are required by the patients of the Hospital. The initial scheme is most cunningly contrived with the view to embracing all ranks within its scope. Those possessed of a surplus of this world's goods may do their part by a fairly generous subscription. Others are asked to give a more modest subscription and contribute a garment each year, while others again are asked to give two garments annually. It is provided that the Mayoress of Accrington for the time being shall be president of the League, whilst the first working officials are Miss Riley, Arden Hall, who is the hon. treasurer, and Mrs. Williamson Lee, Norwood, hon. secretary. The League's object is a most noble one, and I have no doubt that the ladies just mentioned will heartily welcome the aid of any of my readers in making the work of the League a triumphant success.

December 12th

Lady Bullough's donation to the Mayor's Distress Fund is a most generous one. For the last few years Lady Bullough has distributed food during the winter, months to the poor of Accrington, and now to avoid any clashing of her charity with the Mayor's Distress Fund, which has a similar object, she has subscribed £100 to the fund.

* * *

The old folks of Clayton-le-Moors had their eighteenth animal treat last Saturday afternoon at the Mechanics Institute, and right well they enjoyed it. Mrs. Nancy Whittaker, the oldest lady present, was presented with a bonnet and a bouquet of flowers. She was 88 years old, and Mr. Robinson, in presenting the flowers, said that he hoped everybody with whom she came into contact would scatter flowers upon her path and make it pleasant to the finish. Five shillings was presented to Mr. Jones, as being the oldest man present—he will be 92 next February. Mr. and Mrs. Holding, aged 78 and 68 respectively, won the prize for the oldest married couple. They had, been married 34 years. The Vicar of Altham, Rev. J. Robinson, in his address as chairman, suggested that old age pensions ought to be given at 60 or 65, and not at 70. Another defect in the Old Age Pensions Act, to come into operation in January, was that anyone who had received relief during; the present year was not entitled to a pension—so said Mr. Robinson. A number of Clayton ladies presided at the tea trays.

* * *

Not since our Amateurs presented "Erminie" have we had so well-dressed an opera as "Dorothy." The variety of costumes certainly enhance the production, but the constant changes must be very trying to the ladies, for the dressing-rooms behind the stage are anything but commodious. When the three principal ladies retreat to the poky little den allotted to them, there is very little room for the slimmest of dressers. Under such conditions the celerity with which Dorothy and Lydia change their costumes in the last act is wonderful. As it is, the girls have to make four changes of costume, and the chorus girls change three times. Monday night was a record "first night" in the matter of audience. Circle and stalls were booked up early, the gallery was packed, and the pit had its usual "classy" first-nighters, who are only to be seen in this part of the theatre when amateur productions are in progress. It is but a foretaste for many of these of the "state visit" booked later in the week. Long may they so congregate, and help to keep up the enthusiasm which is so necessary a thing to prolong these comic opera efforts in the cause of charity.

December 19th

Enthusiasm ran high in the packed Prince's Theatre, on Saturday, while the last performance of "Dorothy" by the Accrington Amateurs was in progress. Encores were the order of the evening, and nothing less than a double encore would satisfy the audience when Mr. Jack Leitherd was singing his big song, with chorus, in Chanticleer Hall. For Mr. Jack Oldham's "Queen of my heart" also, a double encore was demanded. Assuredly there was no "kid glove" brigade in the Theatre on Saturday. Those who had so cheerfully given their services among the stage crowd lacked nothing in the way of appreciation. The principal ladies were presented with lovely bouquets, the generous gifts, of the president, Mr. William Haworth, J.P. The old custom of presenting the bouquets at the conclusion of a favourite song was abandoned on Saturday. All the bouquets were reserved until the curtain was rung down on the last act. As the curtain rose again the chorus were to be seen grouped to the right of the "Hermit's Oak" on the stage, and the principals came in from the right-hand "wing," bowed in acknowledgement of the applause and bouquets, and passed out, re-entering from the left and forming a semi-circle in front of the grouped chorus. Then Mr. Leffler was called and received quite an ovation.

December 26th

So far as climatic conditions are concerned there is no indication of the close proximity, of the winter festival. Still the calendar is denuded of all but the last slip, and the tradespeople of Accrington are making splendid Christmas shows in their windows, so Christmas must be here. Although laid by the heels by that miserable fiend influenza, I cannot forego the pleasure of wishing my readers, rich and poor alike, a very merry Christmas.

1909

January 2nd

In this, the first issue of the "Observer" and Times" in 1909, my earliest word is to wish every Observerite not merely "A Happy New Year," but, as I heard it most appropriately put several times yesterday "A Happier New Year." Poor old 1908 has gone down to the limbo of the past, by very many people "unwept, unhonoured, and unsung," and of a verity here in Lancashire there were more had ill to say of the year now dead, than were ready to award praise and paens. Perhaps 'twas no fault of friendless 1908 that King Cotton was so seriously indisposed in the year now past; but none the less it will be remembered against that ill-starred period for many a long day to come. Those best able to judge declare that 1909 opens more cheerfully where the cotton outlook is concerned. So may it be! New Year's' Day 1909, will, surely mark an epoch in the care of the aged by the State. There are as yet anomalies to be removed, injustices to be set to rights; but yesterday saw the beginning, and that is indeed much for which to give thanks.

* * *

In view of the serious kitchen boiler explosions in Accrington this week, the instructive and, exhaustive letter by Mr. Hargreaves Riley printed to-day will be read with peculiar interest. Mr. Riley is an expert who has already distinguished himself on the subject involved—plumbing. It is evident from what he says that not one of the three systems in general use is absolutely safe without proper precautions being taken. The most dangerous of all, however, is the push system. It is the cheapest and least elaborate, but a source of constant risk in severe frosts, unless it receives the most careful attention. Hitherto most people giving advice as to how to avoid danger from it have been content to say that one should always try before lighting the fire in the morning whether hot or warm water will run out on turning-the tap at the sink (slopstone it is commonly called hereabouts).

January 9th

"It's an ill wind that blows nobody any good." No doubt the plumbers, the men of the moment last week, would have few regrets that the snow played havoc with nearly every house in town. Apart from these men who make hay while the frost freezes, there was a unanimous sigh of relief as the old year departed, taking with it the keen frost. One would have thought there were plumbers enough in Accrington, but last week's experience proved the supply not equal to the demand. Many a portly paterfamilias had to ascend to the loft to repair the damage himself, lest worse should befall the domestic world below. When the thaw came—ah! then!—all hands were requisitioned to save furniture, carpets, pictures and ornaments from the dripping

ceilings. For when the snow went into liquidation things began to be really "jolly "—
too jolly for the majority of shareholders.

* * *

Mud, like the poor, we have nearly always with us. If occasionally a venturesome
maid, anxious to wash away a portion of the town's mud, throws a pail of water
down the front steps, a Gas and Water Board official, dressed in a little brief
authority and blue uniform, is sure to come up and explain that "swilling at the front
is not allowed by the Gas and Water Board." Jane, indignant argues the point with
him, and is told that swilling in the backyard is allowed to aid sanitation, but not in
the front, and if he "catches her at it again there'll be trouble." Jane, to avoid further
argument, rises early in the mornings now, before the official has donned his
uniform, and swills and scrubs to her heart's content. Can anyone blame her, or the
mistress, who, knowing the contrariness of maids and the ridiculous ways of water
boards, amusedly shuts her eyes to the proceedings? One wouldn't mind such
stringent regulations if the Corporation did the "swilling" of the sidewalks.

* * *

What a mistake it seems to have only one performance of "Second in Command." It
requires as much work to produce a play for one day as for six. Perhaps our Amateurs
could not fill the theatre for a week with one play, but a couple to run alternately
ought to be successful. All the little blemishes inseparable from a first performance
would be obliterated as the week drew to a close. A single performance does not give
the actors a fair chance.

The packed Theatre testified to the diligence of the amateurs in canvassing before the
play. It was felt some time ago that the withdrawal—temporary we all hope—of Mr.
R. W. Kenyon, who for years has worked hard for the annual play, left a big gap, but
Mr. Harry Heap, the new secretary, and a number of helpers, including the actors
themselves, have done their best to make the play successful, and the Victoria
Hospital will once again be presented with a creditable sum of money.

January 16th

An interesting local engagement is that of Dr. A. E. Townley, M.B., Medical Officer
of Health for Oswaldtwistle, and Miss Nellie Dean, youngest daughter of Mr.
Thomas Dean, Carrara Cottage, Accrington.

January 23rd

The "Kentuckies" have once again proved their laughter-provoking proclivities to
some purpose. They have worked hard and deserved the applause accorded them
on Wednesday and Thursday. Local charities will benefit handsomely by these
successes, and their patrons certainly gained two pleasant evenings.

January 30th

Miss L. J. Hargreaves's resignation of her post as head mistress at the Accrington Municipal Secondary School has been received with genuine regret on all sides. Last Friday must have been a proud and happy day for Miss Hargreaves, when the staff and pupils of the Technical School presented her with a solid silver tea service. Miss Hargeaves has retired so that she may reside temporarily in Oxford to pursue postgraduate studies connected with the University. She is already a Bachelor of Science, and no doubt will return from Oxford with still further honours.

* * *

There has been some glorious skating this week. If only the frost continues yet a little while some of us will have the chance of becoming initiated into that fascinating branch "the outside edge." As a rule the frost lasts such a short time that many of us are only able to cut funny figures on the ice. (Friday : Alas! Frost gone!)

* * *

The Accrington Ambulance Drill Hall has been suggested as an admirable place to convert into a roller skating rink. Roller skating is very popular in some big towns and at many seaside resorts, including Blackpool, where several of the places of amusement have recently introduced the new craze. Girls who have not previously roller-skated will be interested in the question of suitable clothes. A most essential item for beginners is a short skirt, which is always more effective worn with a blouse of the same shade. Neat neck bands and trim waist are also of importance. Then, too, nice soft head-gear of the toque variety, well padded at the back, is advised—for these will be found to protect the back of the head when the inevitable falls occur.

Accrington social life seems to have languished somewhat this winter, due partly no doubt to bad trade, so that something new of this kind would brighten things up a bit for the young people. Devotees of the sport assure me that roller-skating, despite the falls, is most fascinating.

* * *

I am reminded that Accrington once had a skating rink. It was on the Peel-street side of the Market Hall, and the late Mr. E. Riley, if I remember rightly, was market lessee at the time. It was thirty years ago, perhaps more, but I recollect it as a girl.

* * *

To Mrs. Walter Higham and the rest of the Higham family I offer my sincere sympathy. Mr. Walter Higham was, at one time, prominently identified with Accrington institutions'—the Choral Society, the Amateurs - how well do I remember his "Gobo" in " Cloches," and the Cricket and Football Clubs.

February 6th

It is pitiful to hear of a boy being before the magistrates for stealing. Still more pitiful is the case of the boy of thirteen, who at the Accrington Police Court, on Monday, was described as the leader of a gang of thieves.

* * *

So Accrington is to have a roller-skating rink after all. Beyond the fact that a local company is being formed for its erection, we know not how or where the rink will appear, but before the end of March the sporting young man of Accrington will probably have the opportunity of indulging in the new craze. His sisters also will no doubt be preparing for the pastime in their own way. Naturally "their" way will include speculations as to suitable costumes to be worn while rinking. As I remarked previously, neatness should be the keynote of a beginner's costume, and knickerbockers must take the place of lace petticoats, if she does not wish to become involved in other difficulties than those common to all beginners.

February 20th

Mr. and Mrs. S. Briggs-Bury, of Bank House, Accrington, suffered a sad bereavement on Friday in the death of their younger son, Derek, aged two and a half years.

The little one, a bright, robust boy, was taken ill about Tuesday, and on Friday it was found that he was suffering from appendicitis in a form so acute as to necessitate immediate operation. This was performed by two Manchester specialists, Dr. Murray and Dr. Thorburne, but death occurred about eight o'clock on Friday night—nine hours after the operation. On all hands much sympathy has been expressed towards Mr. and Mrs. Briggs-Bury in their trouble.

The funeral took place yesterday noon in the family vault at the Accrington Cemetery, the Rev. E. Greensill, vicar of Christ Church, officiating.

* * *

Wednesday's Cunliffe concert audience appeared to be well satisfied with the musical fare provided. Applause was by no means stinted. The music for the orchestra was on the whole well chosen, though perhaps Listz's Rhapsodie might with advantage have been omitted from the programme. I say "perhaps" advisedly, for after all, if the band never attempted anything big they would never advance. There is, maybe, more credit in having tried to conquer music, even though they fell far short of perfection, than not to have tried at all. The earnestness and painstaking care with which each unit of the orchestra attacked this ambitious item was praiseworthy. They worked with such zest that beads of perspiration stood on the brows of many of the instrumentalists before Mr. Hanson lowered his baton. The other orchestral contributions were remarkable for their abrupt endings.

The opening bars of the last musical item used to be the signal for an exodus of people from the concert room. We in Accrington, though, are much improved in these little matters, and we generally keep our seats until the finish now, and don't obstruct a neighbour's view of the artistes with our hats. But some of us still regard the beginning of the last item as a suitable time for putting on hats and adjusting coats and wraps. In fact, we rustle and bustle in a way that is only one degree better than getting up and pushing past other people to gain an early exit.

February 27th

There could be no doubt about it, the Accrington Territorials had a good time last Friday. Those ladies who, led by the Mayoress, arranged the dance, must have viewed with satisfaction the success of their efforts. The Mayor and Mayoress, wearing their mayoralty chains, were early in attendance to receive the guests. It was interesting to watch the arrival of the "Terriers." Some of them walked past the entrance to the ball room utterly oblivious of the fact that the Mayor and Mayoress were standing there smiling a welcome. Others gripped the hands extended to them in a frantic way and then fled speechless to a corner of the room. One young fellow, scarcely more than a boy, behaved beautifully. He displayed none of the discomfiture which was so marked a feature of many of his fellows. Click went his heels together, and he smiled as he raised his arm to salute the Mayor and Mayoress. Several ladies expressed a desire—sotto voce, of course—to kiss that boy because he did not spoil their ideal of a soldier-boy's behaviour.

The uniforms of the men were not nearly so effective as one expected they would be. The scarlet coats of a few officers, and the blue and silver of others supplied attractive colour notes, but on the whole the effect was deadly. Had their ladies all been able to wear evening dresses instead of that abomination at a dance—blouse and skirt costume—adopted by the majority, the effect would have been enhanced.

At intervals the Territorials made raids on the refreshments. The ladies will bear witness to their capacity as "trencher-men." At first a shamefaced shyness prevailed amongst the girls and their cavaliers, and they could not be persuaded to eat much, but as soon as they were seated at a table and the attendants discreetly turned away, the dainties vanished rapidly—so rapidly that before midnight a remnant of a pie and a crust or two were all that remained of the feast. Nearly a thousand meat pies were consumed, thousands of little cakes, hundreds of sandwiches, oranges, and twenty big trifles, to say nothing of the tea, coffee, and aerated water, which flowed merrily all night.

* * *

As soon as the Workers for the Territorial ball had cleared away the debris of flowers etc., on Saturday morning, another batch of workers arrived to make preparations for the Old Folks' Treat. Where on Friday the young ones had pranced and danced, the aged on Saturday quietly enjoyed an entertainment more suited to their advanced years . The contrast between the two gatherings was most marked. The Mayor and Mayoress were again present, both smiling graciously, and chatting amiably with the old folks.

March 6th

The advent of March resembled a Polar bear rather than the proverbial lion this time. The soft thick flakes of snow were almost caressing in their touch as they descended, and as no wind came to drift the snow, the supply was evenly distributed.

On Tuesday one realised that a white world is intensely picturesque. Hill slopes clearly defined for miles round, and trees snow laden take on an unusual aspect.

* * *

At Monday's Council meeting, Mr. Barlow drew attention to the fact that some of the Gas and Water Board officials were going round the town to prevent swilling, especially after foggy weather. His remark that the only thing the water was fit for was swilling, was greeted with laughter. Mr. Barlow further stated that the water was not fit for drinking or washing purposes; and that it took 100 per cent more soap to do the washing at his firm. (More laughter.) Housewives don't regard this hard water and the extra labour and soap it entails as a laughing matter, nor do they approve of the interference of an official when the cleansing of the doorstep to their own houses is in question, as I pointed out a few weeks ago.

March 13th

March may be the month of spring, but it hasn't brought any springlike, balmy weather along yet. The dazzling whiteness of the snow has given place to mud— greasy, slimy, sticky mud. The sullied snow was soon cleared away from Accrington main streets. Compared with one or two other towns, Accrington presented quite a tidy appearance a comparatively short time after the heavy snowstorm. What a pity the mud cannot be dispersed as well. I saw a solitary man with a road-scraper one day this week on one of our public roads. He scraped away diligently for some time, but alas! no fairy came to wave her magic wand, as in Cinderella's time, and the task progressed but slowly. One would have thought that road-scrapers should not work in "single spies but in battalions."

* * *

"Tom Jones" is the opera chosen for the local Amateur Operatic production next season. It is an ambitious choice, as all who have seen the dramatised version of James Fielding's novel will agree. It was first produced in Manchester a couple of years ago, so the Amateurs may consider themselves lucky in having secured the rights of the piece.

* * *

A site in Syke-street, adjoining "Wesley" Chapel has been secured from the Corporation for the erection of a skating rink. The East Lancashire Roller Skating Rink Co., as the new company is called, has a capital of £4,000. The directors, mainly local gentlemen, state that the building will be ready for use before Easter.

* * *

For many years Haslingden tradespeople have been noted for their fondness for long one-day trips at Whitsuntide. This year the chosen place is Ilfracombe, and although Whit-Friday is still many weeks distant, the secretary is booking passengers for the trip—60 of the prospective passengers hailing from Todmorden. Eleven hours in Ilfracombe would not compensate all of us for eighteen hours spent in a railway train. To have travelled 600 miles in one day is something, of course—a feat of endurance.

That an increasing number of people undertake these journeys for the pleasure of a glimpse of far-away beauty spots is testimony that the efforts of the pioneers of these pleasure pilgrimages are keenly appreciated.

March 20th

It is with pleasure that I write this week of the zeal of a young Accrington girl in collecting money for the "Observer and Times" Cot Fund. Miss Alice Warburton's first collection amounted to £7 10s., and her second effort resulted in £1 16s. Thus her two collections total the very creditable sum of £9 6s. Most people when being canvassed in this way subscribe only small sums, so that Miss Warburton must have been most zealous for the causes. Miss Warburton is not yet 14 years of age. Are there not many more girls who would like to emulate Miss Warburton, and do their quota towards providing a cot for the little children? In years to come, when Miss Warburton, and the other collectors I mentioned previously, have grown to womanhood and visit the Victoria Hospital, they will be able to say with pride, "I helped to build that cot." The Editor tells me that less than 1,000 shillings are required now to complete the 10,000 shillings. Now, who of you young lady readers will come forward to help to complete the fund for the endowment of a cot?

March 27th

Romance surrounds the love affairs of the Bulloughs. John Bullough met his first wife—a charming Swiss girl—at the little Swiss village of Thun. His second wife was a fine and beautiful Scotch lassie whom he met quite accidentally—it is said at his bankers. When the late Mr. Bullough died on the 25th February 1891, Ian was a boy under five and not long afterwards his mother married Captain Beech of Cheshire. Both she and her son Ian took an active part in the Conservative Bazaar in the Conservative Club not long ago, and among the stall holders was Lady Bullough who married Sir George under still more romantic cirumstances. And now his half-brother Ian is married, very quietly, in a London Registry Office to an attractive comedy star without any of his relatives being present!

One of the most talked-of events of the week, it follows, is the romantic marriage on Wednesday of Mr. Ian Bullough, to the popular actress, Miss Maudi Darrell. Mr. Ian Bullough is the younger son of the late Mr. John Bullough, who was the head, and practically the founder, of the great Accrington firm of textile machinists now known as Howard and Bullough, Limited. Ian was the son of the second marriage, and consequently half-brother of Sir George Bullough, the present head of the firm, who, was until a week or two ago Conservative candidate for the Accrington Division.

The young bridegroom is only 23 and is the owner of Meggerine Castle, Glen Lyon, Scotland, which he inherited from his father. He is reported to be enormously wealthy. Unlike Sir George, he has never been actively associated with Globe Works, and his visits to Accrington have been comparatively rare, about the best remembered being on the occasion of the last big Conservative bazaar, when he took a prominent part in the proceedings, assisting his mother, who is now the wife of Captain Beach, of Malpas, Cheshire.

After the wedding Mr. and Mrs. Bullough lunched by themselves at the Criterion.

While Mr. and Mrs. Bullough were at lunch after the ceremony, they were seen by a representative of the "Daily Mirror" and that journal thus records what was said. "You can say at once that my wife has left the stage for ever," said Mr. Bullough, who was in high spirits. "We are leaving London directly for a motor-car tour in the South of France and do not know when we shall be back again."

"Yes, I am really saying good-bye forever to the stage,' said Miss Darrell, with a loving glance at her husband."But the public and the critics have been so kind to me that I shall do so quite regretfully."

* * *

The wedding of Miss Alice Macalpine, daughter of Mr. A. Macalpine of Paisley, to Mr. Harry Lupton, son of Mr. Henry Lupton, Accrington, aroused interest among the feminine portion of the population of Accrington on Thursday at Cannon-street Baptist Church. The day was gloomy in the forenoon but rays of sunshine penetrated into the church during the ceremony, and were reflected on the face of the bride as she came out of church. The bride who was given away by her father, looked very sweet, attired in a pretty ivory satin gown with vest of chiffon, draped bodice, and beautifully embroidered silk shaped collar, and folded sleeves. She carried a bouquet of choice white flowers, and her plain net veil was worn over a wreath of orange blossom.

The bride's grandfather, Mr. William Entwisle, J.P., whose age is about 88, was among the guests looking as buoyant as many of the younger ones.

* * *

The Liberal Club is indeed already the scene of considerable activity in connection with the forthcoming bazaar. There is no mistaking the fact that the skirmishers are out, so to speak, as witness the whist drives in aid of this stall or that stall two weeks in succession, and then, on Monday evening, a capital mixed entertainment, in aid of the whole bazaar, with the promise from the chairman, Councillor A. Langham, of more to follow next winter. However, with regard to the entertainment on Monday evening, Councillor Langham, as mentioned, was chairman, and presided over a large attendance, opening the proceedings with a few remarks about the bazaar and its objects. Then followed the entertainment, the first half of which consisted of songs, etc., by children. The various items were very pleasingly rendered by the youthful artistes, whose efforts were a credit both to themselves and the ladies responsible for their training.

The two recitations given by Miss Dorothy Bainbridge were especially good.

April 3rd

With regard to the cost of the present portion of the baths scheme the Borough Engineer has no hesitation in saying that the work can be carried out for the £10,500. Mr. Newton suggested to the committee that, with a view of increasing the accommodation for gentlemen, they might be allowed to use the whole of the sixteen slipper baths, except on certain days of the week, when eight of them might be set apart for ladies. It will be remembered, however, that some members of the Council did not favour this idea. They were under the impression that ladies like to have baths for their exclusive use, and gave that as a reason why the fair sex gave but little patronage to the old Accrington concern before it was burnt down, there being no baths there for ladies' sole use. Experience in other towns rather supports this view. For instance, at the recently-opened, up-to-date Belper-street baths in Blackburn, there are fourteen private, or slipper, baths for ladies, and seventeen for gentlemen. Last year there were 9,103 admissions to the former, while there were only 7,870 to the latter. A considerable proportion of the ladies represented by the nine thousand

The proposed new swimming bath building in St James Street

odd admissions were, as is well known, from Accrington and its district.

In his report to the committee, Mr, Newton stated that should the Council desire to form the floors of the gallery with terrazzo instead of boards (which would be better, from a sanitary and other points of view), and provide 12 additional slipper baths, the extra coat would be £1,500, making £12,000. And he said that accommodation to the extent of 12 further additional baths in the gallery could be provided when necessary at the discretion of the Council for another £1,000; and that this addition could be made during any winter when the swimming bath might be closed. The Council, however, have made up their minds to spend no more than the £10,600 for the present.

April 10th

With decent weather there will be a big exodus from Accrington district to the holiday resorts, for the first play-time of the year. Any amount of facilities are offered by the railways and steamboat companies for travelling practically everywhere that the shortness of the time will permit to be visited. After the long and rigorous winter, and the first scarcely less trying weeks of spring, most of us will be glad to get away, if only for a change of air. Many who successfully negotiated a "go" of influenza are sure to be especially grateful for a chance of bracing up by the seaside, and to leave dull care behind for a while.

April 17th

Seldom in all its long history has the ancient and picturesque church of Altham seen a happier and more brilliant gathering than that which occupied the pretty little church and its precincts on Thursday, on the occasion of the wedding of Mr. Douglas Hewitt Hacking, seventh son of Mr. Joshua Hacking, J.P., C.C., of Henfield

Mr Douglas Hacking and Miss Margery Bolton

House, Clayton-le-Moors, and Miss Margery Allen Bolton, eldest daughter of Mr. H. H. Bolton, J.P., of Highbrake, Huncoat. The bride and bridegroom and their respective families are widely known and highly respected, and the wedding aroused great interest, and was most imposing and attractive. The day was, happily, gloriously fine, with a clear sky and bright sunshine, and the radiant weather lent the final touches to a joyous and animated scene. Altham and the road stretching up to Highbrake being thronged with interested and well-dressed spectators.

The wedding was fixed for one o'clock, and long before that hour crowds of people were wending their way towards the church. The guests being so numerous—about 220— they occupied almost all the seats, and care being taken that the edifice should not be over-crowded, very few outsiders were present at the ceremony. About eighty carriages, with 140 horses, conveyed the guests, the cavalcade stretching for a long distance along the road. It was said that never before had so many people been seen at a wedding at Altham Church, and the number of carriages and horses was quite without precedent.

When the guests had assembled, the bride, leaning on her father's arm, entered the sacred edifice with her six daintily dressed bridesmaids, the bridal procession presenting a very pretty scene, which absorbed the attention of those both outside and inside the church.

The bride was charmingly attired in a white satin charmeuse dress embroidered in pearls, a handsome court train, also embroidered in pearls and lined with chiffon, depending from the shoulders. She wore a dainty tulle veil and wreath of orange blossom, a beautiful diamond pendant, the gift of Mr. and Mrs. Hacking, and a pearl and diamond ring, the bridegroom's present. Her pretty shower bouquet was composed of white roses and white heather.

Six bridesmaids, including three sisters of the bride, formed an attractive retinue. The attendants were Miss Janet Bolton, Miss Muriel Bolton, and Miss Phyllis Bolton, the bride's sisters, Miss Maisie Hacking (sister of the bridegroom), Miss Mabel Wilkinson (cousin of the bride), and Miss Green. The best man was Mr. Arthur Hacking, brother of the bridegroom. The congregation was thoroughly representative, most of the leading gentry and clergy being guests, and the ladies wore charming dresses, several carrying bouquets.

After the ceremony the reception of the 220 guests was held in a large marquee in the grounds at Highbrake, where they were entertained to an excellent repast, a garden party being subsequently held. Mr. George Thornton's Band played selections. As the weather was beautiful, it was a very pleasant affair.

The newly-married couple had hearty send-off for the honeymoon in Switzerland and at the Italian Lakes. The bride's travelling dress was of old rose cloth made in Directoire style, with black satin facings and old rose hat with wreath of roses and osprey.

The workpeople at the East Lancashire Soap Works, Clayton-le-Moors, were treated by the firm to a trip to Blackpool on Thursday, in celebration of the happy event. Mr. Winter, of Preston, photographed the bridal group, and the interior of the church with the floral decorations.

April 24th

After listening to the instrumental and vocal talents of the Misses McCullagh at the Oswaldtwistle Town Hall, on Wednesday evening, one welcomed the knowledge that they are to reside in Accrington for at least three years. When in August their father takes up his duties as superintendent of the Wesleyan circuit we shall have added at least four desirable musicians to our musical circle in Accrington. By the way, Oswaldtwistle audiences are most appreciative. No apathy distinguished their reception of any item on Wednesday; if anything, they were a trifle too impartial, but they succeeded in doubling the programme at any rate. I heard one Accrington young lady remark that she hadn't spent two shillings to such excellent advantage for a long time.

* * *

"Mug's Alley"—I have not coined the inelegant phrase—was not in great request at the Abbey Skating Rink on Wednesday afternoon. Evidently many Accringtonians have graduated in the sport elsewhere, and were able to glide gracefully round and round the rink on the opening day. There were few collisions, and not many undignified collapses earthward. The floor, owing to its newness perhaps, was not very good for skating in the afternoon, but was much improved when evening came. Ladies who eschewed frills and furbelows presented a graceful appearance on the rink, and the gentlemen were quite gallant—for once in a way. Local young gentlemen in a ballroom have become somewhat apathetic this winter, and it is possible that rinking will revive the little courtesies and attentions that require so little effort and are valued by the gentler sex.

May 15th

Mr. Edward Whittaker appears to be following in the footsteps of Mr. William Tattersall, now of Churchtown, Southport, the tutor of his early flights into the realms of things musical. As conductor of the Accrington and Church Co-operative Society's Contest Choir, Mr. Whittaker added still another success to his long list. This choir won the second prize in the competition for mixed voice choirs at the Morecambe Musical Festival on Saturday afternoon. There were nine competing choirs, and Sheffield Congregational Tabernacle Choir won the first prize with 190 marks, just two more than Accrington, who with 188 won second place.

May 22nd

The 2nd of June is the date fixed for the marriage of Miss Muriel Appleby third daughter of the late Mr. Arthur Appleby, and Mr. Burton Hacking, son of Mr. Joshua Hacking, J.P., at Clayton-le-Moors. This year has been quite an eventful one for weddings in the Hacking family; Mr. Burton Hacking will be the third son married within twelve months.

* * *

Nor is this the only happy matrimonial event in which a member of the Appleby family is concerned. To-day I am privileged to be able to announce another most interesting engagement—that of Mr. A. N. Appleby, son of the late Mr. Arthur Appleby, and Miss. Mildred Riley, only daughter of Mr. J. E. Riley, J.P., C.A., of Arden Hall, Accrington. Mr. Appleby recently returned home after an extended tour in India and the East, and the announcement of the engagement will give much pleasure alike to the very many friends of the young lady and gentleman chiefly concerned.

* * *

The Borough Restaurant was much too small to comfortably hold the crowds of people who went to Miss Mary Spencer's pianoforte recital last Friday. Many gentlemen had to prop themselves against the wall, while to other late-comers the only available space was in the open doorway. It is really surprising, with such brilliant pianists as Miss Spencer and a few other ladies one could name in our midst, to say nothing of talented vocalists, that no effort is made to organise a ladies' Clef Club.

June 5th

Seldom have I seen a church so artistically adorned with flowers as was All Saints' for the celebration of the Appleby-Hacking wedding on Wednesday. A more beautiful decorative scheme for a church could not have been wished.

The bride, who was given away by her mother, looked lovely in an ivory satin trained Empire gown, with a very deep round yoke of finely tucked tulle, and a wide berthe of rich fine lace; she carried a bouquet of choice white flowers and wore a floating net veil over a wreath of orange blossom on her pretty hair. The bride was also wearing a beautiful diamond brooch a gift from the bridegroom's father.

Mr. and Mrs. Burton Hacking, I understand are to live at Freshfield, near Southport.

Just before the wedding ceremony commenced on Wednesday a rather startling announcement was made at the Parish Church. The purport of it was that the speaker's attention had been drawn to the fact that several ladies had removed their hats since entering the sacred edifice. "Would the ladies kindly replace their hats, as women are not allowed with uncovered heads in church."

Bridesmaids have appeared at weddings before the new pastor's reign at All Saints' church with nothing save a few flowers in their tresses. They were not forbidden to remain in church, nor was any adverse criticism made about the uncovered state of their heads. Hatless congregations will not be the fashion so long as the majority of women attend church, for hats are a valuable asset to a becoming toilette, but surely a woman in such a modern town as ours would not be debarred from participating in divine service in church should she, from choice or necessity, enter the church without a hat. A woman can be just as devout with or without a hat.

June 12th

Three weddings in little more than a month will be the happy record of the Appleby family. What a busy household their's must be, preparing for a succession of such events in so short a period. It was only last week that Miss Muriel Appleby was married to Mr. Burton Hacking, and now comes the announcement that the wedding of Mr. Noel Appleby and Miss Mildred Riley, only daughter of Mr. J. E. Riley, J.P., C.A., Arden Hall, Accrington, is to take place at Christ Church on Thursday, July 8th. And following closely upon this will come the marriage of Miss Marion Appleby and Mr. H. Fletcher, son of Archdeacon Fletcher, of Chorley, which is fixed for the 20th July, at All Saints', Clayton-le-Moors. In the case of Mr. Noel Appleby and his bride-to-be, they are after the wedding to reside in the South of England. Mr. Fletcher's and Miss Appleby's wedding will be followed by residence in Dublin, where he is engaged in the shipping business.

June 19th

Accrington was en fete on Saturday, when the 34th annual demonstration of the Lancashire Fire Brigades' Friendly Society took place. The weather being fine, the affair was an unqualified success from a spectacular and numerical point of view. Thousands of spectators watched the fine parade, representing nearly one hundred fire brigades from almost all parts of the county. The entire route of over four miles was lined on both sides with people, standing three or four deep in the main thoroughfares. Many watched from the windows of houses, mills and workshops, balconies, tops of arcades and other places from which there was a view. Seldom have more watched a procession in Accrington.

The procession, embracing a thousand firemen, was about a mile long, and was marshalled without a hitch by Chief Constable Sinclair and those assisting him. The

Accrington firemen of the early 1900s

show of bunting in Accrington was the most depressing feature of the whole parade. Much of it was shabby, limp, dirty, and most dejected looking, though there were, of course, pleasing exceptions. The decoration in front of the Town Hall looked as if it had been "Mafficking" on its last appearance, and hadn't recovered, and never would recover, its pristine freshness. Soiled bunting, like soiled dress finery, is unpardonable.

One is glad to hear that when all the expenses of the demonstration are defrayed there will be a nice little balance to hand over to the Lancashire Fire Brigades' Friendly Society and local charities. Street collections alone amounted to £41 5s. 7d. The collections would probably have been doubled had more young ladies taken round the boxes. It is quite impossible to resist the invitation to augment the funds when a dainty young lady presents the collecting box along with a bewitching smile.

July 3rd

What a pity the rain came to mar the crowning of the Rose Queen at Dunkenhalgh last Saturday. The new Rose Queen and her attendants must have been sadly disappointed when they saw all the beautiful finery they had been at so much pains to don, and everything else, spoiled by the heavy downpour. Luckily the procession, a very pretty one by the way, took place before the rain commenced so that the thousands of people who assembled along the route were not robbed of all pleasure in the proceedings.

July 10th

It was not surprising that crowds of people, in addition to the goodly number of invited guests, went to Christ church to witness the marriage of Mr. Noel Appleby to Miss Mildred Riley on Thursday afternoon. Both bride and bridegroom are members of well-known local families. Miss Riley has done much to endear herself to the

Mr Noel Appleby and Miss Mildred Riley

hearts of many Accringtonians. Her unassuming but kindly interest in local charitable organisations was appreciated. Especially was she interested in the good work done by the Victoria Hospital, where she spent a good deal of time entertaining the patients. As treasurer of the Linen League connected with the Hospital—a position she resigned only last week—she was one of the principal workers. We are always sorry to lose the helpers from our midst, but nevertheless our best wishes go out to the bride and bridegroom at the commencement of their new life. May they always be as happy as they deserve!

* * *

One is glad to hear that the Linen League is making such satisfactory progress. It is only six months since that useful work was organised, and the members already number 110. Mrs. Cunliffe, who presided at last Saturday's meeting of the League members, referred in a neat little speech to their inability to procure gentlemen for membership. However, she paid the sex the compliment of saying that she did not think they would be behindhand if money was wanted. It is not quite clear in which department of the League the gentlemen are required, for the strong sex, as a rule, are not clever with the needle, or even cutting out garments. But perhaps I malign them? An annual subscription is much more in their line, surely.

* * *

The Accrington Police Cricket Team of 1909

The cricket match on the Accrington cricket ground on Wednesday, Gentlemen versus Police, resolved itself eventually into a battle between waitresses and the crowd. Before the Gentlemen had finished their innings the rain came down in torrents. Jimmy's score upset the elements, and down the rain came in floods. People rushed helter skelter to the pavilion for shelter. All Mrs. Carter's arrangements for serving tea were set at naught. The people required a diversion. They wanted tea. But the trouble was they all wanted it at once. It was good to see the waitresses in their dainty coloured frocks overcome the difficulty. They pushed their way insidiously through the crowd, and to their credit be it said in a very short time everybody had been served with tea, and even the hungry small boys satisfied.

The umpires walked impressively to the stumps when a break appeared in the weeping skies, and pottered about a bit on the spongy turf, but the result was a foregone conclusion—the match had to be abandoned.

* * *

Any of the 200 crippled little children who joined the motor trip to Lytham last Saturday would tell you what a delightful day they had as guests of some of the Lancashire Automobile Club members. It is almost easy to forget one's infirmities when one is riding for the first time in a beautifully upholstered car, with a nice man driving, and a smiling lady in charge of the rear seats, who has smuggled dainties into the side pockets of the tonneau. Oh, yes, it must have been a happy time, indeed, for the poor little cripples. No wonder their little faces, puckered in some cases with pain, were joyful and smiling as they started from the Town Hall on their trip to Lytham. The mere journey did not by any means include all the delights either; for at Lea Gate Mr. Shorrock supplied light refreshments; at Lytham tea was provided at the Clifton Arms Hotel, and Mrs. Crook, of Hoghton, gave each child a sixpence. Then there was the Pierrot Troupe on the sands. I'm sure the poor little mites will talk, and live over again in thought the splendid day they had with the motorists for many a long day.

July 17th

May it soon come to pass, that the extra hour of priceless daylight will be ours. It would make a wonderful difference to the holiday-maker in August and September. It is possible for a house-party to be a law unto itself as regards daylight saving during holiday periods. A friend of mine tried the experiment last year in a house by the sea, where she and her family were spending a month's holiday. At first the novelty didn't appeal to the servants, who inquired rather tartly whether their mistress expected breakfast at 8-30 by the clock or by the daylight. However, this difficulty was soon overcome by putting all the clocks and watches in the house back one hour, and after that all went smoothly. Twenty-eight extra hours of daylight in a month are worth arranging for. If any of my readers adopt this excellent plan of lengthening the days during the holidays, I should be very pleased to hear the result. Letters addressed to "Stella," "Observer" office, Accrington, will always find me.

July 31st

The latest stimulant for aviators comes from Southport, in the form of an offer of £1,000 made by Sir W. P. Hartley, to the first person who makes a successful flight between Liverpool and Manchester. Now that the Channel has been crossed safely by M. Bleriot in his monoplane, there is hope of more prolonged flights inland. We shall see some funny things aloft by and by.

* * *

On Thursday the employees of the East Lancashire Soap Co. Ltd, had a drive to Higher Hodder to celebrate the wedding of Mr. Burton Hacking, who is a director of the firm. They started out in char-a-banc supplied by J. Moore and Sons, and made Worston the first stopping place, pies and sandwiches being served out. Afterwards they were joined by Mr. Joshua Hacking and Mr. E. Kirkham, both directors, and

Mr. J. Drummond, secretary, and several of the party had a motor drive around the country. The whole party arrived at Higher Hodder about four o'clock, where a splendid tea was awaiting at Higher Hodder Bridge Hotel. The party started on the homeward journey at 8 o'clock, arriving home safely after a most enjoyable outing.

August 7th

Can it be that Accrington and District for once in a very long while is to have a bright and rainless holiday week? It almost seems too good to be true, and especially in such a year as this when it has been rain, rain, rain, and yet more rain. It almost gave one a shock on Wednesday afternoon, for instance, to see folks sitting out on the top of the Blackburn tram cars, basking in the sunshine, instead of having to crowd disconsolately inside out of the rain. And just think of the joys to come if the holidays are accompanied by summer weather—real summer weather. It's well nigh too good to be true!

August 14th

I was asking my venerable friend, the oldest inhabitant one day this week whether he ever remembered such a wonderful August Fair week as this. "No, never," he replied with all the emphasis at his command, and then he sagely added, "and I doubt if ever there'll be such another." Certainly this has been the one great week of the summer—or what stands for summer in the calendar—and if the holiday hosts at the seaside, or wherever else they have betaken themselves, have not had "the time of their lives," then the fault has not lain with the weather.

Bronzed by the breezes, baked by the sun, vastly the gainers in health, I hope, there will to-day be the great homeward trek of returning holiday-makers. Ask almost any railwayman what is the hardest and most "humbugging" job he has in the twelvemonth, and he will tell you it's assisting the return of the native—the great homecoming of the holiday legions. Coming back home somehow leads to far more bustle and confusion, far more noise and trouble, than does the "going off." Perhaps for one thing, there are fewer good trains available for the homeward journey, there is not the same use made of the "luggage in advance" system, and then again so many people make up their minds to return at about the same hour. And among it all passengers and railway folk alike have a decidedly lively time.

September 4th

Airships are very much in evidence—I had almost written "in the air"—just now. Manchester has formed an Aero Club, and Accrington has furnished at least one member in the person of Mr. Harry Bergan, landlord of the Langs Arms Hotel. Yesterday I had a chat with Mr. Bergan, who, by the way, is an ex-engineer, and he informed me that he has the intention of being the first aviator in Accrington. When motoring became popular he became a motorist, but he has decided to forsake flying over the roads for flying in the air.

His motor car is for sale, and its place in the garage will within a month or so be occupied by an aeroplane. For some time he has been studying the science, and his plans are now practically complete. He has been occupied with engines, and has fixed upon one of 12 horsepower, and within a few days hopes to place an order for same. The planes, etc., will be built to Mr. Bergan's own design, on similar lines to those now in use by Bleriot, Latham, and other successful aviators. Whilst following the general methods, Mr. Bergan stated that he has ideas of his own upon which he will experiment, particularly in regard to the raising of the machine from the earth direct, which has so far been one of the problems not successfully solved. Anyhow, Accringtonians will not have long to wait before they see an aeroplane in their own town. I wish Mr. Bergan every success, and, like others, shall watch his experiments with interest.

* * *

All who have taken a hand in the promotion of the Electrical Exhibition at the Town Hall have ample reason to be pleased with the success that has attended the affair. Every night since the Exhibition was opened the hall has been filled to well nigh the limit of its capacity, and visitors have not been slow to admire and appreciate many of the latest products of the electrical world as applied to domestic and other uses.
That was a bright and happy speech Alderman T. E. Higham made at the opening of the Exhibition on Monday afternoon. His references to the little luxuries an electrical supply can now afford—luxuries such as the warming of one's bedroom by the cheap, healthy and cleanly electrical process, the provision of boiling water by the bedside, and electric smoothing irons for laundry purposes—would interest not a few of his hearers.

September 11th

With might and main Blackpool is still working for the attainment of its newly conceived idea of a "flying week." The idea is that the races in the air shall commence on Monday, October 18th, and already it is announced that the authorities are prepared to spend anything up to £15,000, and even more money can be got if it is needed. Bravo Blackpool! Already the organisers have scored one big point. They have had the secretary of the English Aero Club down, in company with another member, and these two were quite agreed with the local committee that the Squire's Gate course was in every way admirable for the purposes of flying.
But the problem still remains, will the best known aviators come to Blackpool? The deputation charged with the task of engaging flying men will not leave for Paris until the week-end, but already it is announced that there is not much likelihood of Latham being persuaded to take part, and Bleriot, too, is regarded as extremely unlikely. But the persuasions and golden bait of the Blackpool deputation may yet work wonders.

* * *

The ill luck which on and off for years has been pursuing the Accrington Conservatives followed them to their garden party at Dunkenhalgh on Saturday. During the persistent rain of the forenoon it was thought probable they would have to fall back upon the alternative of holding their meeting in the Hippodrome. For this the necessary conditional arrangements had been made. However, a deceptive partial clearing-up of the weather after noon induced them to risk the garden party after all. They thought there might be more showers in the course
of the afternoon, but perhaps dry weather enough to make the gathering at least a qualified success. A wet forenoon often precedes a dry afternoon and evening, but seldom when the atmosphere is in the condition it was on Saturday. It was in the state to which we have become accustomed more than formerly, I think, for the past six or seven years—when the air seems to be unable to hold the moisture, which all the time keeps coming down in drops or in heavier measure. There have been very many such days in the summer now drawing to a close, and Saturday was one of the most treacherous of them.

Had there been warmth and sunshine, or even sunshine without the warmth, old Dunkenhalgh Park would have been the scene of a successful, gay and festive function. Even before the appointed time people began coming to it from various parts of the Parliamentary Division. This, despite the threatening nature of the elements. With fine weather such as that of Sunday afternoon their numbers would have been greatly increased. After two o'clock it began to rain again, and probably hundreds, if not thousands, finally made up their minds to stay at home. Still between two and three crowds streamed along the roads leading to the Park. The cars from Accrington were filled, and the receipts of the Tramways Committee must have risen in corresponding measure. And probably more went by the cars—in the rain—from Dunkenhalgh than to it.

Before three o'clock people in the Park were sheltering under the trees from the rain. At that time a goodly assemblage was there, considering the circumstances. Ordinary folk had to pay for admission. It need hardly be said that Sir Robert Hermon-Hodge was the greatest attraction. But apart from him much had been provided to amuse and interest. The programme included dancing from half-past two till seven; performances by a "troupe of refined black and white pierrots"; figure dancing by morris dancers; songs by Bert Terrell, the "garden party favourite," from the Accrington Hippodrome; music by bands, and so on. At a refreshment tent a sandwich was to be had for fourpence, a cup of tea at the same price, and a meat pie for the modest price of twopence. Under apparently unofficial dispensation was a stand at which biscuits, ice cream, ginger beer, and other dainties were offered at, no doubt, reasonable prices. I think it likely, too, that additional facilities for providing solid and liquid refreshments were held in reserve until it would be seen what the weather would do.

Just after three the slight rain thickened, and directly there was a storm. The wind rose, and Jupiter Pluvius set about his work in businesslike fashion. This state of things lasted for over an hour, and at the end of two hours it was still raining.

The scene was depressing, almost pathetic in some ways. There was no shelter, except such as a few trees afforded. Access to the premises of the hall was cut off. If it

A group taken in the entrance hall at Dunkenhalgh, on Saturday. The group, from the left: Mr. John Whittaker, Lady Clifton, Lady Herman-Hodge, Sir R. Hermon-Hodge (ex-Member for the Division), Mrs. Ashton, Mr. Paterson (with little Miss Petre), Captain Petre, Mrs. Paterson, and Mrs. Petre.

had not been many a one would have been glad to take refuge in even an outhouse while the downpour lasted. As it was shift had to be made with overcoats, macintoshes, and umbrellas. A good many had braved the day without any of these. I saw one young man with nothing more weather-proof than a light frock coat, and numbers of men both young and old who had made scarcely better provisions against rain. The ladies, naturally, were in worst case, with their summer dresses, light boots, and the sodden ground. Round the refreshment tent a number of seats (wooden forms) were ranged, mostly lying overturned in the grass. The whole presented as forlorn a spectacle as could well be seen, at a garden party or anything else.

September 18th

Mrs. Robertson-Aikman, who has given the fine collection of butterflies and other insects, worth nearly £2,000, to the Accrington Museum, is a daughter of the late Robert Hargreaves, of Bank House, Accrington, the first chairman of the old Accrington Local Board.

If Mrs. Robertson-Aikman did live at Oak Hill when she was a girl, it would account for the great interest she has always taken in the museum, both personally and in association with Colonel Rimington, who died a few weeks ago, and from whose executors she purchased this collection, getting it at less than half its value. If I am misinformed about her residence at Oak Hill, her memories of it in her childhood and early youth, and the fact that it was her uncle's home, would perhaps be sufficient to explain her warm feeling towards the Museum. And indeed the bare facts that she is a native of Accrington and a member of the Hargreaves family might be enough to do it.

September 25th

The Mayor of Burnley, it is said, has undertaken to be one of the passengers in the new aeroplane purchased by the East Lancashire Motor and Aeroplane Co. on its first flight after reaching Burnley on October 7th. Arrangements for flights of the new aeroplane are also being made in Blackpool and other large towns in Lancashire and Yorkshire.

* * *

Accrington schoolchildren show off their entries in a plant growing competition

Last Saturday's plant-growing exhibition in the Accrington Town Hall proved that the interest in the school competitions is still keen. One could see that the successful girls and boys who received their prizes at the hands of the smiling and gracious Mayoress (Mrs Lupton) were very proud indeed.

Again Green Haworth school secured Mr. G. W. Macalpine's shield for the year. As it was pointed out, Green Haworth children have the advantage of fresher air for their plants, than is possible for competitors who live in the town, where there is smoke from the mills, etc. Mr. Cameron laughingly remarked in his speech that they would have to find a shield for Green Haworth only, as that school repeatedly won the Macalpine shield. On the whole the fair sex held their own on the prize list, though the majority of "special prizes" went to the boys. In promoting these exhibitions and thus inducing school children to take a practical interest in plant life, a very laudable object is being achieved. To instil into the heart of a child a love of the beautiful in nature is to endow him with an interest in life that will develop as he grows, and never pall.

October 2nd

Wednesday was indeed a gala day for Accringtonians. Will the youngsters ever forget the splendid time they had when Peel Park was opened? It was good to see their happy faces, and hear their joking voices raised lustily in song. They made the old Coppice ring again. Their medals, so kindly presented by Mr. and Mrs Peel, too, were a source of pride and pleasure. In fact, during the whole proceedings the children had apparently given themselves up to jollity as only the heart of a child can.

The Mayor too and Mr. Cameron will doubtless treasure the gold medals presented to them as souvenirs of the event. Nobody appeared to know the source whence sprang these golden tokens, though, it was hinted that Mr. Newton, who in his capacity of Borough Engineer had successfully engineered several things connected with the day's proceedings, could solve the mystery of the medals if he chose.

As I gazed on the good natured faces of the councillors and officials grouped round the Peel Memorial on Wednesday, I could not help wondering if they had entirely forgotten their childhoods' picnics. Not one of them, apparently, remembered that the buns of their childhoods' days were all the better when washed down with coffee. Granted there were difficulties in the way of conveying coffee to the top of the hill, they are surely difficulties that might have been surmounted for the nonce. It was whispered that some of the worthy councillors were afraid of being "pulled over the coals" at the November elections for reckless extravagance in spending the ratepayers' money on refreshments for this red-letter day in the annals of Accrington's history. In fact, I am told, that had it not been for the insistence of a strong-minded member of the Corporation, in over-riding all objections, the children would have been deprived of buns also.

Dear! Dear! what a money-saving community we are becoming to be sure.

* * *

Hitherto the privilege of entering the examinations of the Royal College of Surgeons has been withheld from women; but now, if all goes well, after January next a number of women will be qualified to place M.R.C.S. after their names. This is another step in the right direction.

* * *

The musical programme submitted by the Misses McCullagh on Wednesday evening at the Oswaldtwistle Town Hall, was most interesting. The four gifted sisters added considerably to the favourable impression they made in the same hall a year ago. There were several expert musical critics present at the concert who were simply charmed by the musical talent of the McCullaghs.

October 16th

Accrington has just effected one very small but all the same useful public improvement, In the lanterns of the street lamps in the main thoroughfares have been placed little transparencies, so arranged as to indicate the name of the street at the top of which each particular lamp-pillar stands. So that instead of having to wander about making sundry inquiries for the particular street he or she is seeking the stranger finds the task much simplified by the name of each street being clearly displayed upon the street lamp. The idea was well worth adopting.

* * *

October 23rd

It is rather unaccountable that the school girls of Accrington take more kindly and keenly to nature study than the boys. At the prize distribution by the Mayoress on Saturday night there were 46 awards for girls and only 25 for boys. The first prizes (three) were all won by girls. Of the seven seconds only one was obtained by a boy. Even of the thirds (eleven) the girl winners outnumbered those of the other sex by two or three. Last year the disproportion was not so great, 17 awards going to boys and 25 to girls. On that occasion the then Mayor, Alderman Higham, tried to rally the lads out of their comparative apathy, but evidently without success. The present Mayor tried it again this time. He advised the boys to "buck up," and endeavour to do at least as well as the girls. Possibly the lads consider the study too slow, and certainly most of them would vote nature study as not to be compared with cricket on a Saturday afternoon in summer. Besides, the average girl of twelve or thirteen is in the matter of mental and physical development more advanced than the average boy of the same age.

October 30th

The Mayoress of Accrington (Mrs. Lupton) held her last "At home" at the Town Hall yesterday. There was a large and representative attendance, the ladies especially mustering to some purpose. Regret in parting with this year's Mayoress, who has so ably and so kindly discharged the duties allotted to her as the wife of the Chief Magistrate, is inevitable. She, no doubt, will be somewhat relieved to be freed from the many tasks devolving on a Mayoress. The visits, the bazaar openings, the prize distributions, and all the paraphernalia of office must be rather wearisome at times. One can imagine that Mrs. Lupton has often felt that she would much rather stay quietly at home, or in her country cottage at Grindleton, when she has been called upon to appear at some function. Some of us are so apt to forget that a Mayoress is only human after all, and that it requires an amiable and self-sacrificing nature to answer all the calls with gracious mien and smiling face.

* * *

Madame Ada Crossley, the famous contralto, who has just completed a successful tour in Australia, her native land, will appear at the Accrington Town Hall on Wednesday, November 10th. She is not unknown to Accringtonians, for once or twice she has taken a principal part in the Choral concerts here. The concert party she brings is a good one. Miss Edith Evans is quite a favourite locally. She has appeared in Accrington previously at both Choral and Cunliffe concerts.

November 6th

Excitement among young boys and girls reached its zenith yesterday. The glorious "fifth," with its bonfires and fireworks, came at last. For weeks back the youngsters have dragged along every available material that could possibly act as fuel to the blaze. The children dance round the glowing pile, with their mouths stuffed with candy, or roasted potato, or both, while with eager eyes they trace the soaring rocket in its flight, or watch the "pin-wheel" whirl its short vivid life away, nailed to an outhouse door. The years seem many since like joys satisfied us. Do you remember the days, fair reader, when your school satchel was turned into a hamper for fireworks, when your complexion was as naught compared with your first essay into the realms of cookery, the joy of toasting your own potatoes in the bonfire, and eating "the charred-looking objects afterwards; when all the mothers on the terrace "did themselves proud" in the matter of toffy-making, and toffy-giving?

* * *

The impression stamped on one's mind during the Cunliffe concert on Wednesday evening, was that the orchestral contributions would have been improved had some of the passages been more subdued. One likes to hear the full volume of the band at times, but to hear it all the time becomes wearisome. With the exception of the third movement from Luigini's "Russian Ballet," and the opening bars of "The Merry Wives of Windsor," the nuances of expression were of minor consideration. Mr. Hanson, the conductor, is to be complimented on his good work in connection with the band. It wasn't his fault that at times sections of the orchestra failed to grasp the meaning of his raised hand, and eloquent s-s-sh!

The suggestions foregoing are offered in the most kindly spirit. I am among those who think well of the Cunliffe Orchestra, and I am very wishful that every section should strive to still higher standard. The instrumentalists must not feel discouraged because they are reminded of a few blemishes; rather they must be determined that at succeeding concerts these little defects shall be removed.

* * *

Not all the interest was confined to the platform on Wednesday, for Mr. Harold Baker, the prospective Liberal candidate, made his first plunge into the public social life of our little town, in the company of Mr. W. Haworth. Under the circumstances a little curiosity and interest were pardonable, though the interest from the feminine section of the audience was not wholly political.

November 13th

Mr. Johnson's concert party gave us a very pleasurable evening in the Town Hall on Wednesday. If only for the superb singing of Mr. John Harrison it was a night to be remembered.

Madame Ada Crossley was not in her usual voice. Her finished style of singing is always acceptable, however, and her songs gave much pleasures."L'Heureux Vagabond " (Bruneau) was good, but the exceptional beauty of her singing of the sotto voce passages in Brahms' "Sandmannchen" was as charming as it was perfect, and richly earned the applause accorded. It was a great treat.

* * *

The concert in aid of the Accrington and District Institution for the Blind attracted a fairly good audience to the Town Hall on Monday night. We are told that the artistes themselves would be the first to resent any pity for their blindness. Nevertheless, one cannot help feeling how terrible it must be to be deprived of the great gift of sight. Many of them could give us points in cheerfulness, however, and as the Mayor said in his speech, "they know how to enjoy themselves right well." You never see Mr. John Ingham, who has done so much for the cause, for instance with a gloomy face. Whenever you meet "Blind John" his face is like sunshine. One realised as Mr. Wostenholme played piece after piece with great skill, how very precious music must be to the sightless. He is very clever. Mr. Fred Nolan's singing also pleased his audience, for they demanded two encores; and the accompanist, Mr. W. F. O. Preston, did well.

November 27th

A couple of women suffragists, with several allies who remained in the background throughout, attracted a large crowd on the Accrington market ground on Wednesday evening. All told there were five of them, all members of the National Women's Social and Political Union, who are at present "working" the Rossendale valley for the especial benefit of Mr. "Lulu" Harcourt. They made their descent into Accrington on Wednesday evening by car from Rawtenstall, in which town they are staying. The meeting was timed to begin at half-past seven, but the non-arrival of a lurry already engaged delayed matters, till one of the ladies, seized by inspiration perhaps, went and borrowed a chair from a Blackburn-road tobacconist. The crowd, as mentioned, was of very large proportions and some half dozen or more police constables, sergeants, and an inspector were between the crowd and the suffragists all the time. Other officers prowled about on the outskirts of the crowd.

The speaker for the evening was Mrs. Violet Jones, of Clement's Inn, London, and her chairwoman, Miss Helliwell, of Manchester.

The meeting began upon the arrival of the chair, which Miss Helliwell mounted. Miss Helliwell is a young lady of somewhat prepossessing appearance and wore a soft, green felt hat, with pheasant feather rampant, and long, loose waterproof coat of some fawn material. She opened fire by inviting the crowd to come a little closer, which was the signal for a general violent surge forward, the policemen throwing their manly selves into the contest for a little while in vain. Comparative quietude having at length been established, Miss Helliwell briefly introduced Mrs. Jones, and explained the reason of their presence in the Rossendale valley by remarking that "where Cabinet ministers are there also are the suffragettes." Mr. Harcourt, went on Miss Helliwell valiantly, had declared that so long as he was a member of the Liberal Cabinet he would never agree to the giving of the vote to women. Therefore they had to bring him to a proper frame of mind.

Mrs. Jones, a middle aged lady with iron-grey hair, began her address with. "Now friends" and was greeted with confused groans, hoots and cheers. The crowd having quietened down again, Mrs. Jones said she wanted them to understand the suffragists were there to be listened to and then to listen to questions. The vote for women on the same terms as men was only a fair and just demand, because they were only asking for what they had paid for (A voice "Hear, hear.") Continuing, Mrs Jones asserted that the Liberal Government had, always said they believed in people having what they had paid for, and yet when they were so strong that they could bring in any measure they liked, they refused to do justice to the women of the country. That was why they (the suffragists) were there asking electors to see that the Cabinet ministers returned at the next election should keep their promises (Groans.) When the women got votes the men would find they would back them up in seeing that the members returned to Parliament kept their promises. (A voice: "Hes ta done thi weshin'?" and laughter.)

Mrs. Jones continued in the same strain for some time, and at length a second rather unpleasant surge of the large crowd, which threatened to engulf the lady on her chair, occurred.

For some time Mrs. Jones appealed in vain for quietness. "Don't get hurt, friends," shouted she and appealed to those behind the crowd not to push, as there were children in front. "We don't like children to get hurt," she said. "We know what it is to be pushed about. We have experienced it. We know how people get hurt in these crushes." Here the first small stone arrived and was quickly followed by the long-expected lurry.

Mrs Jones and Miss Helliwell having climbed on to the lurry, the former went on to give an address of some length, which was heard with some attention, amid a very desultory fire of small stones, tomatoes, potatoes, etc., which fortunately all went wide of the mark.

At the conclusion of the address Mrs Jones was tackled by various questioners. "What about breaking windows ?" "What about vitriol throwing?" "Do you believe in 'adult' women horsewhipping Mr. Churchill?" "Is the method you're adopting likely to be the most successful in gaining the things you're seeking?" "Why don't you go with the Socialists for universal suffrage?" were among questions put. To one and all Mrs Jones had a ready, a lengthy and fluent reply.

At the conclusion of the meeting the suffragettes stayed chatting with Inspector Ashcroft and a number of other police officers on the Market Ground till the arrival of the nine o'clock Haslingden car, which they boarded in safety, and in which they sailed serenely back to Rawtenstall. Fifty copies of "Votes for Women"—or all the copies they had brought with them—were sold at the end of the meeting, and great was the joy of the suffragists.

December 4th

The weather was not kind to the new Mayoress of Accrington on the occasion of her first "At home" in the Town Hall, on Thursday. Until noon there was no sign of rain, but immediately afterwards a few drops furtively fell from the heavens, and by three o'clock, just as the Mayor and Mayoress were ready to receive their guests, a steady downpour was making everything out of doors look dull and dark and dreary. Doubtless many ladies garbed in delicate toilettes, with be-feathered hats, resolved at the last minute to remain at home. But a crowd of people, mainly ladies, braved the elements and the possible disaster to finery en route to the Town Hall. The assembly room with its plants, carpets, and little

The 1909 Mayor, Alderman Thomas Edward Nuttall

afternoon tea tables spread with dainty fare, looked particularly inviting after the cold and wet outside. The Mayor and Mayoress (Alderman and Mrs. Nuttall) stood just inside the doorway of the assembly-room receiving and welcoming with a handshake and a smile every arrival.

December 11th

That the numerous difficulties in the production of a comic opera like "Tom Jones" are not insurmountable our amateurs have proved beyond a doubt. Some of us gasped with astonishment when the idea of performing such an opera was first mooted. "Can they possibly do it?" was the question heard on all sides. They can, and have done it, and done it well. Each night has witnessed improvements in one character and another, and the climax will be reached to-night.

The request that patrons should wear evening dress at the Hippodrome on Wednesday, Thursday and Friday evenings has caused more comment than the gentlemen who innocently penned the notice would deem possible. It was received by the people of Accrington in various ways. In some quarters the intimation was regarded—very foolishly—as more or less of an insult. One lady remarked as she read it, "'Humph I've gone to every performance given by the Amateurs since "Les Cloches de Corneville", but I never yet thought it necessary to be told what to put on." Another young lady said, "Oh, how nice; then I can give my lace evening gown another turn, and wear my new gold head-dress." Several gentlemen objected on the score of "changing to an evening suit being an awful fag." Still another gentleman was heard asking an Accringtonian, "Say, old chap, what's your 'dress' night at the opera because that's the night I'm not "going?" Again some who had booked for other nights resented the distinction that one night should be more "classy" than another, as all the patrons and subscribers paid the same price for tickets. It has been a regular storm-in-a- teacup, and the wisest people of all have been those who pleased themselves in the matter of dress without any questioning or heart-burning. The desire of the originators of this innovation locally was, no doubt, to see the auditorium as beautiful and well-dressed as the stage. From a picturesque point of view the idea was excellent. And, as I have heard a member of the committee say, some of the men who object to evening dress in Accrington would not dream of going to a theatre in another town in any other dress.

December 18th

Trade may be bad and dividends low but however gloomy the outlook we shall all happily have some Christmas presents to buy. Some of us may grumble, and declare that present giving is a tax, and that we cannot afford to buy gifts, but we shall give them all the same. The spirit of Christmas is irresistible and who would have it otherwise?

December 25th

Yet once again it is my pleasure and privilege to wish Observerites everywhere "A Merry Christmas." May health, happiness and plenty abound in every home.
When Wednesday's early morning blizzard had done its worst and we were wallowing boot-top deep in slushy snow, we began to realise that "a real old-fashioned Christmas" might after all have its drawbacks as well as it's delights, and I don't think most of us were in the least sorry when that double-quick thaw set in and carried off with wonderful celerity the evidences of one of the heaviest downfalls of recent years. Snowy Christmas is all very well, but there are limits.
Before Wednesday morning's icy bombardment Sunday's storm paled into insignificance. Such a scene as met the eye in the early hours of Wednesday has not been encountered for many a long day, nor will a good many people want to repeat

the experience for many a long day to come. I know of instances where girl and women factory operatives living in the more exposed parts of the town pluckily turned out with the intention of getting to work at the usual hour, but after an unequal contest against the beating snow, the piercing wind, and the great drifts that faced the pedestrian like an impassable barrier, they had to turn back home, chilled, dispirited and soaked with the icy mixture. Worse still was the plight of those snowed up on the road or on the railway. There were some lively tramcar experiences, and the railway provided incidents of the storm in plenty. It was nearly noon when passengers who had set out to travel by the early morning trains from Burnley reached Accrington, and then they had had to travel round by Blackburn. Trains became stuck fast in the snow in almost every direction, and the railway officials were afforded a most unenviable task. Farmers had to dig their way through the great drifts, and some never got to town with their milk at all. And one sincerely pitied the plight of those who had to tramp about among it all day long—the postmen, the policemen and all the other people whose occupation takes them out of doors. No wonder we were all thankful for the rain and the rapid thaw.

December 31st

The improved atmospheric conditions of Christmas Eve gave a great impetus to shopping and made the hearts of the traders glad. The business outlook up to past the middle of the week was not by any means bright, but Friday made up for much of the leeway. A curious state of affairs was developed with regard to that special article of Christmas fare, the turkey. The previous week Irish turkeys were selling on the farms at elevenpence a pound, and very few foreign birds were reaching the market. In consequence the stocks were being held back, in expectation of last year's high prices being touched again, and at the beginning of last week it appeared quite probable this would happen.

But the frosts and snows of the first half of Christmas week interfered with buying, though the retail price was still kept up to at least a shilling a pound. When the almost spring-like mildness of Thursday, and especially of Friday, came it was recognised that the birds must be got on the market at any price. Consequently in Manchester on Christmas Eve the choicest English and Irish turkeys were sold at eight-pence halfpenny a pound, while the inferior Continental sorts were hardly saleable at sixpence. This affected, of course, every other section of the poultry market, and prices all round were extremely low, with supplies a good deal more than equal to requirements. The worst of it is that country town's like those in East Lancashire practically never get the advantage of these collapses in prices, which always take place too late to have the birds distributed, and after the dealers have got their stocks. Prime turkeys were sold in the Accrington, Blackburn, or Burnley districts up to last Friday evening at 1s. 2d. a pound.

1910

January 1st

A Happy New Year to you all, kind readers! May health and happiness be yours in abundance during 1910. In the industrial sense, at least, we are looking to 1910 to afford us a measure of prosperity which the year just gone denied to Lancashire and its cotton trade, and, it follows, to many kindred industries also. May all our best anticipations be realised!

* * *

Christmastide appeared and brought in its train the usual, festivities, and a wealth of "tips". Both joys are inseparable from the season. "Pay up and look cheerful," would be an excellent motto for Christmas time. It would be interesting to know how much money some small boys have received in "tips" this last fortnight.

Every parcel delivered by a tradesman's boy, be he confectioner, draper, tailor, or boot-maker, or any other maker in embryo, a tip is expected, and generally received on delivery. One has to be very "thick skinned" indeed not to see the obvious hesitation of the parcels' boy who is waiting for his tip, regardless of the fact that he is probably the twentieth pensioner of the day. But even this is preferable to the lad who without the slightest claim on one's generosity for services rendered during the past year, unblushingly hands to you a book in which you find the request for a Christmas box. One such was handed in to me last week. On enquiry I found that this boy came from an establishment where I had never previously purchased anything. One wonders if many of the firms know of this wholesale "trading" on the customers. It is a pleasure to give to those who really have contributed some little duty in the past, but for a boy to demand a donation on his first visit is surely the limit.

January 8th

New Year's day would for a good many Accringtonians have something lacking were they by any unlucky chance to be denied the pleasure and privilege of seeing the dramatic performance given annually on the first day of the new year by that talented little band of local Amateurs at Prince's Theatre. Excellent as is the primary object —to benefit the funds of the Victoria Hospital—these New Year s Day performances have also a value over and above that expressed in mere monetary results. With a confidence borne of past experience we know when we book our seats for "The Amateurs" that we are to have a most excellent afternoon's entertainment. And never in all their nine plays have our Amateurs failed to meet the fullest measure of our anticipations.

This year it was "All-of-a-sudden Peggy" they gave, and never did they make a better or more popular choice of play.

* * *

January 29th

One is not sorry that the excitement of political warfare has subsided locally. The comparatively quiet aftermath is infinitely preferable to the strife—in many quarters, very bitter strife—which obtained during election week, and for many weeks previous.

A disagreeable feature of the election most manifest on the polling days was the utter lack of restraint exercised by some ladies. I came across several groups of ladies who were discussing the political question in loud, excited tones, and wearing party colours, on the afternoon of the election. They even waved small banners and cheered passing motor cars if they sported the approved colours, and sang snatches of election songs. They were "ladies," too, of some social standing in our little community, from whom one naturally expected decorous behaviour. When one sees ladies throwing reserve entirely to the winds in this fashion one feels less respect for the sex.

* * *

The best of good wishes to Mr. and Mrs. (Miss Bessie Moore) Phil Broadley, who were married at the Church of the Sacred Heart, Accrington, on Wednesday. The wedding was a very pretty one. The bride, attired in ivory satin, with a train several yards long, looked very striking as she walked down the aisle.

In attendance were Miss Lily Kirkman Miss Hannah Higham, and Miss Phyllis Broadley.

February 5th

I must not forget to pay a well-deserved tribute to those who had to arrange for the clearing of our streets after the heavy snowfall last week. Compared with other towns round about Accrington, our streets were cleared of snow with surprising celerity. An organised scheme of labour for men and horses was required before this feat was successfully accomplished. It was well and quickly done. In my jouneyings this week I have encountered snow—which in many country districts still lies several feet deep—in such quantities that it was a relief to come back to a place where the head of affairs had contrived to annul the unpleasantness of walking out of doors.

February 12th

Long speeches were not the order of the day at the opening of the Liberal bazaar on Wednesday. Lord Lucas, the chairman Mr. Baker, M.P., and the other speakers were commendably brief.

Personally, I do not see any reason why the gentlemen should monopolise the platform, as they did on Wednesday, and again on Thursday. Quite apart from the fact that the ladies have done the lion's share of the work in connection with the bazaar, there is the decorative aspect to think of. How much prettier Thursday's platform would have been, for instance, if the Mayoress had accompanied the Mayor; Miss Haworth had been seated by Mr. Haworth; Mrs. A. Bury with her husband, Mrs. J. H. Lupton alongside Mr. Lupton, and so on. Gentlemen, one thinks you have been rather remiss in your platform arrangement this time!

February 19th

Wednesday's Cunliffe Concert was a great success. In general tone and accuracy the orchestra has greatly improved during the last year or two. If they continue to improve as much in the next few years, Accrington will be very proud indeed of the Cunliffe orchestra, which we must not forget was founded by him whose name it still bears. Mr. Hanson as wielder of the baton is doing splendid work. He has not always the command of the orchestra one would like perhaps, but considering all things he does very well, and certainly works, hard.

February 26th

There was a gratifyingly large attendance—mostly ladies—at the opening of the first day proceedings in connection with the sale of work at Huncoat Wesleyan School on Wednesday afternoon. The proceeds are to go towards the "fund" for defraying the cost of a new organ for use in the chapel and also for alterations in the interior of the edifice. The affair on Wednesday was favoured with splendid weather. By hard work extending over a year the ladies connected with the place have, by holding sewing meetings, etc., done much to make the affair a success.

March 5th

The annual meeting of the Accrington and District Branch of the National Society for the Prevention of Cruelty to Children, held in the Town Hall on Wednesday afternoon, was quite a nice affair. Many ladies were present, and a few gentlemen.
The care of children is essentially a woman's interest, both in a private and public capacity. In the nineteen years since the Accrington Branch of the Society was formed—the Society has just entered on its twentieth year's work—many cases of neglect have been investigated; to be exact 2,500 cases affecting upwards of 6,500 children in Accrington district. It seems incredible that in these advanced days mothers still neglect, or are callous of the well-being of their offspring. But such unfortunately is the case, as the detailed report of the Society's work in recent years too plainly proves.

March 12th

Queer sounds issued from the garden last week, followed by violent peals at the hall door bell. On investigating matters I discovered a crowd of youngsters tricked out in funny garments howling some music hall ditty to the strains of tin whistles and tambourines. One small boy, evidently a leader of the band, stepped forward and presented his tambourine. He had a boy-scout hat with a Chanticler feather arrangement at the side, perched above a blackened face, a fancy vest, sash and skirt—supposed to be a kilt evidently. Another youngster was attired in a girl's pinafore, and hat with blue ribbons. The rest of the party also wore curious clothes, "We're seggers," piped the voice of the leader. In mystification I wondered what "seggers" were, and waited. "We're pay-seggers" they chimed in chorus. I tendered a few coppers in the tambourine, and found that my guess was correct. They were certainly, to put it in vulgar parlance, "out on the make," for as the band turned away questions of "Heaw much?" and "Wod's ta' getten?" were plainly audible. This is essentially a money-making age, even the small fry seem to have acute business capabilities, entirely misapplied, but still there.

March 19th

As I sat in the stalls at the Hippodrome one night this week, watching the performance, of "The Silver King," I began to wonder what magic there could be in Accrington that so much histrionic talent should flourish here. It was prophesied when the Garrick Society was first thought of that there was absolutely no opening for it in Accrington, as the other amateur societies, already in good working order, absorbed all public interest locally. This week has proved that prophecy quite wrong. People are apparently just as keen to see "The Silver King" as they were to hear "Tom Jones" and "All-of-a-sudden Peggy" earlier this winter. It is said that we in Accrington hold a record for successful bazaars; the same may be said with equal truth of plays and players.

April 2nd

From a musical standpoint Wednesday's Choral concert was disappointing. Great expectations centred round the engagement of Mr. Francis Harford, but his singing of the baritone passages was one of the keenest disappointments of the evening. It was said that Mr. Harford was suffering from a wretched cold—principals often are at Accrington concerts—and this, no doubt, accounted in some measure for his disappointing singing, for he was manifestly working under difficulties. Even apart from the bad cold, it was apparent that this arrangement of "Hiawatha" was in much too high a key for his range of voice. He shirked the F in the closing bar of "Love is all Iago tells us," etc, and once or twice besides substituted lower notes than those of the score. His voice occasionally "broke" in a way that must have been as annoying to himself, as it was surprising to other people. It is to be hoped that Mr. Harford will come again to Accrington in the near future, to wipe out the altogether wrong impression formed by some people of his voice and ability on Wednesday. Although young, Mr. Harford has made a name for himself in the musical world, and one would really like to hear him at his best here.

Miss Ethel Wood worked hard to make the soprano part a success. She sang the most exacting passages with confidence, moderately good tone, and intense dramatic power. "Spring has come with all its splendour" was beautifully delivered.

Mr. Anderson Nichol did not give an inspiring interpretation of "Onaway, awake beloved." This, one feels to be an unpardonable omission on the part of a tenor who sings "Hiawatha," for it is the predominant gem of the whole composition. Later he was more successful, but never artistically perfect.

"Sing to us, O Chibiabos" was tastefully given by the choir. It was expressive, and beautifully modulated. The chorus singing was more faulty than usual in the matter of attack. Several times the choir were quite half a beat behind in taking up the phrases. They did not interpret the quieter passages properly, either. For this, a musical friend of mine who is a member of the choir assured me, the instrumentalists were to blame. "Who can sing pianissimo parts properly, when the band is determined to play fortissimo?" As it was, the ends of many phrases were lost behind the wall of sound raised by the players. Strange to say, when the choir were not singing the music of the band was more subdued; the advent of any chorus work seemed to be the signal for unrestrained ardour on the part of the instrumentalists. It was a great pity to thus minimise the results of months of rehearsal by the choir, under their capable instructor, Mr. W. S. Walker.

April 9th

People from the South say truly that Lancashire has no equal for successful bazaars. And Accrington heads the list, even in Lancashire, The "May flower" Bazaar, which is now having a five days run at the Accrington Town Hall, is no exception to the golden rule. On Wednesday, the opening day, the proceeds amounted to nearly £2,000. It really is wonderful in these days of bad trade where all the money comes from. There seems little doubt that before the bazaar closes next Monday evening the workers will have succeeded in raising the desired £3,500.

April 23rd

This is a proud week, indeed, for the lady Guardians of Pike Law. At Wednesday's meeting of the Haslingden Board of Guardians, Miss Higham, of Accrington, was appointed the first lady chairman of the Board, and Mrs. Mountain, of Bacup, became vice-chairman. For two ladies to hold office as chairman and vice-chairman at the same time is, I should imagine, unique in Poor Law annals throughout the country. May the two ladies enjoy good health during their term of office!

April 30th

The coming Shopping Festival for Accrington is sure to have great attractions for the ladies. Especially will this be so in relation to the establishments of drapers, milliners, jewellers, and high-class grocers, but there are few shops of any kind in which ladies do not take an interest. There will certainly be plenty to please the eye and claim the attention during the Festival, which begins with Saturday, 4th June, and ends with the 11th, so that there are two Saturdays in it. Prizes are to be offered for the best window displays. These include a special prize, which takes the form of a shield, given by the "Observer and Times." Four prizes, from £2 downwards, are to be divided among the public for the best forecasts of the judges decisions as to the window shows. Each elementary school in the borough will have two prizes allotted to its children for the best essays on the subject of Accrington shops. In addition, a special prize is to be provided for the best essay from scholars residing either in or outside Accrington.

May 7th

The news coming through from London late last night concerning the illness of the King was of the gravest description.
The later bulletins indicated that the condition of His Majesty had grown still more serious, and the news could scarcely have been less hopeful.
The Prince and Princess of Wales and the whole of the members of the Royal Family were in attendance at Buckingham Palace, and the Attorney General and Home Secretary received hasty summonses to the Palace.
At 11 p.m. the message came through: "His Majesty's condition is extremely critical."
Later: His Majesty passed away shortly after midnight.

May 14th

"The King is dead." Which of us that did not feel a thrill of deep emotion, a sense of personal loss, a feeling that something material alike to our individual well-being and our sense of national security had passed out of our lives when we heard or read those four short words, so simple, yet of such vast import to the nation, to the Empire, to the world? Some of us had been keeping vigil far into the night waiting, 'twixt hopes and fears, for every fresh scrap of news from that Royal Palace in London upon which the mental gaze of the whole world was centred. And then as the climax to a night of waiting that will long be remembered, there came over the wires those four direful words, so brief, so highly tragic in the message they brought—"The King is dead."
That phase of this great loss with which the nation finds itself confronted struck me forcibly on Sunday, when in three different churches, all of them widely divergent in creed and in thought, I heard in three different parts of the day heartfelt eulogies of the mighty dead, and afterwards stood there while in grandly solemn tones the organ pealed forth that haunting, awesome tribute to him from whose worthy hand the sceptre has fallen, the Dead March in "Saul." Here at least, thought I, over the dead body of its King, is a united people, of one mind, of one voice, of one purpose. Volumes could not say more for him who is gone; and there is in it, too, I think,

much hope for the future. England is as sound and loyal and steadfast and true and patriotic to-day as ever she was. This great unbaring of the national heart shows it so. There was a strange sense of the new, the unaccustomed, a feeling that one had suddenly stepped into another epoch, as on Sunday one heard the clergyman of the Church of England offer his prayer for "George, our King, the Queen, the Queen Dowager Alexandra, and all the Royal Family." How strangely the unfamiliar words fell upon the listening ear. And appealing to the senses and the emotions in another way were the muffled peals of the church bells. How solemn the sound; how mournful the tale they had to tell!

* * *

The King's death has such far-reaching effects that to many tradespeople will spell financial disaster. Even in Accrington it has been considered wise to postpone the shopping festival arranged for June, until October, on account of the mourning period. What must it mean to the big shops in London and in the big cities? It may only be that grey, mauve, or black and white will be substituted for the brighter colours of summer finery, but this will make a tremendous difference to shopkeepers who have laid in a stock of pink, blue, yellow, green and red materials. The loss to trade, especially in the City, is bound to be enormous. Many of the big firms are, of course, insured against loss by the death of a monarch, but this is by no means general.

* * *

It has been touching this week to observe the little tributes to the dead King in the shape of clothing. Gentlemen have with common consent donned mourning in one form or another. Those who had no black suits, or did not choose to put them on, have worn black ties, and in some cases black gloves, and some had mourning bands on their shiny hats going to church on Sunday. Ladies have not the same opportunity of changing their attire so quickly, which perhaps is just as well, all things considered. Many of them, though, wore a touch of black, either a black hat, or a bow of black ribbon, to show their loyalty to the dead King. Black hats trimmed with flowers have been fashionable lately, and it was an easy matter to substitute ribbon or black feathers for the flowers. Some form of mourning will be adopted generally for some days to come.

* * *

To me the most surprising feature of the proclamation on the Market Ground, on Monday evening, was the apparently apathetic manner of many of the men in the vast crowd. A large number of them never even took the trouble to doff their hats. Of course this may have been due to ignorance of what was expected, but Lancashire men as a rule are not slow in the "uptak," and the fact that the public men on the platform had all removed their hats should have been indication enough to the bystanders. Preceding the Mayor's proclamation speech in a neighbouring town a voice from the platform was heard commanding "All hats off." Evidently in that borough they were taking no risks. We in Accrington are by no means disloyal, and the fact that hats were not removed should perhaps not be taken altogether as a sign of indifference, for many of the offenders against good form in this way wore black ties or other signs of mourning. Also the people who rush home from work, wash, dress, have tea, and are down town ready to listen to the proclamation in a drizzling

The Mayor of Accrington, Alderman Thomas Nuttall, proclaims King George V as King

rain, have not earned the title "indifferent."

"Knowing so well the feelings of my beloved father, I am sure that it would be contrary to his wishes if there were any interruption in the enjoyment of the public during the Whitsuntide holiday. I, therefore, hope that the general mourning will not prevent my people from taking the usual advantages of the various opportunities afforded them for rest, relaxation, and amusement in the coming days."

Such is the generous and thoughtful message given to the nation this week by His Majesty King George. Friday next, the day of the funeral, stands out, of course, as one apart from the rest. Friday is to be observed as a day of national mourning with, as far as possible, a complete cessation from work. It follows that not only will all the local industrial concerns be closed on that day, but, the tradespeople will close their establishments also.

* * *

This closing of mills and workshops on the day of the King's funeral has brought about, in very many cases, a re-arrangement of the Whitsuntide holidays. Messrs. Howard and Bullough, for instance, instead of stopping for Whit-Monday and Tuesday, will close Monday only, and will work Tuesday, stopping again on Thursday night until the following Monday morning. At Messrs. Steiner's works Whit Monday, with Friday and Saturday, are the days on which the works are to be closed, and this arrangement will also apply to many of the cotton mills in Accrington

and district. Broad Oak Works are closed to-day and Whit-Monday, and will again
stop for Friday and Saturday.

* * *

All the trees are wearing their first fresh suits of green, and the spring flowers are in,
full glory. Even the less endowed among us have these pleasures within easy reach,
for the country beyond Whalley just now is very beautiful, and well worth a long
walk to see. It is pleasant, at this season of the year, to stretch our limbs and expand
our lungs on the top of Pendle, or that easier vantage ground Waddington Fell, or to
see the wealth of primroses and cowslips, with their more humble sisters beloved of
the children, the daisies and buttercups, alongside the gleaming river at Brungerley
Bridge; one can almost smell the wood violets and bluebells at Hodder and sniff the
breeze on the top of Kemple End, where it is possible to get such a magnificent
panoramic view of the surrounding country. Oh! Yes. We in Accrington are
fortunate indeed in having so much beautiful country to explore at our very doors, so
to speak. None of us need grumble that there is nowhere to go and nothing to do this
Whitsuntide; if only the sun will shine on our holiday plans.

May 21st

Accrington and district yesterday worthily sustained its part in the memorable
national requiem over the body of "Edward the Peacemaker." It was a day
observed as one of public mourning, and associated with it were scenes and incidents
that will live long in the memories of many who witnessed them. Loom and spindle,
lathe and chisel, all were silenced in token of the great and mournful event of the day.
Shops closed their doors, and drew down their blinds, unwilling to desecrate the day
of the dead King's funeral by trade and barter, and even on the railways the service
was reduced to well nigh the lowest possible minimum, the trains running only at
lengthened intervals.

It was surprising, and was a supreme testimony to the affection his people bore their
King to find that practically every one among the great masses of people one met in
the streets displayed some outward token and semblance of mourning. Very many
were clad in black from head to foot, others wore merely a tie of black or purple, but
in greater or less degree the subdued colours associated with death and mourning
were everywhere. It seemed strange to see all those thousands of people "on holiday"
out in the warmth of the beautiful sunshine, and yet keeping themselves under a
marked and unmistakable restraint. It was truly a great day of national mourning.

* * *

The slowly moving and well ordered procession from the Accrington Town Hall to
St. James' Church at noon was watched by thousands of spectators. In it joined the
Mayor, Magistrates, members of the Town Council, Board of Guardians, Officials,
Police, Fire Brigade, Boy Scouts, and very many townspeople who wished to thus
associate themselves with the official visit to the State church. One disappointment

for very many among the great crowds of onlookers there was—nobody seemed to know beforehand the route of procession, and thousands of people had taken up a position in streets which the processionists never traversed at all, and to catch even a glimpse they had to hurry to some vantage point. It would have been much better could the townspeople have known exactly the way that was to be taken. In the Church the solemn and sacred proceedings were marked by a reverence, and impressiveness most fitting to the occasion.

May 28th

Tradesmen will be grateful for the curtailment of the period of general mourning. The King has considerably modified the original order for mourning. Full mourning has to continue until Friday, June 17th, and half-mourning onward until June 30th. Assuredly a very sensible amendment, for many ladies who consider any infringement of a Royal command a form of disloyalty. On the other hand many people whose dress allowance permits only of one or two outfits per year, having adopted mourning, will now be obliged to wear black until the end of the summer season. I think I may safely claim to be as loyal as most folk, but to be continually meeting ladies attired in deep mourning is depressing. There is no doubt that, colour affects the mind, so it is probable we should all have been a most serious people before the end of the summer had the first Imperial mandate held good. One feels sure that King Edward would have been the last to uphold a scheme for many months of mourning by which many tradespeople would suffer. One can be really loyal at heart without going about for a whole summer in funeral garb.

June 11th

Quite one of the latest ideas is to have electric lights fixed in the doors of wardrobes and hanging cupboards. As the doors open and close, the lights switch on and off automatically. It looks as if the family skeleton by and by will have no gloomy abode wherein to dwell.

June 18th

The birth of triplets in a family so well known is such an unusual event that it would be almost unpardonable were I to fail to chronicle the fact that Mrs. Hubert Blake (Whalley-road), presented her husband with three fine boys on Wednesday morning. Mr. and Mrs. Blake have received numerous congratulations, and it is safe to say that they have been in the thoughts of all Accrington this week. The latest report I had was that mother and children were well.

June 25th

Thousands of people turned out to view the crowning of the Rose Queen at Dunkenhalgh last Saturday. It was a gloriously fine day for the ceremony, and everything went swimmingly. The Rose Queen, Miss Margaret Foster, looked very sweet in her soft white eolienne dress, with its Court train of purple velvet. Her twelve attendant maids of honour and pages also looked charming in their festive attire.

July 2nd

The woman before the Accrington magistrates the other day, whom the Chief Constable described as "a perfect nuisance," is a type of her class. She had been out of gaol only about two days when again locked up, for drunkenness. Over twenty times has she been before the Blackburn and Accrington justices, and came out of an Inebriates' Home not long ago, after three years' detention. Her case, like those of many others, proves how little use such institutions are for the reform of drunkards. Some medical men will tell you they never knew a case of a habitual woman drunkard being cured. Personally, I know of one only, and she was a young woman who got into the hands of the Salvation Army.

* * *

How delightful Miss Higham's treat to the elderly women inmates of the Workhouse must have appeared to them is suggested by the exclamation of one of them, who said she thought she would never again have such a pleasant outing and entertainment. Miss Higham is not one who does things in a half-hearted way, as the women found by her hospitality. That tea will live in the old creatures' memory. The nice things they had at it, the beautiful surroundings, following the stroll in Oak Hill Park, decked out in all its summer loveliness, with the charming weather to grace it all, must have seemed in their eyes like another world in comparison with the environment of the workhouse. Like many another kindly person in a position to confer favours, Miss Higham doubtless felt how much sweeter it is to make others happy than to minister to merely selfish pleasure.

* * *

One of the outdoor events slightly marred by bad weather was the cricket match on the Accrington ground on Wednesday, Gentlemen versus Police. One member of the Force made a splendid score, and, indeed, taking them all round, the Police were a capable lot. Several of the "Gentlemen" went and returned from the wickets quickly, looking rather crestfallen, and holding limply the bat that should have hit the ball — and didn't. The poor show they made only goes to prove that a college cap and cricket "get-up" do not make a cricketer, without training.

It was rather cold for spectators on the pavilion, and one felt that it was unkind of the Weather Clerk to send a chill November day in lieu of the glorious June weather hoped for. It is quite impossible to feel completely happy watching a cricket match with teeth chattering with cold, and a nose getting bluer every minute.

Mrs. James Carter, who for several years now has been at the head of the tea department, had not an easy task on Wednesday. She overcame the difficulties, though, and with her little band of helpers came successfully through the ordeal of supplying tea to a large number of people who, apparently, wanted it all at one time. Soon after six o'clock the match ended, in the Police's favour, the strawberries were all sold, and the last cup of tea disposed of. Next year we hope the weather will be more ideal

July 9th

The full debate at the monthly meeting of the Accrington Town Council on Monday supplied most interesting reading. Whether the debate will have the desired result of ensuring a softening of the water from Altham is quite another matter. Monday was a day when a woman councillor who was also a housewife would have been useful. However, Mr. Barlow was not a bad substitute. He drew a pathetic and quite truthful picture of a family of girls and their mother washing their pretty summer frocks with the hard water.

Mr. James Whittaker, in his speech, enlarged upon the evil smell of the water, and argued that water that wouldn't wash was not fit for either cooking or drinking. Messrs. Langham, Waddington, Higham, Lupton, Bury and Dr. Bolton also supported the resolution moved by Mr. Barlow that "the Gas and Water Board be urged to put down plant or take such other steps as may be necessary for softening the hard water pumped from the Altham Works." Mr. Cameron likened the purity of the water to mountain dew. Mountain dew may be excellent, but if it is anything like the water it is not good enough for washing or drinking, and we have no use for it. Perhaps it was a dew Mr. Cameron intended to take the place of oil on troubled waters, but it didn't calm the storm.

July 16th

I was especially glad to see a fine day on Wednesday, if only because of the motor trip thirty-three of Accrington's crippled children were afforded—thanks to the kindly feeling and sympathy which prompted so many local motorists to place their cars at the disposal of the Mayor and those who organised the outing. Fine weather meant so much to the little crippled ones, who are not likely to forget in a hurry the glories of gliding through the country all the way to Blackpool and back in a motor car, and being entertained to a scrumptious tea at St. Annes in the bargain. Why, there's scarcely a youngster in Accrington who would not envy the little guests at Wednesday's motor trip. It's not everybody has ridden in a motor car.

* * *

It was good to see Wednesday's blazing sunshine, too, for the sake of "Bobby" Riley, an old Enfield cricketer, who, with ill health to add to his trials, has encountered more than his share of "the slings and arrows of outrageous fortune." On the Enfield ground on Wednesday local cricketers foregathered to play a benefit match for "Bobby," and if for nothing else the game was noteworthy from the fact that it brought out of his retirement Mr. Tom Lancaster, who, albeit he had never previously handled bat or ball this season, demonstrated that his hand had not lost its cunning by doing the "hat trick," and getting seven wickets for 47 runs. No wonder the Enfielders sigh for the return of their old favourite.

July 23rd

At the Hippodrome, Accrington, a matinee was held on Wednesday afternoon of a rather unusual type, all the artistes being amateurs desirous of demonstrating their abilities to entertain and amuse. There was a large entry, the programme containing 34 turns, of which about 25 were presented. There was a very large attendance, and the audience were well pleased with the quality of the afternoon's entertainment. Some of the artistes made a decidedly good impression, whilst the audience were indulgent to some of the others in allowing them to conclude. Amongst those who acquitted themselves well as vocalists were the Landli Trio from Blackburn, who proved themselves superior to many other trios travelling the country, the baritone revealing exceptional abilities in the Toreador song from "Carmen." He is the possessor of a voice of fine quality, and displayed some culture. A boy soprano, S. Worswick, of Accrington, also won approval by his rendering of a song of the type which especially appeals to music hall audiences. Four young men were billed as bass vocalists, but they were only moderate.

Jack Knowles, Accrington, proved himself a very clever and finished dancer, and compared favourably with many professionals. Geo. Warren, Accrington, surprised everybody with his first-class musical act, and Mr. Brennand, of the Arcade, played well on the bagpipes, zonophone, and bells. Donald and Belle, a Rishton couple, presented a sketch, "Scottie and Damsel," which is capable of being considerably improved. Both showed promising ability. One of the hits of the afternoon was the imitation of George Formby by Tom Cody, of Church, whose facial expressions and antics were decidedly funny. Geo. Emms, the local humorist, sang a comic song in his usual style. Robert Arthur, of Rawtenstall, played a selection on the concertina very pleasingly, and A. Lightbown, of Accrington, revealed much ability as a bone soloist.

One of the most amusing incidents was the wrestling donkey owned by a local young man and introduced by Jack Broadbent. The effort of two young men to wrestle the donkey created roars of laughter, but the attendant showed that the trick could be performed.

July 30th

Another part of the scheme of the Accrington and Church Co-operative Society for celebrating their jubilee year was fulfilled on Saturday, when young Accrington was entertained. The proceedings took the form of a procession, presentation, and field day. The procession was doubtless the largest juvenile parade that has ever passed through the streets of Accrington, the children numbering about 7,000. The adults who lined the streets wondered where they all came from as the children, ranging from about three to thirteen years of age, tripped along. The processionists were not confined to Accrington, nor to the children of members of the Co-operative Society. Five bands figured in the procession, and they were none too many, for the procession beyond a demonstration of the strength of Co-operation in Accrington, possessed few attractions. Starting from Oak-street, the route taken was Blackburn-road, King-street, Bull Bridge, Castle-street, Whalley-road, Avenue-parade, across Washington-street, and along Cobham-street, to Mr. Harrison's farm.

A section of the 7,000 processionists in the Co-operative Society celebrations

The arrangements for the enjoyment of the children on reaching the meadow were admirable, and after the processionists had filed in at the gate the scene was an animated one. Each youngster received a bun and a souvenir mug, and after partaking of coffee and buns they gave themselves over to field games. Balls and skipping- ropes were distributed, the bands in turn played spirited music, and the Society's Morris dancers displayed their graceful dances. There were shoe-blacking and spoon cleaning competitions, and keen efforts were put forth to secure the prizes. A Punch and Judy show was a source of delight to hundreds. Ice cream, fruit, sweets, etc., were obtainable, and the elder people, who were present in great force, could obtain tea in a large marquee capable of holding 600 people at once.

Ten fifty-six gallon barrels of coffee were consumed and over 7,000 buns distributed, and also the same number of mugs. Nearly 10,000 were on the field at one time, and 1,600 were served with tea, besides 300 in the tent for delegates

On the mugs, which were decorated with roses, was inscribed: " Accrington and Church Industrial Co-operative Society. Jubilee souvenir, 1910." In the middle were two clasped hands with the words "Unity is strength."

August 6th

Accrington was on Saturday night, in the very busiest hour of the busiest day of the week, visited by one of the most appalling and disastrous outbreaks of fire the town has ever known.

The scene of the tragically fatal outburst of all-devouring flame was the extensive establishment of Messrs. Williams, Limited, drapers and outfitters, whose premises in Church-street and Holme-street formed one of the attractions of the shopping centre of the town. In what seemed little more than an instant the whole of this big establishment was swept from end to end, from bottom to top, by an all-consuming and devastating fire, and when, a little past midnight, search was made amid the rain and wreckage, there, closely huddled together in a tiny room at the rear of the premises lay buried neath the still smouldering debris the dead bodies of five women. It was a discovery to send a tremor to the stoutest heart, to blanch the cheeks of men brave, strong and fearless who yet have a spark of tenderness in their make-up. In

William's Church St. Accrington. Fire July 30th 1910.

People gather to gaze on the scene of the fatal fire

many an eye there was tears.

The names of the five victims are:

Martha Glasgow (17), shop assistant, 28, Hindpool-road, Barrow-in-Furness.

Eva Roberts (27); shop assistant, Waterloo Park, Liverpool.

Alice Ion (23), shop assistant, 17, Wordsworth-terrace, Penrith.

Amelia R. Morgan (36) weaver, 42 Albert-street, Oswaldtwistle.

Mrs. Mary Martha Barnes (40), 42. Albert- street, Oswaldtwistle.

The two last-named were sisters, and were among the customers in the shop at the time of the outbreak.

* * *

The funeral of the two sisters, Mrs. Barnes and Miss Morgan, of Albert-street, Oswaldtwistle, who met their death so tragically in the great fire at Messrs.

Williams, Limited, Accrington, on Saturday evening, took place on Thursday. The sad fate of the two sisters evoked heartfelt sorrow in the district, both being very highly respected. Long before the hour of the departure of the cortege people began to assemble in the vicinity, and at New-lane Baptist church, in large numbers. The tramcars between two and three o'clock were packed with passengers, mostly women. In Albert-street and Union- road blinds were drawn.

The cortege consisted of two hearses and seven coaches, the bearers walking alongside the hearses. Prior to leaving the bereaved home, the Rev. T. B. Hainsworth, pastor of Ernest-street Baptist church, which the deceased women attended, offered prayer, and he also conducted the burial service. The gates at the entrance to the churchyard were kept locked until the interments concluded—a wise and respectful precaution.

August 13th

Pots! Pots! Pots! Many an Accrington housewife has been tremendously busy and positively happy this week spending leisure hours at the pot fair and there securing some of those tremendous bargains, the disposal of which at such ruinous prices, the despairing salesmen will tell you, is fast driving them towards the bankruptcy court and the workhouse. And yet it's astonishing how these gentlemen seem to thrive off their nightly losses. They take these ever-recurring reversals of fortune quite philosophically—after business hours. For some of these pot fair auctioneers this much shall be said— they are real artistes. Notice how tenderly and lovingly they take up a piece of crockery, how daintily they handle it and turn the full blaze of the light upon it, while they dilate in glowing periods upon its incomparable excellences, its great intrinsic value, its superlative qualities from a purely artistic and ornamental point of view. Surely there never was such crockery! Oh, yes, the pot fair holds a great fascination, and especially for the ladies. Why, some of them would rather go to the pot fair than have a week at Blackpool.

I have heard it suggested—and very heartily do I hope it is true—that within the next few weeks something is likely to be done in the direction or forming a Tree Planting Association, or some kindred organisation, for Accrington. Such a movement, once it is set on foot, ought to have the undivided approval and support of the whole town. Nothing makes a town and its surroundings so beautiful as foliage. A few thousand trees planted in and about such a town as Accrington could indeed work wonders in enhancing its beauty and attractiveness. Anyone who on a hot summer's day has walked up Manchester-road will at once have noted the sense of coolness and restfulness there is when one gains the shelter and the pleasing greenery of the overhanging trees, and Observerites will remember with what regret very many people recently regarded the uprooting of some of the trees in the lower part of the road, and will recall the efforts that were made to save the trees that yet remain.

Suppose Accrington, instead of having a mere leafy patch just here and there—and after all our trees are few and far between— could be embowered in woodland beauty. What a difference it would make to the borough and its inhabitants. How much it would add to our pleasure and perhaps even to our health, because what pleases the eye and appeals to our aesthetic tastes must be good for body as well as for mind. Why not, by a combined effort on the part of the inhabitants of the town, clothe the Coppice in that verdure which the planting of trees could impart.
Why, that alone would in time work a veritable transformation. Trees grew there once; they could be made to grow there again. And so with other parts of the town and its environs to which the public have access.
Here is a splendid work for a Tree Planting Association, or a Beautiful Accrington Society, or whatever we might choose to call it. There are, I feel confident, those in plenty who in no naggardly spirit would support such a movement.

August 20th

A well attended and successful concert in aid of the Mayor's fund for the sufferers through the fire at Messrs Williams' shop was held in the Town Hall on Wednesday evening. The Accrington Military Band, conducted by Mr. George Thornton, played selections and Mr. T. Greenwood gave a cornet solo, and Mr. J. Duckworth a clarionette solo. Turns were given by Miss Winifred Ward, Nash and Noel, from Accrington Hippodrome and Les Saldos from the Burnley Empire. Songs were rendered by Miss Janie Kenton, Mr. Harold Harwood, Master Sam Worswick and Mr. W. H. Day (humorist). Selections were also given by Church Kirk Quartette. Mr. H. O. Pickard, who was one of the accompanists, played pianoforte solos and Mr. R. Fletcher a violin solo. Other artistes were Mr. Tom Hamer and Messrs Cosgrove and Knowles and Claude Standring (dancers), Mr. C. R. Rigby (comedian), Mr. A. Lightbound (bone soloist), and Master Hugh Walmsley. The other accompanist was Mr. F. Dalloway.

August 27th

Once more we have to go away from home to learn the news:—"A representative of the 'Pall Mall Gazette' states that the impregnating of cigarettes with opium is rampant, especially, it is asserted, among the mill girls of Lancashire, who find it irresistible as a solace and means of obtaining temporary relief from the weariness and pain attendant on a life of toil." Just imagine that now! And where on earth would the mill girls get their cigarettes "impregnated with opium"? Where is the shop they sell 'em at? How are they going to proceed about the "impregnating" business, I should like to know? Fudge! The merest fudge! What terrible creatures they would have us believe the Lancashire mill lasses are. Everybody knows—certainly everybody in Lancashire—that our mill girls as a class do not smoke either cigarettes or anything else—they leave that to the exalted members of their sex, those who move in "high society."

September 10th

There's no doubt about it, the Accrington Market Shopping Festival is more than justifying itself. The promoters have every reason to be gratified with the results, so far as they have gone. The affair has given a decided fillip to shopping in the Market Hall, and has attracted hundreds of people there who in the ordinary way would never think of walking through the Market. On Saturday—at night especially—the place was crowded.

Quite the tit-bit among the Market Festival attractions is the decorated and illuminated tramcar, which comes in for unstinted admiration wherever it goes. In all it carries some 300 electric lights, most effectively arranged as to device and colour, and these and the other decorations of the car make a very pretty and striking picture indeed as the car is driven over the local tram routes. Those responsible for the adornment of the car have done their work exceedingly well. It is about as nice as anything I have ever seen in the way of a specially decorated tram car.

* * *

That was a pretty and animated scene at Oak Hill Park on Sunday afternoon, the occasion of the massed bands' Concert for the benefit of those employees of Messrs. Williams's who lost their belongings in the fire. It could scarcely have been a more beautiful day for such an event, with its bright sunshine and its comfortable temperature. The ladies put on their prettiest frocks and most bewitching hats, the men folk made themselves as spruce and debonair as they knew how, and off they went in their thousands to the concert. There must have been anywhere from ten to twelve thousand folk at Oak Hill while the bands were, with rare volume and pleasing effect, playing their well-selected music, and a happier-looking, more contented, well-dressed crowd one never need wish for.

September 24th

After covering something like a distance of 18,000 miles, in her capacity as Spiritualist missionary to South Africa, Mrs. Millicent Thompson recently returned to her home in Accrington. Mrs. Thompson has for over 22 years been associated with Spiritualism, and her undoubted attainments secured for her the position of vice-president of the British Mediums' Union.

Though thousands of miles away from home, Mrs. Thompson had many pleasant reminders of Accrington and its associations. For one thing, she was surprised and delighted to find almost wherever she went that copies of the "Observer and Times" were available, from which to learn something of affairs and events at home. Over and over again she found the "Observer" in the hands of folks from the old country.

October 8th

Today marks the commencement of Accrington's great shopping festival. All this week a feeling of suppressed excitement has permeated the town in the vicinity of the shops. On Monday one encountered numerous workmen busily engaged in repainting shop fronts, while in entering one or two shops one ran the risk of upsetting paint pots and being dabbed with a whitewash brush. Nearly everybody in the shop line appeared to be "Spring cleaning," or having some part of the premises re-gilded, or re-decorated. Monday, usually a quiet day in town, had become for the nonce a scene of bustle and industry. For where no workmen had foregathered, one saw drawn blinds jealously concealing the display-in-the-making that is to dazzle shop-gazers today and during next week. And so, like a hive of busy bees, the tradesmen worked, and the arrangements have progressed towards perfection. On Wednesday half-holiday was taboo by many shop-keepers, and the hours after noon till late at night were spent in planning, and arranging the windows. Here, one could see through lighted panes great cases of goods ready for use in the display, and enthusiastic shop-hands watching with breathless interest the genius of the establishment preparing to arrange the goods to the best advantage.

There, with the light of battle in his eyes, was a small tradesman draping yards of ribbon to enhance the glory of his little stock; and here again were women shop-keepers gracefully hanging pretty trinkets and knick- knacks to charm the shop-gazer, and perchance the judges who shall adjudicate in favour of the finest displays.

October 15th

I trust Accrington tradesmen have not sought in vain to attract local as well as general trade by their special displays during the week. Ladies sometimes need to be reminded that the more purchases they make in their own town, the more they are helping to build up its success. Money spent locally is always a help, to the tradesmen, and after all is it not more or less of a duty for the wives of business men to spend at least a portion of their incomes in the town where it is made. Naturally if a big proportion of the money is spent outside our little Community, the town will not be as prosperous. We have all, I hope, the welfare of our growing town at heart, and it is often nothing more than mere thoughtlessness that causes us to ignore our responsibilities in this respect.

October 22nd

Mr. J. Kitching and Mr. G. E. Slack will be proud men this week, for it was. announced at the whist drive on Wednesday that the former had succeeded in winning the cup for best outside decorations, and to the latter was awarded the "Observer" Shield and souvenir medal for the best window display.

There is no doubt that many tradespeople reaped a golden harvest during the shopping week. One hears of confectioners with not a cake left after the incoming crowds were fed; and of butchers who revelled in the unprecedented sale of meat hours before closing time arrived. Why, some of them were sitting with folded arms at nine o'clock on the first Saturday night, with not so much as a mutton chop left to dispose of! Then there were the clothiers, and other tradespeople who have done remarkably well. And the success does not end here, for probably many people will have mentally ticked off a list of desirable goods that shall be theirs before the New Year dawns.

* * *

Seldom have I seen a prettier wedding than that of Miss Katherine Birtwistle, eldest daughter of Mr. Arthur Birtwistle, J.P., of Cliffe House, Great Harwood, and William Lawrence, second son of Mr. James Lawrence, J.P., of Northbrook, St. Annes-on- the-Sea, which took place at Great Harwood Parish Church on Wednesday afternoon. The bride had a full court train to her beautiful white silk gown and to the regulation white lace veil and sprays of orange blossom was added a quaint Indian cap of pearls. She carried a choice shower bouquet of lilies of the valley, and wore a diamond brooch and a pearl necklet with pendant, gifts of the bridegroom.

Eight prettily dressed maids attended the bride. Six of the eight bridesmaids wore gowns composed of white satin, with tunics of silver net, and their white satin hats were trimmed with pretty rose-shaded ostrich feathers. The two children looked sweet in their Empire frocks of white satin and befeathered white hats trimmed white cord, and they carried dainty posies, and wore proudly horse-shoe patterned brooches, the gift of the bridegroom. The gifts to the elder bridesmaids were gold and tortoise-shell brooches.

A reception was held in a large marquee erected in the grounds of Cliffe House, after the wedding ceremony, over two hundred guests being present. The wedding tour will be spent in London and the South, and eventually Mr. and Mrs. W. Lawrence will reside at "The Woodlands," Cherry Tree, Blackburn.

* * *

On Wednesday afternoon next it will be our pleasant duty to visit the Mayoress, Mrs. Nuttall, who will be "at home" in the Town Hall Accrington. This will be almost the last social function at which Dr. and Mrs. Nuttall will entertain in the capacity of Mayor and Mayoress, as with November comes their release from these, we will hope, not entirely irksome duties. While perhaps not altogether agreeing with some of the rigid doctrines expounded by the Mayor and Mayoress during the term of Mayoralty, one admires their genuine earnestness for the causes they both love.

Certainly we never had a Mayoress who could speak so fluently on public platforms, nor one who grasped and marshalled facts so cleverly. Strange, is it not, that so many ladies have this gift at home—a fact the gentlemen will verify—and fail to deliver even the simplest speeches with any degree of confidence in public? However, this deficiency is never in evidence at Mayoral "at homes" where there is always a feast of cakes and a flow of talk. It is a pleasant task, this welcoming of the newly elected, and speeding the parting Mayor and Mayoress.

October 29th

More than once it has been my pleasure to refer to the talented daughters of the Rev. H. McCullagh, the Wesleyan superintendent at present stationed at Accrington. The Misses Isabel and Mary McCullagh (second violin and violoncello) took part in a quartet of young ladies—"from Manchester"— in the Bechstein Hall, London, this week, and won the plaudits of the audience as well as the praises of the newspaper critics. Miss Mary McCullagh, I notice, is to play at the Cunliffe concert on Wednesday.

November 5th

For such "a feast of music and a flow of soul"—to slightly alter the quotation—as that we were afforded at the Accrington Town Hall on Wednesday night, we may very properly return our heartiest thanks to the Robert Cunliffe Orchestra. I have seldom enjoyed a Cunliffe concert so much. Everything went off so well. For one thing there was a crowded audience. Money was actually being turned away at the doors, and many who would have entered had to be denied. A new experience this, in recent seasons at all events, for the Cunliffe Orchestra. Chiefly, I fancy, the great magnet that attracted so many of those present was the announcement that Miss Phyllis Lett was to sing. A more fortunate choice of artiste the committee have never made.

On Wednesday night Miss Lett simply took the Town Hall by storm. From the first few notes of her initial song she had completely captured her audience, and for the rest of the evening they were hers most devotedly.

And of course I must not forget the band. Theirs was a well devised programme for a popular audience, and take it all in all, I have seldom heard them play better. Obvious blemishes there were here and there —that in an amateur organisation such as this is, I suppose, inevitable. People who institute comparisons, say, with Halle's, are unjust and unreasonable. But the performance afforded very much upon which they were entitled to congratulation.

November 19th

What a wretched morning Alderman Bury had for Mayor's Sunday. Taking the weather into account, there was a fairly good turn-up. On such a day one feels inclined to stay by a warm fire, reading a good book. Many friends I know never troubled to put on their boots on Sunday. All honour to those who braved the elements. Oak-street has been singularly fortunate in providing so many civic fathers— a number out of all proportion to the importance of the community measured purely by numerical strength. Four of Alderman Bury's predecessors have been prominently identified with Oak-street—the late Alderman Lee, Alderman Duckworth, Mr. John S. Higham, M.P., and Alderman Higham, and three of them were able to accompany him to church. The Rev. Mr. Brook has had the distinction of preaching to our local senators—collectively, I mean—oftener than any other minister, and his sermon on Sunday was as appropriate as it was eloquent. The service altogether was inspiriting. I hope Mr. Brook may remain among us for many years to come, and that he will have the pleasure of speaking to future Mayors from Oak-street pulpit.

Arthur Smith-Bury, Accrington's Mayor
1910-11

November 26th

The Mayoress's "At Homes" at Accrington become more and more democratic. Time was when only the "elete" accepted the invitation to take tea with the consort of the First Magistrate, but now the assemblies are much larger, and on Wednesday Mrs. Bury had the satisfaction of receiving 600 friends or more. And she seemed as radiant as any of her guests—she appeared to be supremely happy to be surrounded by such hosts. There was a considerable sprinkling of the sterner sex, though the ladies, some accompanied by little ones, largely predominated. It is no light task to entertain such a big company, and if there was an occasional rush for tables, that was perhaps not surprising. The decorations were on an unusually lavish scale, but everything harmonised, and Mrs. Bury's first "At Home" may be voted an unqualified success. Standing with the Mayor—both wearing insignia of office—she received her guests in a very homely fashion, doing her best to make everyone feel at ease. She was attired in a rich gown of apricot-coloured satin with an overskirt of chiffon ninon, edged with bronze velvet. The bodice was draped with tucked chiffon ninon and gold lace, finished at the waist with gold cord girdle. She wore a black beaver hat, trimmed with black tulle, and mounted with black ostrich feather.

* * *

The Mayor's Old Folks' Treat has to be discontinued. This decision has been come to this week by a committee of the Council. The reasons for this step seem cogent enough. Every citizen over a certain age is entitled to attend, and in years past many aged, but comparatively well-to-do people, have presented themselves for the annual "feed." Since the Old Age Pensions came into operation, the aged people have not fared so badly as they did at one time, and there is no longer the necessity for this annual festival. It must not be assumed that the old people will be uncared for. The Mayor's Poor Fund will be continued, and cases of distress will receive attention. Every year local patients are sent to convalescent homes, and this beneficent work will be continued, and, it is hoped, its scope enlarged.

December 10th

Let me hasten to congratulate "Our Amateurs"—otherwise the Accrington Amateur Operatic Society—upon this week's performances of "Princess Ida" at the Accrington Hippodrome. And I should like, if I may, to commiserate with them also. Of all the weeks in the years that could have been chosen for opera week, this was surely the most unfortunate. Of course, the officials of the society are not to blame for that. If anyone is to blame at all it is His Majesty's late Government for daring to plunge the country into the "stress and turmoil of a general election" just on the very week when the Accrington Amateurs were to give "Princess Ida."

But what about the performance? It was excellent. I am not going to say the Amateurs have never done anything better. I think they have. But it is nevertheless a capital show, highly creditable to everybody concerned.

December 17th

Her many friends in East Lancashire will join in extending their felicitations to Mrs. Pound (Miss Dorothy Barr), daughter of Dr. J. Barr and Mrs. Barr, of Rishton, who was married to Lieut. Pound, of H.M.S. "Diana," at Malta, on Monday. It was a naval wedding, and as such was a particularly picturesque affair, with all the officers of the bridegroom's ship in attendance. The bride has a large circle of friends in our own neighbourhood. She is an enthusiastic Badminton player, and has been a member of the Rishton and Accrington clubs. Occasionally she has contributed stories to newspapers and magazines. Lieut. Pound, who has been in this district on several occasions, is a son of the late Mr. Alfred Pound, barrister-at-law, and his mother, who resides at Ealing, is a cousin of Mr. Joseph. Chamberlain.

Miss Barr had a rather trying experience on her way from Rishton to Malta. She left Liverpool on December 1st by the steamship "Seti," and had for her companion a lady who is the wife of a brother officer of Lieut. Pound, of the "Diana," who was also on her way to Malta. In a letter home from Gibraltar, Miss Barr relates that on arriving at "Gib," she and her lady friend left the "Seti" to have a look round "Gib." Whilst they were ashore a storm arose, and meantime the "Seti" had to depart hastily to Algeciras, a considerable distance away, for shelter. The feelings of Miss Barr may be better imagined than described when she was informed that the storms sometimes lasted for considerable periods and that there would not be another boat for Malta for two or three days. However, her wedding day was fixed, and the "Seti" was then in possession of all her personal belongings and trousseau, as well as the many beautiful wedding presents she had received before leaving Rishton, and she was determined to catch the boat if at all possible. The two ladies actually braved the rough sea in a steam launch, but were beaten back, and all seemed hopeless when Capt. Rimington, the King's Harbour Master at Gibraltar, came to the rescue by ordering out the largest Admiralty tug, and in that the ladies were taken to Algeciras, where they joined the "Seti."

December 24th

For the two delightful receptions held at the Town Hall on Wednesday and Thursday evenings those of us who were privileged to attend owe, I think we shall everyone feel, a debt of gratitude to Accrington's Mayor and Mayoress, Alderman A. S. Bury and Mrs. Bury. I have never seen the Town Hall look prettier than it did on Wednesday evening. The Mayor and Mayoress had left nothing undone that could contribute to the pleasure and entertainment of their guests, and doubtless after an arduous couple of days, since the weight of arranging the hundred and one details fell largely upon their shoulders—and particularly does that apply to the Mayoress—they will be happy in the reflection that they have added materially to the Christmas joys of the 800 fortunate folk who enjoyed their hospitality.

December 31st

"New Year." With the end of the old year and the beginning of the new, comes a time of retrospect and of resolution.

If the year which closes to-day has not been, from the local standpoint, entirely a time of fatness and of uninterrupted industrial and commercial prosperity, there has at all events been much for which we may still be thankful. Accrington and district has come through the time of depression in the cotton trade better than some weaving centres one could name, and if there has not been the fullest measure of work and wages, at least there has been very little in the way of acute want or distress among those who depend upon our great staple trade for their livelihood. Happily the indications point to better days for Lancashire's main industry, and with the distinct revival in the cotton trade may come also, it is hoped, a brisker demand for textile machinery, with, it would follow, increased employment for those engaged in that important branch of our local industries.